HERBAL THERAPEUTICS:
SPECIFIC INDICATIONS
FOR
HERBS & HERBAL FORMULAS

By
DAVID WINSTON, RH (AHG)

Agrimony

THIS INFORMATION IS INTENDED FOR
EDUCATIONAL PURPOSES ONLY.

Many thanks to my Editing Team: Elizabeth Lambert, Cynthia Troy Pollak, Karen Tuorto and Hannah Lee

Cover Layout by Anne Lambert

Published by:
Herbal Therapeutics Research Library
P.O. Box 417
Riegelsville, PA 18077
www.herbaltherapeutics.net

TABLE OF CONTENTS

ABOUT HERBAL FORMULAS

History - Animals and humans since their origin have relied on plants for both food and medicine; thus our bodies have evolved an ability to assimilate the bio-active compounds in plants. This evolutionary relationship is important to herbal medicine because the body is accustomed to assimilating the more potent chemicals of herbs within the matrix of the whole plant. When properly and carefully used, herbal medicines can often work with a high degree of efficacy without many of the side-effects common with prescription drugs or over-the-counter medications. While a few cultures have used herbs as simples (one herb at a time) the history of herbal medicine and traditional systems of medicine reflect a focus on polypharmacy. This means most herbs are given in complex formulas to create a unique synergy of action. A well constructed formula can increase activity of some herbs, decrease toxicity of others, decrease risk of herb-drug interactions and improve patient outcomes. This concept of synergy, using a whole plant extract rather than an isolated constituent or a well chosen formula rather than a single herb for a single disease, is one of the foundational elements of good herbal medicine. Over the last 15 years researchers have provided numerous examples of the validity of this concept, in both animal and human studies (Liao, et al., 2010, Gao, et al., 2009).

Clinical Experience - The following formulas are based on over 45 years of clinical experience as well as extensive research. Herbs from around the world were chosen for their safety and efficacy. The formulations are based on a theory of balance found in most herbal medicine systems (Traditional Chinese Medicine/ TCM, Ayurveda, Japanese Kampo, Tibetan medicine, etc.). Each contains herbs that strengthen or nourish a tissue or organ, some that tonify or normalize function, and others that relax or gently cleanse the tissue. In this way proper function of an organ or system can be achieved without additional stress or "dis-ease" occurring.

Holistic Approach - All medicines are most effective as a part of a comprehensive, holistic treatment program including diet and lifestyle changes, as well as stress reduction techniques. Foods, like medicines, are best used in their natural matrix, so whole foods are the most nutritious and assimilable. Regular exercise is also important - it not only keeps the muscles and heart strong, but promotes good circulation of blood, lymph and energy (*qi*). A positive frame of mind and sensible lifestyle that minimizes stress are also essential elements of good health. Adequate sleep, good nutrition, and a healthy lifestyle including exercise, community, and a purpose filled life are foundations for health.

Such a holistic program is most effective when it addresses the underlying causes of imbalance in the body (the terrain) rather than simply treating symptoms of a disease or pathology. By educating ourselves and understanding the differences between healthy choices/lifestyle and those that cause disease, we make an important step towards true health and healing.

THE SAFE USE OF HERBS

There are a few simple guidelines for safe use of these formulas and herbs in general:

1. When using an herb or formula for the first time, it is wise to take only 1/4 of

the recommended dose to make sure you will not have an adverse reaction to it. If such a reaction occurs, immediately discontinue using the herb or herbal product. Usually herbs are well tolerated, and it is suggested that the dose be slowly increased over 2 weeks until you are at the recommended dose level.

2. Always pay careful attention to recommended use or dosage. "If a little is good, more must be better" does not apply here. Many herbs, particularly the stronger medicines used to treat chronic problems, are best used in small doses taken over an extended period of time.

3. There are few herbs that have been clinically tested and definitely found to be safe during pregnancy, although many herbs have a long history of apparent safe use during pregnancy. If you have a history of miscarriage or problem pregnancy consult a midwife or knowledgeable physician before trying herbs. See the herbal contra-indications section on the following pages.

4. Know yourself! There are conditions that are mild and self limiting and safe to self treat. While more serious illnesses require the knowledge and services of a health professional. Always use common sense and careful discretion to choose the appropriate remedies for yourself. If you try something and it doesn't work for you, you may have misinterpreted your symptoms and probably should consult a health care practitioner. With minor complaints you may want to be patient, the actions of many herbs are subtle and only manifest when used over time.

5. If you are taking prescription drugs, interactions between some herbs and pharmaceuticals are possible. Discussing these possibilities with a clinical herbalist, professional member of the American Herbalists Guild, [RH (AHG)], knowledgeable pharmacist or physician is advised.

6. Another source of authoritative information on herb safety, the use of herbs during pregnancy and lactation and herb/drug interactions is the recently published Botanical Safety Handbook (Gardner, Z & McGuffin, M, 2013). As a member of the team that created this exhaustive work, I am proud to say that it is an essential and much needed resource.

HERBAL CONTRAINDICATIONS

Classification System - Many traditions of herbal medicine have systems for classifying plants by their relative safety. For example, *Food herbs* are herbs that can be used as daily tonics with little or no potential for problems. *Medicines* are herbs that are used for a specific purpose for a specific duration because they are more powerful in their activity. *Poisons* are herbs only used in tiny doses under the supervision of experienced and competent practitioners. Traditional Chinese Medicine uses the terms *Superior remedies* for food-like or very safe herbs and *Inferior remedies* for those with a strong potential for toxicity or adverse effects.

Examples of food or superior herbs are Dandelion, Nettles, Hawthorn, Codonopsis, Red Clover, Lemon Balm and Peppermint. Medicines would include Osha, Goldenseal, Horse Chestnut and Valerian. Inferior or potentially poisonous herbs would include Mayapple, Gelsemium and Aconite. Most commonly used botanical medicines fall into the food or milder medicine categories and these should always be a person's first choice for a remedy. Don't be fooled into thinking an herb is not helpful because its action is not immediate or drastic. Often the subtlest herbs prove the most profound in the long run. Violet leaves, Red Clover blossoms and Dandelion roots are very common and gentle herbs yet they are important ingredients in some of the most famous and commonly used alterative formulas.

Energetics - It is important to keep in mind the energetic properties of herbs in relationship to the condition being treated. For example, when treating a hot condition - red, inflamed tissue that is hot to the touch - a cool, soothing herb like marshmallow will be most helpful. Using a hot herb like Cayenne could further irritate the tissue.

Pregnancy - During pregnancy and nursing one must consider the dose of any medicine that the baby may receive through the placenta or milk. For simple home remedies a pregnant or nursing mother would be wise to limit her choices to food or superior herbs taken in teas. Teas are assimilated more slowly than extracts and would therefore have less chance of an impact on the fetus.

Herbs to be used with caution during pregnancy -

Angelica root	Feverfew herb	Pleurisy root
California Poppy	He Huan Pi/Mimosa bark	Tienqi Ginseng root
Dang Gui root	Horse Chestnut seed	Tribulus seed
Fenugreek seed	Motherwort herb	

Herbs not to be used internally during pregnancy -

Andrographis herb	Ephedra twigs	Poke root
Arnica flowers	Germander herb	Pulsatilla herb
Asafoetida gum	Goldenseal rhizome/root	Quassia wood
Barberry Root	Gravel Root	Rauwolfia
Bethroot	Gum Guggul resin	Rosemary herb❖
Bitter Melon fruit	Huai Niu Xi root	Rue herb
Black Cohosh root ❖ ❖	Hyssop herb	Sage herb❖
Blue Cohosh root	Indian Madder root	Scotch Broom herb
Blue Flag rhizome	Jamaica Dogwood bark	Shepherd's Purse herb
Blue Vervain herb	Juniper berry	Spikenard root ❖ ❖
Boldo herb	Lesser Periwinkle leaf	Stillingia root
Borage herb	Licorice root	Sweet Annie herb
Buchu herb	Life Root	Tansy herb
Bugleweed herb	Ligusticum root	Thuja leaf
Butterbur root	Lobelia herb	Tricosanthis root
Calamus rhizome	Lomatium herb	Uva Ursi leaf
Cat's Claw bark	Mistletoe herb	Wild Carrot seed
Celandine herb	Mugwort herb	Wild Ginger rhizome
Celery seed	Myrrh gum	Wormwood herb
Chaparral herb	Neem leaf, bark, or seed	Yellow Root
Chinese Coptis root	Oregon Grape root	Yi Yi Ren/Coix seed
Chinese Peony root	Osha root	Yohimbe bark
Coltsfoot herb	Parsley tincture or EO	
Comfrey root or leaf	Pau d'Arco wood	
Corydalis tuber	Pennyroyal herb or EO	
Cotton root bark	Petasites/Butterbur	
Devil's Club root	Picrorhiza root	

Herbs with potential for serious toxicity such as Mayapple, Bloodroot, Belladonna, Veratrum, Gelsemium, Aconite/Dan Fu Zi, Wormseed and Pink Root should not be used during pregnancy.

Herbs not to be used while breast-feeding -

Aloe	Mayapple	Rue
Boneset	Petasites/Butterbur	Sage ❖
Borage	Poke	Senna
Comfrey Root	Pulsatilla	Wild Ginger
Ephedra	Rhubarb	White Sage

Herbs not to be used with young children -

Blue Flag	Comfrey Root	Petasites/Butterbur
Boneset	Ephedra	Poke
Celandine	Mayapple	Quassia

❖ Medicinal dosage, food amounts are safe

❖ ❖ Under physician's recommendation may be used during the last 2 weeks of pregnancy.

HERB/DRUG INTERACTIONS

With the increase in people taking both herbs and drugs, the potential for herb-drug interactions does exist, but we need to put the issue into perspective.

Food/drug interactions are far more common, as we consume far greater quantities of food than herbal medicines. Grapefruit juice inhibits Phase 1 liver detoxification (CYP3A4) and can increase serum levels of some drugs including calcium antagonists and antihistamines. Milk interferes with absorption of Tetracycline by 50-90%. Green leafy vegetables (spinach, cabbage, beet greens, kale), as well as broccoli, peas and cucumbers, can alter coagulation and interact with anticoagulant medications such as Warfarin.

Drug/drug interactions are even more common. Even seemingly benign antacids with polyvalent minerals (Ca, Fe, Mg, Zn, Al) can interfere with cycline and mycin antibiotics. The common blood thinner Warfarin can interact with NSAIDs, aspirin, antiretrovirals, some antidepressants, Capecitabine, antibiotics and glucocorticoids. Other medications that have a strong potential for drug/drug interactions include Phenytoin (Dilantin), Carbamazepine (Tegretol), Phenobarbitol, Lithium, acid blockers, Statins, SSRIs, Lithium, oral contraceptives and Cisapride (Ament, et al., 2000). According to Zubrina Mawji, MD (1998), the potential for drug/drug interaction for those patients taking multiple drugs (6 or more) is close to 100%.

Herb/drug interactions can occur, but significant reactions are relatively rare (Butterweck, et al., 2004). In addition some herb drug interactions are actually *positive* and could result in the ability to decrease drug dosage:
1. Decreased bioavailability of medicine - decreased absorption (Psyllium Seed, Flax Seed, Slippery Elm), enhanced metabolism (Brassicas), or enhanced elimination (Senna, Coffee).

2. Increased bioavailability of medicine - increased absorption (Ginger, Cayenne, Prickly Ash, Black Pepper), decreased metabolism (Grapefruit juice), or decreased elimination (Licorice).
3. Potentiation of a drug's effects - via a different but complementary action (Siberian Ginseng and antibiotics).
4. Potentiation of drug's effects via similar activity (Lasix and Dandelion Leaf, Digoxin and Lily of the Valley).
5. Protection from adverse drug effects (Milk Thistle and hepatotoxic/ nephrotoxic herbs, Licorice and corticosteroids).
6. Antagonistic or incompatible activities (laxatives and astringents, CNS stimulants and sedatives).

Simple Guidelines - When evaluating a potential interaction:
1. Be specific about
   a. herb product dose, form (tea, extract, capsule), brand, other ingredients
   b. any medications taken
   c. foods consumed
2. Record timing of occurence-plausible pharmacological timing is more likely to be within a few hours or a day or two rather than weeks or months later.
3. Does reaction occur on re-challenge? (Do not attempt this without clinical supervision.)
4. Does reaction cease on stopping herb?

Predicting/Preventing Interactions - The following are a few simple rules:
1. Follow traditional knowledge of herb activity to predict and prevent possible synergies or antagonisms with prescription drugs.
- Hawthorn may potentiate beta-blockers (I have seen this twice in my practice, but it seems to be rare.).
- Diuretics such as Buchu, Goldenrod, Juniper, etc. are contra-indicated while taking Lithium.
- Herbs with Vitamin K such as Shepherd's Purse and Nettles should not be added to the diet in large amounts if taking blood thinners.
- Garlic (large amounts), Red Root, Hong Hua (Safflower flos) and Chinese Salvia should be avoided with prescription blood thinners (Warfarin) or anti-platelet medications.
- Large doses of Valerian, Hops and Kava may potentiate the effects of benzo-diazepines, barbiturates or alcohol.
- Mucilaginous herbs like Slippery Elm and Marshmallow may reduce absorption of other medications, when taken concurrently. It is best to separate ingestion of mucilagenous herbs from pharmaceutical medications by 2-3 hours.
- Laxative and diuretic herbs may increase potassium loss, therefore increasing the toxicity of cardiac glycosides present in Digoxin, or Lanoxin.
- Herbs with high levels of tannins - Oak Bark, Bayberry root bark, Wild Geranium, etc. can interfere with mineral absorption, (especially iron) and

inhibit absorption of alkalodial medication such as Theophylline if taken within 2-3 hours of each other.

2. Use formulas and lower dosages of herbs with potential problems - a recent study of St. John's wort showed that its ability to provoke a herb/drug interaction was dose dependent. In traditional herbal medicine, herbs are usually used in formulas, thus reducing the amount of any one herb ingested.

3. Take herbs and drugs separately (by 2-3 hours).

4. When adding herbs to already established drug regimens, start at low dose and gradually increase the dose. Monitor patients carefully.

5. Avoid starting or stopping medications and herbs suddenly. Subtle changes may not create a problem but substantial changes may trigger a major response.

6. Avoid red flags - Warfarin is known to interact with over 200 foods, pharmaceuticals and herbs. Other problematic drugs include protease inhibitors, Lithium, Cyclosporine, and Digoxin. Use care combining herbs, drugs, or supplements with medications that have a narrow therapeutic index.

7. Avoid using herbs that have been reported to cause hepatoxicity (Kava, Black Cohosh, Chaparral) with hepatotoxic medications (tetracycline, statin drugs, excessive alcohol, acetaminophen).

8. Studies indicate St. John's wort has the ability to strongly stimulate or inhibit Phase I liver detoxification (cyclic P-450 activity-CYP3A4, CYP2D6, CYP2E1, CYP2C9 and CYP1A2) and P-Glycoprotein (P-gp) activity in the gut and kidney. Medications known to be metabolized via these pathways can have reduced or increased blood levels if taken with St. John's wort. Avoid using St. John's wort with protease inhibitors, Cyclosporine, Irinotecan, Digoxin, Warfarin, Imatinab, Alprazolam, Tacrolimus, Verapamil, Ivabradine, Talinolol, Clopidogrel, Clozapine, and possibly contraceptive pills. (Rahimi & Abdollahi, 2012) Discuss using this herb with a knowledgeable practitioner before combining it with any pharmaceutical medications.

HERBAL REPERTORY - A Guide to Therapeutic Formulas and Herbs by Body Systems.

* Indicates to use only with Practitioner's Guidance

Cardiovascular System

Anemia (Iron deficient)	Iron Extract™, Women's Adapt™, Stinging Nettle leaf, Yellow Dock, Parsley, Ashwagandha, Processed Rehmannia, Dong Quai, Amla, Lycium fruit, Watercress, Artichoke leaf, Alfalfa
Arteriosclerosis	Ginkgo/Horsechestnut Compound™, Healthy Heart Compound™, Garlic, Gum Guggul, Chrysanthemum flower, Myrrh, Linden flower, Rosemary, Amla, Pomegranate-Goji Berry Solid Extract™, Horsetail, Blueberry Solid Extract™, Hawthorn Solid Extract™, Hawthorn, Cayenne, Gotu Kola
Bleeding, passive	Reckless Blood Tonic™, Cinnamon, Agrimony, Unprocessed Rehmannia, Yarrow, Shepherd's Purse, Bugleweed
Circulation (impaired) *Cerebral*	Ginkgo/Horsechestnut Compound™, Lemon Balm, Rosemary, Blueberry Solid Extract™, Holy Basil, Gotu Kola, Ginger, Bacopa, Lavender, Chinese Peony, Sage, Damiana
Peripheral	Ginkgo/Horsechestnut Compound™, Healthy Heart Compound™, Hawthorn Solid Extract™, Blueberry Solid Extract™, Pomegranate-Goji Berry Solid Extract™, Cinnamon, Prickly Ash, Cayenne, Lycium fruit, Horse Chestnut, Yarrow, Amla, Gotu Kola
Heart *Angina*	Healthy Heart Compound™, Dong Quai, Chinese Salvia, Astragalus, Corydalis yanhusuo, Kudzu, Lobelia, Cyperus, Khella, Hawthorn Solid Extract™
Congestive heart failure (mild)	Healthy Heart Compound™, Chinese Salvia, Dong Quai, Kudzu, Astragalus, Hawthorn Solid Extract™, Night Blooming Cereus

17

Mitral valve prolapse (mild)	Hawthorn with Night Blooming Cereus and Collinsonia, Hawthorn Solid Extract™, Gotu-Kola
Palpitations/Nervous tachycardia	Healthy Heart Compound™, Women's Calmpound™ (menopausal), Motherwort, Bugleweed (Thyroid-induced), Polygala (stress-induced), Tension Relief™
Hypertension	Healthy Heart Compound™, Cardio Calmpound™, Black Haw, Garlic, Olive Leaf, Chrysanthemum Flower, European Mistletoe (use with 5% Eleuthero for increased synergistic effect), Huang Qin, Kudzu, Eucommia Bark/Du Zhong decoction, Motherwort, Linden flower, Reishi, Chinese Salvia, Dandelion leaf
Raynaud's disease	Ginkgo/Horse Chestnut Compound™, St. John's wort, Yellow Sweetclover, Prickly Ash, Ginger, Cinnamon, Hypericum Oil (topically), Lycium fruit
Varicose Veins	Ginkgo/Horse Chestnut Compound™, Healthy Heart Compound™, Collinsonia, Blueberry Solid Extract™, Cayenne, Gotu Kola, Lycium fruit, Pomegranate-Goji Berry Solid Extract™, Amla, Hawthorn Solid Extract™, Horse Chestnut, Cinnamon

Digestive System

Achlorhydria (hypochlorhydia)	Original Bitters™, Bitter Roots™, Old World Bitters™, Spiced Bitters™, Orange Peel, Angelica root, Juniper berry, Prickly Ash, Ginger, Cayenne, Cinnamon, Dandelion root
Antacid (hyperchlorhydria)	Meadowsweet, Marshmallow, Chamomile, Licorice, Slippery Elm (tea only), Fresh Aloe gel, Lemon Balm
Assimilation of Nutrients (impaired)	Original Bitters™, Bitter Roots™, Old World Bitters™, Spiced Bitters™, Carminative Compound™, Metabolic Support™, Artichoke leaf, Orange Peel, Angelica, Gentian root, Black Pepper, Prickly Ash, Long Pepper, Bitter Melon

Belching	Original Bitters™, Bitter Roots™, Old World Bitters™, Spiced Bitters™, Carminative Compound™, Artichoke, Orange Peel, Gentian, Wild Yam
Cholagogue/Choleretic	Thistles Compound™, Original Bitters™, Bitter Roots™, Old World Bitters™, Spiced Bitters™, Dandelion root, Artichoke, Gentian, Watercress, Mugwort, Barberry, Yellow Root, Oregon Grape Root, Red Alder Bark, Wormwoood, Blessed Thistle, Culver's Root, Tumeric
Cholesterol (elevated)	Original Bitters™, Bitter Roots™, Old World Bitters™, Spiced Bitters™, Thistles Compound™, Metabolic Support™, Gum Guggul, Garlic, Artichoke leaf, Gymnema, Reishi, Fenugreek, soluble fiber, Shiitake, Bitter Melon
Fat Digestion (impaired)	Original Bitters™, Bitter Roots™, Old World Bitters™, Spiced Bitters™, Thistles Compound™, Gentian, Dandelion root, Mugwort, Watercress, Artichoke leaf, Blessed Thistle, Wormwood, Horehound, Red Alder Bark, Turmeric
Gastroesophageal Reflux Disease (GERD)	Original Bitters™*, Bitter Roots™, Old World Bitters™*, Spiced Bitters™*, Chamomile, Wild Yam, Catnip, Black Haw, Blessed Thistle, Cyperus
Hepatitis (A,B, or C)	Thistles Compound™, Turmeric, Milk Thistle, Schisandra, Seven Precious Mushrooms™, Reishi, Artichoke, Huang Qin, Shiitake, Licorice, Bupleurum (do not use with Interferon), Isatis, Chinese Salvia
Hiatal Hernia	Wild Yam, Original Bitters™, Bitter Roots™, Old World Bitters™, Spiced Bitters™, Catnip, Chamomile, Meadowsweet

Indigestion (dyspepsia)	Original Bitters™, Bitter Roots™, Old World Bitters™, Spiced Bitters™, Carminative Compound™, Kid's Tummy Relief™, Fennel seed, Ginger, Chamomile, Peppermint, Rosemary, Holy Basil, Cilantro, Damiana, Cardamom, Bai-Zhu Atractylodes, Artichoke leaf, Roman Chamomile, Fenugreek, Meadowsweet, Catnip, Linden flower, Lemon Balm, Lavender, Thyme
Liver Support	Thistles Compound™, Milk Thistle, Turmeric, Schisandra, Dandelion root, Watercress, Blessed Thistle, Bupleurum, Artichoke leaf
Motion Sickness	Carminative Compound™, Kid's Tummy Relief™, Ginger
Nausea	Carminative Compound™, Immune Adapt™ (Chemotherapy-induced), Fennel, Chamomile, Ginger, Catnip, Anise-Hyssop, Cyperus, Artichoke leaf, Wild Yam
Nervous Stomach	Hops, Catnip, Valerian, Chamomile, Kid's Calmpound Glycerite™, Wild Yam, Meadowsweet
SIBO *(Small intestine bacterial overgrowth)* SBBO *(Small bowel bacterial overgrowth)*	AP Compound™, Andrographis, Neem, Thyme, Garlic, Usnea, Goldenseal, Yellow Root, Bai-Zhu Atractylodes, Angelica
Ulcers, Gastric/Duodenal	Meadowsweet, Yarrow, Goldenseal, Licorice, Plantain, Aloe Gel, raw Cabbage juice, Yarrow, Marshmallow, Turmeric, Cat's Claw, Calendula (to inhibit adhesion of H. pylori)

Ear, Eyes, Nose, Throat

Ear Infection, (Otitis media)	Ultimate Echinacea™, Compound Mullein Oil™ (intra-aurally), Sinus Support Compound™, Eyebright
Eyes *Itchy and irritated (hayfever)*	Sinus Support Compound™, Eyebright

Poor vision	Insight Compound™, Blueberry Solid Extract™, Chrysanthemum flower, Lycium fruit, Ginkgo, Pomegranate-Goji Solid Extract™, Amla, Elderberry, Blueberry Solid Extract™
Wet Macular degeneration	Insight Compound™, Blueberry Solid Extract™, Calendula (contains Lutein), Chrysanthemum flower, Lycium fruit, Elderberry, Ginkgo, Amla
Cataracts (to slow progression)	Blueberry Solid Extract™, Insight Compound™, Lycium Fruit, Chrysanthemum flower, Pomegranate-Goji Berry Solid Extract™, Amla,
Diabetic Retinopathy (to help prevent)	Blueberry Solid Extract™, Insight Compound™, Lycium Fruit, Chrysanthemum flower, Pomegranate-Goji Berry Solid Extract™, Amla,
Gum disease	Phytodent™, Myrrh, Goldenseal, Calendula, Spilanthes, Yellow Root, Huang Qin, Propolis, White Sage, Ultimate Echinacea™, Echinacea, Thyme, Sage, Witch Hazel, Oregon Grape Root, Barberry, Yellow Root
Halitosis	Phytodent™, Spilanthes, Cinnamon, Cardamom
Laryngitis	Herbal Relief Botanical Throat Spray™, Echinacea/Goldenseal Compound™, Ultimate Echinacea™, White Sage, Calendula, Myrrh, Collinsonia, Sage, Propolis, Marshmallow
Sinusitis	Echinacea/Goldenseal Compound™, Sinus Support Compound™, Ultimate Echinacea™, VX Immune Support™, Andrographis, Isatis
Strep Throat	Echinacea/Goldenseal Compound™, Ultimate Echinacea™, White Sage, Usnea, Japanese Honeysuckle, Herbal Relief Botanical Throat Spray™, Andrographis, Sage, Isatis
Thrush	AF Compound™, Phytodent™, Yellow Root, Spilanthes, Myrrh, Calendula, Barberry, Oregon Grape Root, Thyme, Herbal Relief Botanical Throat Spray™, Goldenseal, Cardamom

Eliminatory System

Cholagogue/Choleretic	Gentlelax™, Original Bitters™, Bitter Roots™, Old World Bitters™, Spiced Bitters™, Dandelion root, Artichoke leaf, Gentian, Culver's Root, Red Alder Bark, Thistles Compound™, Mugwort, Barberry, Yellow Root, Oregon Grape Root, Wormwood
Constipation	Gentlelax™, Original Bitters™, Bitter Roots™, Old World Bitters™, Spiced Bitters™, Butternut bark, Culver's Root, Red Alder bark, Psyllium seed, Soluble Fiber, Buckthorn
Diarrhea	Intestinal Calmpound™, Kid's Tummy Relief™, Bayberry root bark, Bai-Zhu Atractylodes, Cinnamon, Red Root, Slippery Elm (tea only), Myrrh, White Pond Lily, Chamomile
Diverticulitis	Intestinal Calmpound™, Chamomile, Kudzu, Slippery Elm (tea only), Sarsaparilla, Turmeric, Yarrow, Licorice, Marshmallow
Dysbiosis (intestinal)	Original Bitters™, Bitter Roots™, Old World Bitters™, Spiced Bitters™, Artichoke, Gentian, Dandelion root, Elecampane, Lavender, Bai-Zhu Atractylodes, Quassia, Burdock root
Gallbladder (sluggish)	Original Bitters™, Bitter Roots™, Old World Bitters™, Spiced Bitters™, Intestinal Calmpound™, Gentlelax™, Celandine, Wild Yam, Wormwood
Gas/Flatulence	Original Bitters™, Bitter Roots™, Old World Bitters™, Spiced Bitters™, Carminative Compound™, Intestinal Calmpound™, Kid's Tummy Relief™, Fennel seed, Ginger, Cilantro, Lavender, Damiana, Orange Peel, Chamomile, Cardamom, Cinnamon, Sage, Thyme, Catnip, Peppermint, Cyperus, Rosemary, Pippali Long Pepper
Hemorrhoids	Ginkgo/Horsechestnut Compound™, Collinsonia, Figwort, Yarrow

Ileitis	Intestinal Calmpound™, Kudzu, Chamomile, Sarsaparilla, Turmeric
Inflammatory Bowel Disease (IBD)/ Crohn's disease/Ulcerative Colitis *To inhibit excessive immune response*	Intestinal Calmpound™, Immune Adapt™, Seven Precious Mushrooms™, Immune Balance Compound™, Unprocessed Rehmannia, Huang Qin, Chinese Salvia, Licorice, Cat's Claw, Turmeric, Gotu Kola, Reishi, Maitake
To heal the gut mucosa	Chamomile, White Pond Lily, Wormwood, Turmeric, Cat's Claw, Yarrow, Licorice, Gotu Kola, Slippery Elm (tea only), Marshmallow, Plantain, Calendula, Myrrh
Irritable Bowel Syndrome (IBS)	Intestinal Calmpound™, Serenity Compound™ (stress-induced), Turmeric, Kudzu, Chamomile, Roman Chamomile, Wild Yam, Sarsaparilla, Cyperus, Wormwood, Catnip, Hops, Valerian
Laxative	Gentlelax™, Butternut bark, Buckthorn, Red Alder bark, Culver's Root, Violet, Original Bitters™ (aperient), Bitter Roots™, (aperient), Old World Bitters™ (aperient), Spiced Bitters™ (aperient)
Leaky Gut Syndrome	Intestinal Calmpound™, Sarsaparilla, Turmeric, Cat's Claw, Original Bitters™, Bitter Roots™, Old World Bitters™, Spiced Bitters™, Fenugreek, Bayberry, Chamomile, Yarrow, Huang Qin, Licorice, Plantain, Calendula, Myrrh, Marshmallow, Gotu Kola
Parasites (amoebic)	AP Compound™, Andrographis, Quassia, Elecampane, Black Walnut hull, Sweet Annie, Garlic, Neem, Wormwood, Long Pepper
Spasm (Intestinal)	Intestinal Calmpound™, Black Haw, Full Moon - Women's Anti-Spasmodic Compound™, Kudzu, Chamomile, Ginger, Usnea, Wild Yam, Roman Chamomile, Cyperus, Valerian, Hops, Catnip

Endocrine System

Adaptogens (HPA axis regulators)	Daily Adapt™, Fit Adapt™, Calm Adapt™, Energy Adapt™,Women's Adapt™, Men's Adapt™, Immune Adapt™, Adrenal Balance Compound™, Holy Basil, Rhodiola, Codonopsis, Eleuthero, Ashwagandha, Prince Seng, American Ginseng, Licorice, Reishi, Cordyceps, Red Ginseng, Shatavari, Schisandra
Athletic Performance (to improve)	Daily Adapt™, Fit Adapt™, Adrenal Balance Compound™, Hawthorn, Ashwagandha, American Ginseng, Cordyceps, Rhodiola, Red Ginseng
Blood Sugar (mildly elevated)	Pancreaid™, Original Bitters™, Bitter Roots™, Old World Bitters™, Spiced Bitters™, Fenugreek, Blueberry Solid Extract™, Bitter Melon, Gymnema, Holy Basil, Red Ginseng, American Ginseng, Olive leaf, Cinnamon, Platycodon, Lycium fruit, Kudzu, Devil's Club
Endocrine dysfunction - *Pancreas*	Pancreaid™, Metabolic Support™, Original Bitters™, Bitter Roots™, Old World Bitters™, Spiced Bitters™, Fenugreek, Devil's Club, Gum Guggul, Cinnamon, Gymnema, Holy Basil
Hypothalamic/Pituitary/Adrenal Axis	Daily Adapt™, Energy Adapt™, Calm Adapt™, Women's Adapt™, Men's Adapt™, Immune Adapt™, Adrenal Balance Compound™, Rhodiola, Holy Basil, Eleuthero, Codonopsis, Reishi, Licorice, Ashwagandha, American Ginseng, Cordyceps, Red Ginseng, Schisandra
Ovaries	Women's Transition Compound™, Licorice, Shatavari, Rhodiola
Fatigue *Mental*	Clarity Compound™, Focus Formula™, Daily Adapt™, Energy Adapt™, Calm Adapt™, Women's Adapt™, Holy Basil, Fresh Oat, Gotu Kola, Bacopa, Rosemary, Sage, Lavender, Damiana

	Physical	Immune Adapt™, Daily Adapt™, Seven Precious Mushrooms™, Cordyceps, Reishi, Rhodiola, Codonopsis, Eleuthero, Ashwagandha
Grave's Disease		Thyroid Calmpound™, Seven Precious Mushrooms™ (for autoimmune causation), Motherwort, Self Heal, Immune Balance Compound™, Huang Qin
Hormonal Balance	*Men*	Men's Adapt™, Saw Palmetto, Stinging Nettle root, Ashwagandha, Red Ginseng, Maca, Cordyceps, Cynomorium
	Women	Women's Formula™, Women's Calmpound™, Women's Transition Compound™, Women's Adapt™, Licorice, Shatavari, Chaste Tree, Rhodiola, Cordyceps
Hyperthyroid		Thyroid Calmpound™, Self Heal, Bugleweed, Motherwort (Hyperthyroid-induced palpitations), Huang Qin
Hypothyroid		Ashwagandha, Bacopa, Gum Guggul, Myrrh, Bladderwrack
Metabolic Syndrome		Original Bitters™, Bitter Roots™, Old World Bitters™, Spiced Bitters™, Metabolic Support™, Artichoke, Gentian, Cinnamon, American Ginseng, Fenugreek, Jiaogulan, Bitter Melon, Eleuthero, Blueberry Solid Extract™
Obesity		Metabolic Support™, Bitter Melon, Gum Guggul with Triphala, Stinging Nettle leaf, Bladderwrack, Dandelion leaf, Chickweed

Female Reproductive System

Anxiety (PMS or Menopausal)	Women's Calmpound™, Motherwort, Kava, Women's Transition Compound™, Serenity Compound™, Bacopa, Chinese Polygala, Tension Relief™, Blue Vervain, Pulsatilla*, Fresh Oat, Chamomile
Bacterial Vaginosis (intravaginal use)	Usnea, Pipsissewa (orally), Garlic

Circulation (Uterine)	Uterine Tonic™, Dong Quai, Raspberry leaf, Ginger, Chinese Peony
Infertility (Female)	Women's Formula™, Shatavari, Dong Quai, Licorice, Cordyceps, Rhodiola
Menopausal symptoms *Hot flashes*	Women's Transition Compound™, Chaste Tree, Black Cohosh, Licorice, Sage, Chinese Peony, Motherwort, Ligustrum berry
Night Sweats	Sage, Women's Transition Compound™, Chaste Tree, Black Cohosh, Chinese Peony
Anxiety	Women's Calmpound™, Motherwort, Kava, Blue Vervain, Fresh Oat, Night Blooming Cereus, Chinese Polygala, Tension Relief™, Bacopa, Pulsatilla*, Chamomile, Linden flower
Insomnia	Serenity Compound™, Phytocalm™, Passionflower, Motherwort, Fresh Oat, Valerian, Hops, Chamomile
Cloudy Thinking	Focus Formula™, Women's Adapt™, Holy Basil, Rosemary, Gotu Kola, Ginkgo, Lavender, Bacopa, Chinese Peony
Menstrual Cramps	Aspirea Compound™, Full Moon - Women's Anti-Spasmodic Compound™, J. Kloss Anti-Spasmodic Compound, Black Haw, Roman Chamomile, Cyperus, Corydalis yanhusuo, Cramp Bark, Chinese Peony, Motherwort, Valerian, Jamaica Dogwood, Kava
Premenstrual Syndrome (general)	Women's Calmpound™, Serenity Compound™, Women's Formula™, Chaste Tree
PMS-A (anxiety)	Chaste Tree, Motherwort, Blue Vervain, Women's Calmpound™, Fresh Oat, Chamomile, Tension Relief™, Chinese Polygala, Bacopa, Pulsatilla*, Linden flower
PMS-D (depression)	Women's Adapt™, Black Cohosh, St. John's wort, Rosemary, Lavender, Damiana, Licorice, Night Blooming Cereus, Mimosa

26

PMS-C (cravings)	Original Bitters™, Bitter Roots™, Old World Bitters™, Spiced Bitters™, Fresh Oat, Artichoke, Mugwort, Gentian
PMS-H (hyperhydration)	Dandelion leaf, Stinging Nettle leaf, Parsley, Juniper berry, Kidney Relief Compound™
Profuse Menstrual Bleeding (menorrhagia)	Reckless Blood Tonic™, Uterine Tonic™, Raspberry leaf, Yarrow, Shepherd's Purse, Unprocessed Rehmannia, Cinnamon
Uterine Fibroids	Uterine Tonic™, Saw Palmetto, Chinese Peony, Shepherd's Purse (bleeding associated with fibroids), Chaste Tree, Dong Quai
Vaginal Dryness	Replenish Compound™, Women's Adapt™, Shatavari, Fresh Oat, Chinese Asparagus, Licorice, Processed Rehmannia, White Pond Lily, Dong Quai
Polycystic Ovarian Syndrome (PCOS)	Saw Palmetto, Stinging Nettle root, Chaste Tree, Chinese Peony with Licorice

Immune System

Allergies (Hayfever)	Sinus Support Compound™, Reishi, Maitake, Chinese Salvia, Huang Qin, Bayberry, Kudzu, Licorice (animal dander), Immune Balance Compound™, Osha, Amla, Eyebright, Cordyceps, Cat's Claw, Blueberry Solid Extract™, Lung Relief Cold/Damp™ or Hot/Damp™
Auto-immune Conditions *Immune amphoterics*	Immune Adapt™, Seven Precious Mushrooms™, Ashwagandha, American or Red Ginseng, Cat's Claw, Astragalus, Holy Basil, Licorice, Reishi, Maitake, Schisandra, Cordyceps
Immuno-regulators	Turmeric, Sarsaparilla, Gotu Kola, Cinnamon, Chinese Salvia, Bupleurum, Huang Qin, Immune Balance Compound™, Unprocessed Rehmannia

Cancer *(general supportive therapies)*	Alterative Compound™, Immune Adapt™, Burdock/Red Root Compound™, Seven Precious Mushrooms™, Chaga, Turmeric, Cat's Claw, Ligustrum berry, Boswellia, Astragalus, Milk Thistle, Scudder's Alterative*, Eli Jones' Compound Syrup of Scrophularia*
Breast Cancer (specific additions)	Red Clover, Poke Root*, Cleavers, Violet
Colon Cancer (specific additions)	Turmeric, Sarsaparilla, Violet
Prostate Cancer (specific additions)	Saw Palmetto, Stinging Nettle root, Green Tea
Candida (local overgrowth)	AF Compound™, Echinacea/Goldenseal Compound™, Spilanthes, Cardamom, Yellow Root, Barberry, Oregon Grape Root, Myrrh, Pau d'Arco, Calendula, Thyme, Goldenseal
Chronic Fatigue Immune Deficiency Syndrome (CFIDS)	Immune Adapt™, Seven Precious Mushrooms™, Daily Adapt™, Energy Adapt™, Fresh Oat, Reishi, Maitake, American Ginseng, Ashwagandha, Rhodiola, Codonopsis, Eleuthero, Red Ginseng, Holy Basil, Cordyceps
Colds	Astragalus/Echinacea Compound™, Echinacea/Goldenseal Compound™, Sinus Support Compound™, Ultimate Echinacea™, Andrographis, Isatis, Honeysuckle flower, Elderflower, Lemon Balm, Thyme, Yarrow, Myrrh, Houttuynia, Burdock Seed, Lung Relief Cold/Damp™ or Hot/Damp™
Epstein-Barr Virus (EBV)	Astragalus/Echinacea Compound™, Immune Adapt™ (Compound), Seven Precious Mushrooms™, VX Immune Support™, Isatis, Andrographis
Immune Amphoterics	Adrenal Balance Compound™, American Ginseng, Ashwagandha, Cordyceps, Eleuthero, Daily Adapt™, Holy Basil, Immune Adapt™, Licorice, Maitake, Red Ginseng, Reishi, Schisandra, Seven Precious Mushrooms™

Immunity (decreased) *Surface or secretory immune system* *(i.e., macrophage activity)*	Ultimate Echinacea™, Calendula, Elderberry, Red Clover, Myrrh, Garlic, Yarrow, Marshmallow, Usnea, Astragalus, Thyme, Horehound, Andrographis
Deep immune system *(K, NK, T4, T8 cells)*	Isatis, Poke*, Astragalus Thuja, Ligustrum berry, Shiitake, Cordyceps, Cat's Claw, Lomatium, Andrographis, Chaga, Seven Precious Mushrooms™
Non-Specific immune system *(Adaptogens)*	Daily Adapt™, Licorice, Red Ginseng, Codonopsis, American Ginseng, Licorice, Holy Basil, Rhodiola, Eleuthero, Ashwagandha, Cordyceps, Immune Adapt™
Immune reservoir *(Bone Marrow & Immune Potential)*	Immune Adapt™, Seven Precious Mushrooms™, Licorice, Astragalus, Ligustrum berry, Reishi, Maitake, Cordyceps, Shiitake, Ashwagandha, Adrenal Balance Compound™, Chaga
Infection *Bacterial*	Astragalus/Echinacea Compound™, Echinacea/ Goldenseal Compound™, Phytodent™ (mouth/ gums), Ultimate Echinacea™, UT Compound™ (urinary), Herbal Relief Botanical Throat Spray™ (throat), Elecampane (respiratory), Thyme (respiratory), Garlic, Usnea (respira-tory), Lung Relief Hot/Damp™ (respiratory), Lung Relief Hot/Dry™ (respiratory), Myrrh, Japanese Honeysuckle, Cinnamon, Isatis, Barberry, Oregon Grape Root, Yellow Root, Osha
Viral	Astragalus/Echinacea Compound™, VX Immune Support™, Ultimate Echinacea™, Andrographis, Isatis, Hyssop, Ground Ivy, Thuja, St. John's wort, Holy Basil, Rosemary, Lemon Balm, Thyme, Oregano, Licorice, Osha, Lomatium, Japanese Honeysuckle

Influenza	Astragalus/Echinacea Compound™, Ultimate Echinacea™, Healthy Kid's Compound, Echinacea/Goldenseal Compound™, VX Immune Support™, Yarrow, Isatis, Japanese Honeysuckle, Andrographis, Lomatium, Chrysanthemum, Houttuynia, Elderflower, Ginger
Lupus	Alterative Compound™, Immune Adapt™, Seven Precious Mushrooms™, Chinese Salvia, Huang Qin, Licorice, Immune Balance Compound™, Sarsaparilla, Turmeric, Gotu Kola, Bupleurum, Unprocessed Rehmannia, Reishi, Maitake
Mononucleosis	Astragalus/Echinacea Compound™, Echinacea/ Goldenseal Compound™, Burdock/ Red Root Compound™, Immune Adapt™, Codonopsis
Rheumatoid Arthritis	Alterative Compound™, Immune Adapt™, Seven Precious Mushrooms™, Immune Balance Compound™, Sarsaparilla, Boswellia, Gotu Kola, Reishi, Maitake, Huang Qin, Chinese Salvia, Ashwagandha, Turmeric, Licorice, Gum Guggul, Unprocessed Rehmannia, Feverfew

Liver, see Digestion

Lymphatic System

Cysts	Burdock/Red Root Compound™, Healthy Skin Tonic™, Red Clover, Cleavers, Self Heal. Figwort, Chickweed, Burdock Root, Gotu Kola
Cystic Breast Disease	Burdock/Red Root Compound™, Red Clover, Violet leaf, Poke Root*, Figwort, Self Heal, Chaste Tree, Cleavers
Lymphatic - Congestion	Alterative Compound™, Burdock/Red Root Compound™, Echinacea, Calendula, Violet leaf, Cleavers, Red Clover, Figwort, Self Heal, Horse Chestnut, Sarsaparilla, Gotu Kola, Red Root, Chickweed

Lymphedema		Burdock/Red Root Compound™, Cleavers, Violet leaf, Red Root, Horse Chestnut, Gotu Kola, Figwort

Male Reproductive System

Impotence	*Impaired circulation*	Ginkgo/Horse Chestnut Compound™, Men's Adapt™, Red Ginseng, Epimedium, Rhodiola, Ginkgo
	Low testosterone	Ashwagandha, Cordyceps, Rou Cong Rong, Red Ginseng, Cynomorium, Maca, Epimedium
Infertility		Men's Adapt™, Ashwagandha, Cordyceps, Maca, Red Ginseng, Cynomorium
Prostate	*BPH*	Men's Prostate Tonic™, White Sage, Collinsonia, Agrimony, Saw Palmetto, Nettle root, Horsetail, Hydrangea, Buchu, Schisandra
	Prostatitis (bacterial)	Thuja, Echinacea, Pipsissewa, Buchu, Agrimony, UT Compound™, Oregon Grape Root, Goldenrod, Barberry, Uva Ursi, Yellow Root, Ultimate Echinacea™, Kidney Relief Compound™

Musculo-Skeletal System

Anti-Inflammatory	Fit Adapt™, Muscle/Joint Tonic™, Ginger, Gum Guggul, Blueberry Solid Extract™, Turmeric, Sarsaparilla, Amla, Immune Balance Compound™, Pomegranate-Goji Berry Solid Extract™, Bupleurum, Willow, Yucca, Unprocessed Rehmannia, Chinese Salvia, Cat's Claw, Huang Qin, Gotu Kola, Devil's Claw, Wintergreen, Meadowsweet, Sichuan Teasel
Bone Fractures	OsteoHerb™, HerbCal™, Horsetail, Stinging Nettle leaf, Alfalfa, Processed Rehmannia, Sichuan Teasel, Comfrey leaf (topical use), Amla, Kudzu, Epimedium

Bursitis		Muscle/Joint Tonic™, St. John's wort, Compound Arnica Oil™ (topically), Turmeric, Sarsaparilla, Gotu Kola, Hypericum Oil (topically)
Fibromyalgia		Immune Adapt™, Seven Precious Mushrooms™, Muscle/Joint Tonic™, Kava, Black Cohosh, Ashwagandha, Wood Betony, Compound Arnica Oil™ (topically), Chinese Peony
Neuralgia		Aspirea Compound™, J. Kloss Anti-Spasmodic Compound™, St. John's wort, Yellow Sweetclover, Prickly Ash
Osteoarthritis		Muscle/Joint Tonic™, Alterative Compound™, Burdock/Red Root Compound™, Boswellia, Ginger, Meadowsweet, Devil's Claw, Devil's Club, Guaiac, Gum Guggul, Yucca, Ashwagandha, Turmeric, Sarsaparilla, Willow, Sichuan Teasel, Compound Arnica Oil™ (topically)
Osteoporosis		OsteoHerb™, HerbCal™, Horsetail, Stinging Nettle leaf, Alfalfa, Kudzu, Amla, Processed Rehmannia, Sichuan Teasel, Epimedium
Pain	*General*	Aspirea Compound™, Full Moon - Women's Anti-Spasmodic Compound™, J. Kloss Anti-Spasmodic Compound, Phytocalm™, Meadowsweet, Willow, Valerian, California Poppy, Cyperus, Indian Pipe, Corydalis yanhusuo, Jamaica Dogwood, Horse Chestnut, Yellow Sweet Clover
	Muscular pain	Aspirea Compound™, Black Cohosh, Kava, Wood Betony, Ashwagandha, Compound Arnica Oil™ (topically), Dragon's Dream™ (topically), Chinese Peony, Hypericum Oil (topically)
	Spasmodic pain	J. Kloss Antispasmodic Compound, Respiratory Calmpound™, (lungs or ribs), Full Moon - Womens Antispasmodic Compound™, (uterine pain) Kudzu, Black Haw, Cramp Bark, Jamaica Dogwood, Wild Yam, Skullcap, Cyperus

Sharp stabbing pain	Yellow Sweetclover
Joint pain	Muscle/Joint Tonic™, Compound Arnica Oil™ (topically), Dragon's Dream™ (topically)
Nerve pain	St. John's wort, Yellow Sweetclover, Prickly Ash
Dull throbbing pain	Horse Chestnut, Gotu Kola, Aspirea Compound™
Peripheral Neuropathy	Ginkgo/Horsechestnut Compound™, Blueberry Solid Extract™, St. John's wort, Cinnamon, Ginger, Prickly Ash
Restless Leg Syndrome	Skullcap, Kava, Chinese Peony, Cramp Bark, Black Haw, Ashwagandha, J. Kloss Antispasmodic Compound, Chinese Peony
Sciatica	Aspirea Compound™, St. John's wort, Yellow Sweetclover, Compound Arnica Oil™ (topically), Prickly Ash, Horse Chestnut, Sichuan Teasel
Rheumatoid Arthritis	Alterative Compound™, Immune Adapt™, Seven Precious Mushrooms™, Immune Balance Compound™, Sarsaparilla, Boswellia, Gotu Kola, Reishi, Maitake, Huang Qin, Chinese Salvia, Ashwagandha, Turmeric, Licorice, Gum Guggul, Unprocessed Rehmannia, Feverfew
Spasm, muscular	Aspirea Compound™, Full Moon - Women's Anti-Spasmodic Compound™, J. Kloss Anti-Spasmodic Compound, Kudzu, Black Cohosh, Skullcap, Cramp Bark, Cyperus, Chinese Peony, Black Haw, Kava, Lobelia
TMJ pain	Aspirea Compound™, Jamaica Dogwood, St. John's wort, Blue Vervain,

Nervous System

Alzheimer's disease (to slow the progression)	Clarity Compound™, Ginkgo/Horsechestnut Compound™, Healthy Heart Compound™, Holy Basil, Rosemary, Eleuthero, Bacopa, Chinese Polygala, Chinese Peony, Lavender, Gotu Kola, Turmeric

33

Anxiety		Tension Relief™, Phytocalm™, Serenity Compound™, Blue Vervain, Motherwort, Kava, Chamomile, Fresh Oat, Chinese Polygala, Bacopa, Linden flower, Pulsatilla*, Skullcap, Women's Calmpound™
Attention Deficit Hyperactivity Disorder (ADHD)		Focus Formula™, Hawthorn, Ginkgo, Lemon Balm, Holy Basil, Fresh Oat, Gotu Kola, Eleuthero, Linden flower, Bacopa, Skullcap, Chamomile, Hawthorn Solid Extract™
Circulation, Cerebral (*impaired*)		Clarity Compound™, Focus Formula™, Holy Basil, Blueberry Solid Extract™, Gotu Kola, Bacopa, Rosemary, Sage, Ginkgo, Lemon Balm, Lavender
Depression (mild to moderate)	*General*	Emotional Relief™, Clarity Compound™, St. John's wort, Rhodiola, Mimosa, Lemon Balm
	Hormonal	Emotional Relief™, Women's Adapt™, Black Cohosh, Night Blooming Cereus, Pulsatilla*
	Stagnant depression *(chronic situational depression)*	Lavender, Damiana, Rosemary, Grief Relief™. Rose Petal, Rhodiola, Holy Basil, Mimosa
Seasonal affective disorder (SAD)		St. John's wort with Lemon Balm, Holy Basil
	GI or hepatic depression	Rosemary, St. John's wort, Culver's Root, Evening Primrose herb, Wormwood
	Old-age depression	Night-Blooming Cereus, Damiana, Ginkgo
Fatigue (Mental)		Clarity Compound™, Focus Formula™, Immune Adapt™, Daily Adapt™, Rosemary, Holy Basil, Gotu Kola, Fresh Oat, Lavender, Bacopa
Headaches	*Vasodilative*	Aspirea Compound™, Serenity Compound™, Women's Calmpound™, Feverfew, Chrysanthemum
	Vasoconstrictive	Clarity Compound™, Ginkgo, Rosemary, Holy Basil, Lavender

	Spasmodic	J. Kloss Anti-Spasmodic Compound, Phytocalm™, Skullcap, Ligusticum root, Yellow Sweet Clover, Kudzu, Chinese Peony
	Migraines	Chinese Peony root, Feverfew, Kudzu, Jamaica Dogwood
	Stress-induced	Phytocalm™, Aspirea Compound™, Wild Lettuce, Passionflower, Chamomile, Linden flower, Skullcap, Motherwort, Blue Vervain, Kava, Lemon Balm, Wood Betony
	Menstrual	Cyperus, Motherwort, Blue Vervain
Hyperactivity (ADHD)		Focus Formula™, Kid's Calmpound Glycerite™, Phytocalm™, Serenity Compound™, Skullcap, Hawthorn, Bacopa, Ashwagandha, Fresh Oat, Chamomile, Hawthorn Solid Extract™
Insomnia	*General*	Phytocalm™, Serenity Compound™, Chrysanthemum, Valerian, Hops, Chamomile, Wild Lettuce, Chinese Salvia, Passionflower
	Difficulty falling asleep (long sleep latency)	California Poppy, Lavender, Lemon Balm, Passionflower
	Menopausal insomnia	Motherwort, Passionflower, Hops
	Caused by circular thinking	Passionflower
	Caused by pain	Cyperus, Corydalis yanhusuo, Indian Pipe, Aspirea Compound™, Jamaica Dogwood, Willow
Memory (impaired)		Clarity Compound™, Holy Basil, Bacopa, Rosemary, Lemon Balm, Ginkgo, Gotu Kola, Chinese Peony
Restlessness		Phytocalm™, Focus Formula™, Serenity Compound™, Kid's Tummy Relief™, Motherwort, Passionflower, Chamomile, Fresh Oat, Skullcap, Linden flower, Lemon Balm

Smoking Cessation *(withdrawal symptoms)*	Smoker's ResQ™, Licorice, Lobelia, Fresh Oat, Plantain
Stress (to relieve)	Daily Adapt™, Immune Adapt™, Clarity Compound™, Kid's Tummy Relief™, Cardio Calmpound™, Phytocalm™, Serenity Compound™, Seven Precious Mushrooms™, Fresh Oat, Lemon Balm, Lavender, Skullcap, Hawthorn, Ashwagandha, Reishi, Hops

Respiratory System

Allergy, Respiratory	Sinus Support Compound™, Immune Adapt™ , Respiratory Calmpound™, Seven Precious Mushrooms™, Kudzu, Ginkgo, Schisandra, Horseradish, Blueberry Solid Extract™, Eyebright, Osha, Amla
Asthma	Respiratory Calmpound™, Khella, Lobelia, Unprocessed Rehmannia, Thyme, Ginkgo, Schisandra, Grindelia, Lung Relief™ Anti-spasmodic™, Cordyceps, Licorice, Reishi, Passionflower, J. Kloss Antispasmodic Compound
Bronchitis	Astragalus/Echinacea Compound™, Echinacea/ Goldenseal Compound™, Lung Relief™ Hot/ Dry, Lung Relief™ Hot/Damp, Thyme, Pleurisy Root, Usnea, Ground Ivy, Thuja, Propolis, Garlic, Elecampane, Isatis, Myrrh, Platycodon
Coughs *General*	Respiratory Calmpound™, J. Kloss Anti-Spasmodic Compound, Mullein leaf, Horehound
Hot/Dry *(little or no mucus, yellow or* *green in color, fever)*	Lung Relief Hot/Dry™, Marshmallow, Horehound, Elecampane, Slippery Elm (tea only) Mullein, Platycodon, Solomon's Seal
Hot/Damp *(excessive mucus, yellow or green* *in color, fever)*	Lung Relief Hot/Damp™, Usnea, Horehound, Ground Ivy, Elecampane, Houttuynia, Mullein, Sage, Huang Qin, Isatis, Japanese Honeysuckle
Cold/Dry *(little or no mucus, clear* *or white in color, no fever)*	Lung Relief Cold/Dry™, Solomon's Seal, Prince Seng, Licorice, Chinese Asparagus, Shatavari, Red Clover, Spikenard, Angelica, Platycodon

	Cold/Damp *(excessive mucus, clear or white in color, little or no fever)*	Osha, Thyme, Yerba Santa, Grindelia, Cinnamon, Lomatium, Ginger, Horseradish, Thuja, Garlic, Orange Peel, Lung Relief Cold/Damp™, Cardamom
	Spasmodic	Lung Relief Antispasmodic™, Wild Cherry bark, J. Kloss Anti-Spasmodic Compound, Skunk Cabbage*, Licorice, Lobelia, Wild Lettuce, Khella, Ashwagandha, California Poppy, Pleurisy Root, Jamaica Dogwood, Passionflower
Pneumonia		Astragalus/Echinacea Compound™, Ultimate Echinacea™, Thyme, Elecampane, Pleurisy Root, Grindelia, Ground Ivy, Garlic, Usnea, Japanese Honeysuckle, Lung Relief™ (depending on the energetics of the pneumonia), Huang Qin, Isatis
Spasm, bronchial		Respiratory Calmpound™, J Kloss Anti-Spasmodic Compound, Wild Lettuce, Wild Cherry bark, Sundew, Khella, Lung Relief Antispasmodic™, Pleurisy Root, Ashwagandha, California Poppy, Horse Chestnut, Passionflower

Skin

Acne	*General*	Burdock/Red Root Compound™, Healthy Skin Tonic™, Figwort, Yellow Dock
	Hormonal	Chaste Tree, Saw Palmetto
	Deep cystic	Saw Palmetto, Chaste Tree, Oregon Grape Root, Sarsaparilla, Figwort, Butternut bark, Calendula
	Rosacea	Red Alder Bark (internally & topically), Oregon Grape Root (internally & topically), Isatis, Sarsaparilla, Gotu Kola
	Comedones (Large red pimples on the back, neck or buttocks)	Oregon Grape Root, Red Alder Bark, Isatis, Figwort

Athlete's Foot	AF Compound™ (topically), Black Walnut, Yellow Root
Insect bites (topical applications)	Ultimate Echinacea™, Plantain, St. John's wort/ Sage Ointment™, Comfrey/Calendula Ointment™
Jock Itch	AF Compound™ (diluted for topical use), Yellow Root
Ringworm (all topically)	AF Compound™, Back Walnut hull (diluted for topical use), Usnea
Shingles	St. John's wort (topically & internally), Licorice (topically), Lemon Balm (topically), Aspirea Compound™ (for pain), Hypericum Oil (topically), Self Heal (topically), Hyssop
Skin conditions *General*	Burdock/Red Root Compound™, Healthy Skin Tonic™
Hot, red, inflamed	Sarsaparilla, Gotu Kola, Figwort, Turmeric, Isatis, Honeysuckle
Dry, itchy, crusty or scaly	Burdock seed, Milk Thistle, Cleavers
Damp, oozing	Yellow Dock, Red Alder bark, Elderflower
Skin like paper (tears easily)	Stinging Nettle leaf, Horsetail
Greasy Skin	Butternut bark, Oregon Grape Root
Itchy Skin	Ligusticum root, Siler root, Burdock seed, Comfrey/Calendula Ointment™ (topically)

Urinary System

Bed Wetting (due to irritation)	Agrimony, St. John's wort, Marshmallow
Cystitis	UT Compound™, Astragalus/Echinacea Compound™, Echinacea/Goldenseal Compound™, Cleavers, Corn Silk, Pipsissewa, Stinging Nettle leaf, Agrimony, Horsetail, Oregon Grape Root, Shepherd's Purse, Buchu, Goldenrod, Isatis, Huang Qin, Japanese Honeysuckle

Gout (to increase uric acid excretion)	Kidney Relief Compound™, Celery Seed, Parsley, Pipsissewa, Pellitory-of-the-Wall, Corn Silk, Buchu, Spilanthes, Stinging Nettle leaf
Edema	Dandelion leaf, Hawthorn, Stinging Nettle leaf, Parsley, Kidney Relief Compound™, Green Tea, Poria, Goldenrod, Juniper berry, Celery seed
Impaired Kidney Function	Kidney Support Compound™, Stinging Nettle seed, Cordyceps, Processed Rehmannia, Pellitory-of-the-Wall, Stinging Nettle leaf, Chinese Salvia, Astragalus, Kidney Relief Compound™
Interstitial Cystitis	UT Compound™, Saw Palmetto, Corn Silk, Marshmallow, Kava (pain), Plantain, Agrimony, Chickweed, Eryngo, Hydrangea (for pain), Shatavari, Cleavers
Urethritis	UT Compound™, Echinacea/Goldenseal Compound™, Uva-Ursi, Buchu, Oregon Grape Root, Pipsissewa, Barberry, Yellow Root, Isatis, Huang Qin, Japanese Honeysuckle
Urinary Pain	Kava, Hydrangea, Khella
Urinary Tract Infection	UT Compound™, Echinacea/Goldenseal Compound™, , Pipsissewa, Uva-ursi, Buchu, Horsetail, Corn Silk, Oregon Grape Root, Shepherd's Purse, Yarrow, Isatis, Huang Qin, Japanese Honeysuckle, Barberry, Yellow Root,

DAVID WINSTON'S THERAPEUTIC FORMULAS
DERIVED FROM OVER 40 YEARS
IN CLINICAL PRACTICE
KEY TO ABBREVIATIONS
BID = two times per day
TID = three times per day
QID = four times per day
* = Use only with a practitioner's guidance

ADRENAL BALANCE COMPOUND™

CONTAINS: Hydroalcoholic extracts of Eleuthero root (Eleutherococcus senticosus), Schisandra fruit (Schisandra chinensis), fresh Oat milky seed (Avena sativa), Holy Basil herb (Ocimum tenuiflorum), Devil's Club root bark (Oplopanax horridus), Sarsaparilla root (Smilax regelii) and vegetable glycerin.

INDICATIONS: This formula strengthens the adrenal glands and helps to restore normal endocrine function. It is most effective for chronic adrenal stress or exhaustion (fatigue, dark circles under the eyes), depressed HPA Axis function, fibromyalgia, chronic fatigue syndrome and for insulin resistance/metabolic syndrome. I frequently use this formula for people with mildly elevated blood sugar and excessive cortisol levels.

ACTIVITY: Eleuthero, Schisandra, and Holy Basil are adaptogens which normalize the body's stress response and strengthen the endocrine, immune and nervous systems. Holy Basil as well as Devil's Club have hypoglycemic activity and helps inhibit insulin resistance. Oat is a cerebral tonic and nervine that reduces stress and anxiety. Sarsaparilla and Devil's Club are anti-inflammatory agents that reduce muscle pain (fibromyalgia) and inhibit pro-inflammatory prostaglandins and cytokines.

CONTRAINDICATIONS: None.

SUGGESTED USE: 40-60 drops (2-3 ml) TID. Long-term use (4-6 months) is indicated, especially for chronic conditions.

ADDITIONAL RECOMMENDATIONS: Adequate sleep, exercise and stress reduction techniques such as meditation, deep breathing exercises, Tai Chi or biofeedback can be beneficial. Eliminating simple carbohydrates and excess caffeine are also useful.

ADDITIONAL USEFUL HERBS: Adaptogens such as Rhodiola, Licorice, Red Ginseng, American Ginseng, Cordyceps, Codonopsis, Reishi or Ashwagandha may be indicated. Other beneficial nervines include St. John's wort, Linden flower, Skullcap, Wood Betony and Chamomile.

AF COMPOUND™

CONTAINS: Hydroalcoholic extracts of fresh Black Walnut hull (Juglans nigra), Yellow Root (Xanthorrhiza simplicissima), fresh Spilanthes herb (Spilanthes spp.), Usnea (Usnea barbata), Myrrh (Commiphora molmol), Cardamom seed (Elettaria cardamomum) and vegetable glycerin.

INDICATIONS: This formula is used as a systemic anti-fungal for chronic or acute candidiasis including thrush or vaginal candidiasis. It can also be applied topically in diluted form for athlete's foot, ringworm and jock itch.

ACTIVITY: The herbs in this formula have broad spectrum anti-fungal activity. The fresh green hulls of Black Walnut have long been used for topical and internal fungal and yeast infections. Yellow Root contains the alkaloid berberine which is active against yeasts, fungi and bacteria. The lichen Usnea contains usnic acid which has shown activity against various fungal strains including those that cause ringworm and athlete's foot. Spilanthes and Cardamom are also rich in phytochemicals that inhibit yeasts and fungi.

CONTRAINDICATIONS: Not to be used internally during pregnancy or lactation. Discontinue topical use if skin irritation develops, and avoid contact with sensitive mucous membrane tissue.

SUGGESTED USE: 30-40 drops (1.5-2 ml) TID while symptoms persist.

ADDITIONAL RECOMMENDATIONS: Add fresh garlic to the diet. Avoid sugars and refined carbohydrates.

ADDITIONAL USEFUL HERBS: For topical fungal infections a combination of Lavender and Tea Tree essential oil can be useful.

ALTERATIVE COMPOUND™

CONTAINS: Hydroalcoholic extracts of aged Buckthorn bark (Frangula alnus), Burdock root (Arctium lappa), Red Clover blossoms (Trifolium pratense), Bladderwrack seaweed (Fucus vesiculosus), Licorice root (Glycyrrhiza glabra), Oregon Grape root (Mahonia nervosa), fresh Poke root (Phytolacca americana), Turmeric rhizome (Curcuma longa), Prickly Ash bark (Zanthoxylum clavaherculis) and Quassia wood (Picraena excelsa).

INDICATIONS: This is a classic alterative formula used to enhance normal elimination via the major eliminatory organs (liver, kidneys, bowel, skin, lymph, lungs). This compound is based on the Hoxsey formula and Parke Davis' Trifolium Compound which were primarily used for treating cancer and other degenerative diseases. It is indicated as one part of a holistic approach for cancer treatment as well as for other chronic degenerative diseases such as autoimmune diseases, arthritis, chronic skin conditions and obesity.

ACTIVITY: Red Clover and Licorice contain isoflavones including genistein, daidzein, biochanin A, and formonenetin which have been shown to help prevent metastases of tumor cells and inhibit hormonally sensitive cancers. Licorice is also a possible adaptogen, an immune amphoteric and it prevents the stronger herbs from irritating the GI tract. Burdock root contains lignans which have active antimutagenic and antitumor activity. Phytolacca has a long tradition of use as a powerful alterative, increasing elimination via the lymph, liver and bowel. It also contains compounds which have cytotoxic, antiviral and antitumor activity. Bladderwrack, Prickly Ash and Oregon Grape root contain active antiviral, antifungal, and antibacterial compounds. The alkaloid berberine found in Oregon Grape root also stimulates the immune system and has been shown in in vitro studies to inhibit cancer metastasis, promote apoptosis and down-regulate pro-cancer cell signaling pathways such as MMP-9, COX-2, prostaglandin E_2 +

E_3, MAPK and VEGF. Turmeric and Buckthorn enhance bowel and liver function and have compounds that have been found in laboratory studies to have antileukemic and cytotoxic effects. Bladderwrack is a rich source of minerals especially potassium iodide, long used to enhance thyroid function and prevent radioactive iodine-induced thyroid cancer. This seaweed is also a good source of the essential nutrient iodine. In low doses it has been shown to inhibit tumor growth (Aleksander, et al., 1991) and thyroid nodules. In India regular consumption of turmeric is linked to reduced systemic and cerebral inflammation, lower levels of cancer (bowel, stomach, lung and liver) and better liver health. Turmeric has been shown to down-regulate over 70 pre-cancer signaling molecules, while enhancing immune response, reducing serum glucose levels and inhibiting Reactive Oxygen Species (ROS).

CONTRAINDICATIONS: Pregnancy, lactation, hyperthyroidism.

NOTICE: This formula contains Buckthorn. Do not use if you have or develop diarrhea, loose stools, or abdominal pain because Buckthorn may worsen these conditions and be harmful to your health. Consult your physician if you have frequent diarrhea or are taking medication, or have a medical condition.

SUGGESTED USE: 20-30 drops (1-1.5 ml) BID/TID as part of a long-term treatment protocol.

ADDITIONAL RECOMMENDATIONS: Dietary supplementation of mixed carotenoids, vitamins C, E and K may be useful. Green Tea, Brassica family vegetables such as broccoli, kale, watercress or cauliflower, and Allium family vegetables such as garlic, scallions and onions are healthy dietary additions.

ADDITIONAL USEFUL HERBS: Immune Adapt™, Red Clover, Maitake, Shiitake, Chaga, Eli Jones' Compound Syrup of Scrophularia, Scudder's Alterative, Turmeric and Milk Thistle have all been used to treat cancer and other chronic degenerative illnesses.

AP COMPOUND™

CONTAINS: Hydroalcoholic extracts of Black Walnut hulls (Juglans nigra), fresh Elecampane root (Inula helenium), Long Pepper (Piper longum), Quassia wood (Picraena excelsa), fresh Sweet Annie herb (Artemisia annua), and vegetable glycerin.

INDICATIONS: This formula is useful for a variety of intestinal parasites. It is effective for amoebic or protozoal infections caused by Blastocystis hominis, Crytosporidium, Dientamoeba fragilis, Giardia or Entamoeba histolytica. Use it with Gentlelax™ formula for nematodes such as pinworms or roundworms.

ACTIVITY: Research conducted on Sweet Annie in China and at the Walter Reed Army Research Institute in Washington, DC, has shown it to be useful in treating amoebas as well as malaria. The intensely bitter Quassia has been successfully used throughout Central America for treating amoebas, flagella and protozoal infections. Elecampane contains three effective anti-amoebic compounds: alantolactone, isoalantolactone and helinin which shows activity at 1 part in 500,000 against amoebas. The fresh green hulls of Black Walnut have a long history of use by Native Peoples, the Thompsonians, Physiomedicalists, and

Eclectics for treating a variety of intestinal parasites and Long Pepper has been found to inhibit several types of amoebic infections including giardia (Triphathi, et al., 1999). This formula can also be used to treat SIBO (Small Intestine Bacterial Overgrowth).

CONTRAINDICATIONS: Do not use during pregnancy or lactation. Long pepper may increase blood levels of other herbs and medications. Consult your physician if you are taking other medications.

SUGGESTED USE: 30-40 drops (1.5-2 ml) TID while the condition persists.

ADDITIONAL RECOMMENDATIONS: Include fresh garlic and bitters in the diet.

ADDITIONAL USEFUL HERBS: Andrographis or Neem may also be helpful, especially if treating SIBO. If nausea occurs, use AP Compound™ with carminative herbs or Carminative Compound™.

ASPIREA COMPOUND™

CONTAINS: Hydroalcoholic extracts of Meadowsweet herb (Filipendula ulmaria), St. John's wort flowering tops (Hypericum perforatum), Willow bark (Salix spp.), Corydalis yanhusuo root (Corydalis yanhusuo), fresh Indian Pipe whole plant (Monotropa uniflora), Jamaica Dogwood bark (Piscidia piscipula) and vegetable glycerin.

INDICATIONS: This formula is used as an herbal analgesic (painkiller). It combines anti-inflammatory herbs such as Willow, Meadowsweet and St. John's wort with two powerful antispasmodic/analgesic herbs, Jamaica Dogwood and Corydalis. It also has Indian Pipe which is an antinociceptive, an herb which raises the pain threshold. It is indicated as a general pain reliever useful for conditions such as headaches, menstrual cramps, neuralgia, sciatica, bursitis, arthritic and muscular pain.

ACTIVITY: The aspirin-like compounds methyl salicylate found in Meadowsweet and salacin in Willow act as gentle pain relievers and anti-inflammatories without the G. I. tract irritation that aspirin can cause. St. John's wort is an anti-inflammatory agent especially for nerve pain including sciatica. It also acts as a mood elevator. Jamaica Dogwood is a strong antispasmodic and analgesic especially useful for dysmenorrhea, facial nerve pain and muscle spasms. Corydalis is used in TCM for treating headaches, menstrual or abdominal pain, pain-induced insomnia, torticollis and back pain. Indian Pipe is an antinociceptive which means it increases a persons pain threshold making them less sensitive to pain.

CONTRAINDICATIONS: Do not use this product while taking any prescription drugs without the advice of your prescribing physician. Avoid excessive exposure to UV irradiation (e.g. sunlight, tanning) when using this product. Use cautiously during pregnancy.

SUGGESTED USE: 20-40 drops (1-2 ml) TID as needed.

ADDITIONAL RECOMMENDATIONS: Anti-inflammatory herbs such as Turmeric, Sarsaparilla, Devil's Claw, Muscle/Joint Tonic™ and antispasmodics like Roman Chamomile, J. Kloss Anti-Spasmodic Compound, or Cyperus root may offer additional benefits.

ASTRAGALUS/ECHINACEA COMPOUND™

CONTAINS: Hydroalcoholic extracts of fresh Echinacea root and flower (Echinacea purpurea), Andrographis herb (Andrographis paniculata), Astragalus root (Astragalus membranaceus), Eleuthero root (Eleutherococcus senticosus), Echinacea flower (Echinacea purpurea), Oregon Grape Root (Mahonia nervosa) and Myrrh gum (Commiphora molmol).

INDICATIONS: This formula is indicated for enhancing immune function and treating viral or bacterial diseases, such as colds, influenza, mononucleosis, bronchitis, pneumonia, cystitis, Epstein-Barr virus, sore throat, as well as promoting immune competence in people who frequently get sick. This formula can be taken in small amounts to potentiate immune activity or larger amounts when dealing with acute viral or bacterial illness.

ACTIVITY: This formula is designed to increase the secretory immune system (macrophage activity) as well as stimulate deep immune activity (T-cells, K and NK cells, Interferon, Interleukins). It also strengthens the "immune reservoir" (a concept I developed to describe the body's ability to mount an immune response) creating a greater immune potential. Echinacea root and flower, as well as Andrographis stimulate macrophage activity and have a long history of use for treating colds, influenza and sore throats. Oregon Grape Root and Myrrh have antibacterial, anti-inflammatory and antiviral activity. Astragalus enhances immune response as does Eleuthero, which is also an adaptogen which promotes endocrine function.

CONTRAINDICATIONS: Use with caution during pregnancy.

SUGGESTED USE: 40-60 drops (2-3 ml) TID/QID while symptoms persist.

ADDITIONAL RECOMMENDATIONS: Humidifiers (cleaned regularly) help to reduce respiratory infections as does regular handwashing and tongue brushing. Increase intake of vitamin C and D, mixed carotenoids and zinc to stimulate the immune system and help prevent infection.

ADDITIONAL HERBS: Reishi, Echinacea/Goldenseal Compound™, Ultimate Echinacea Compound™, Maitake, Cat's Claw and Garlic may offer additional benefits. Add Elecampane or the appropriate Lung Relief™ formula for respiratory infections.

BITTER ROOTS™

CONTAINS: Hydroalcoholic extracts of fresh Burdock Root (Arctium lappa), Dandelion root (Taraxacum officinale), Gentian root (Gentiana lutea), Turmeric rhizome (Curcuma longa), Yellow Dock root (Rumex crispus), Elecampane root (Inula helenium)

INDICATIONS: This formula stimulates the entire process of digestion, absorption and elimination by increasing production of gastric hydrochloric acid as well as liver, pancreatic and small intestine digestive enzymes and juices. By stimulating bile production this formula also enhances fat metabolism and acts as a natural aperient/ laxative. Indications include achlorhydria/hypochlorhydria, malabsorption, chronic gas, belching, indigestion and abdominal bloating. Bitter Roots™ is a useful adjunct for any protocol addressing GI dysbiosis or food sensitivities caused by leaky gut

syndrome. Many chronic conditions such as arthritis, auto-immune disorders, skin conditions, etc. will benefit from enhancing digestive and liver/gallbladder function.
ACTIVITY: This "earthy" bitters formula is comprised of the bitter roots of herbs traditionally used to enhance digestion, absorption and elimination. It combines cooling bitters such as Dandelion root, Gentian and Yellow Dock, with warming bitters such as the aromatic Elecampane and Turmeric. This creates a bitter formula that can be used everyday to not only promote digestion, but also enhance liver and gallbladder function. Turmeric, Dandelion root and Yellow Dock offer hepatoprotective activity and act as choleretics/cholagogues, thus impoving bile secretion and bile excretion. Herbs such as Burdock Root, Dandelion root and Elecampane are rich sources of inulin (fructo-oligsaccharides/FOS) which also enhance the growth of healthy bowel flora. This formula may also mildly lower blood sugar levels, calm rebellious Qi (GERD), improve bowel function, and reduce systemic inflammation.
CONTRAINDICATIONS: Do not use if you have hyperchlorhydria. Use cautiously if you have gastric ulcers or gastritis.
SUGGESTED USE: 15-30 drops (.75-1.5 ml) taken 10-15 minutes before meals. Shake well before using.
Sprayer suggested use: 1-2 sprays on the tongue 10-15 minutes before meals. Shake well before using.
ADDITIONAL RECOMMENDATIONS: Eat slowly, chew thoroughly and eat simple meals. Avoid drinking large amounts of cold liquids with meals. Relax at meals; do not eat while standing up, watching TV or when you are upset.
ADDITIONAL USEFUL HERBS: For flatulence add Fennel, Ginger, Lavender or Carminative Compound™. Plant enzymes or Papaya tablets may help improve protein digestion.

BURDOCK/RED ROOT COMPOUND™

CONTAINS: Hydroalcoholic extracts of Burdock root (Arctium lappa), fresh Echinacea root (Echinacea purpurea), Figwort herb (Scrophularia nodosa), Red Clover blossoms (Trifolium pratense), fresh Red Root (Ceanothus americanus), fresh Violet herb (Viola sororia), and vegetable glycerin.
INDICATIONS: This is an alterative formula, alteratives are used to gently enhance normal elimination via the major eliminatory organs (liver, kidneys, bowel, skin, lymph, lungs). It is indicated for lymphatic stagnation, lymphedema, acne, recurrent boils, poor resistance to infections, fluid-filled cysts or lipomas, cystic breast disease, arthritis, mononucleosis, and chronic infections such as Epstein-Barr virus, or Cytomegalovirus (CMV).
ACTIVITY: This formula thins the lymphatic fluid, allowing it to flow more easily thus facilitating elimination via the lymphatic system. Burdock, Figwort, Violet and Red Clover have long histories of use for cysts, tumors, enlarged lymph nodes, arthralgias, cystic breast disease and chronic skin conditions. Red Root is a traditional remedy for detoxifying the lymphatic system, mildly thinning the blood and promoting the immune function of the spleen. Echinacea enhances lymphatic and immune function. Violet acts as a mild laxative and Burdock root is a rich source of inulin which acts as a prebiotic. Burdock and Figwort also mildly promote liver

and kidney function.

SUGGESTED USE: Long term use is recommended. For chronic situations use 30-40 drops (1.5-2 ml) TID, for acute cases 60-80 drops (3-4 ml) TID.

ADDITIONAL RECOMMENDATIONS: Regular exercise, massage, saunas, dry skin brushing and hydrotherapy may also be helpful for promoting lymphatic circulation. Eliminating dairy products from the diet can also relieve lymphatic stagnation.

ADDITIONAL USEFUL HERBS: Cleavers, Calendula, Chickweed, Self Heal and Horse Chestnut can all be useful for promoting lymphatic drainage. This formula is part of David Winston's rejuvinative cleanse protocol and is used with Gentlelax™, Thistles Compound™ and Healthy Skin Tonic™ to create a well rounded and effective protocol to enhance elimination of metabolic wastes.

CALM ADAPT™

CONTAINS: Hydroalcoholic extracts of Ashwagandha root (Withania somnifera), Linden flower and leaf (Tilia sp.), Oat milky seed (Avena sativa), Reishi mushroom and mycelium (Ganoderma spp.), and Schisandra berry (Schisandra chinensis).

INDICATIONS: This formula is appropriate for high-strung people who cannot seem to relax. It helps provide a serene, calm mindset; reducing anxiety, agitation, irritability, nervousness and anger. At the same time it improves sleep quality and mental focus, and reduces inflammation, stress and headaches.

ACTIVITY: This unique formula combines calming adaptogens (Ashwagandha, Reishi, Schisandra) with nervines (Oat and Linden flower). Ashwagandha is an adaptogen, anti-inflammatory, anxiolytic, immune amphoteric and mild analgesic. Clinically I use it for treating fibromyalgia, anxiety, arthritic pain, excess insomnia, perfomance anxiety, hypothyroidism and nervous exhaustion. Reishi is used in Chinese medicine to "calm the shen". It is a mild adaptogen, nervine, immune amphoteric, cardiotonic and anit-inflammatory agent. It is used for anxiety, bad dreams, isominia and stress-industed hypertension. Schisandra is unique in that it is calming, yet gives a person a clear, focused mind. It was traditionally used in Eastern monastories before prayer. It also has anti-inflammatory, hepatoprotective, anti-asthmatic and and immune balancing effects. Fresh Oat and Linden flower are two of my favorite nervines. There are herbs that help to re-establish a healthy emotional foundation relieving cravings, irritability, anxiety, emotional overreations and agitation.

CONTRAINDICATIONS: Do not take if you have mushroom allergies.

SUGGESTED USE: 60-80 drops (3-4 ml) in juice or water. Take 2-3 times per day. Shake well before using..

ADDITIONAL RECOMMENDATIONS: Get adequate sleep, learn relaxation techniques (mindful meditation, yoga, tai qi, qi gong), avoid the use of stimulates.

ADDITIONAL USEFUL HERBS: Other nervine herbs such as Skullcap, Passionflower, Chamomile, Motherwort, Blue Vervain, Hawthorn, Catnip, may be useful.

CARDIO CALMPOUND™

CONTAINS: Hydroalcoholic extracts of Olive leaf (Olea europea), Hawthorn fruit, leaf and flower (Crataegus spp.), Linden flower (Tilia sp.), fresh Motherwort herb (Leonurus cardiaca), European Mistletoe herb (Viscum album) and vegetable glycerin.

INDICATIONS: This formula is designed to help alleviate mild to moderate hypertension. In addition it helps promote cardiovascular health and helps to relieve emotional stress.

ACTIVITY: Linden, Hawthorn and Motherwort have long been used in Europe as nervines, mild hypotensive agents and cardiac tonics. They are beneficial for treating "white coat" or stress-induced hypertension as well as mildly elevated blood pressure. Olive leaf contains Oleuropein which acts as a spasmolytic on the smooth musculature and a hypotensive agent for labile or mild to moderate hypertension. (Susalit, et al., 2011, Perrinjaquet-Moccetti, et al., 2008) Olive leaf also decreased LDL cholesterol levels and reduced oxidative stress. European Mistletoe is used to gradually reduce blood pressure and the unpleasant symptoms associated with hypertension, especially headaches, dizziness, fatigue and irritability.

CONTRAINDICATIONS: Pregnancy. Do not use with prescription blood pressure lowering medication (ACE Inhibitors, Beta-blockers or Calcium channel blockers).

SUGGESTED USE: 30-60 drops (1.5-3 ml) TID.

ADDITIONAL RECOMMENDATIONS: Hypertension is associated with obesity, metabolic syndrome, diabetes, chronic stress, overuse of stimulants (coffee, tea, ephedra), excessive sodium consumption, cigarette smoking, as well as lack of exercise and a familial history of cardiovascular disease. Quitting smoking, reducing sodium intake and consumption of refined carbohydrates, as well as weight loss can be very beneficial. A healthy diet low in saturated fats and refined carbohydrates and rich in soluble fiber, whole grains, legumes, dark green leafy vegetables, olive oil and cocoa is very helpful. Supplementing calcium, magnesium, potassium, Co-Q10 and omega 3 fatty acids (fish oil) can also help reduce blood pressure. Stress reduction techniques such as meditation, yoga and deep breathing exercises are also beneficial.

ADDITIONAL USEFUL HERBS: Garlic as a fresh herb or in pill form is mildly useful for lowering blood pressure, as are Du Zhong (Eucommia) tea, Cramp Bark, Chrysanthemum flower or Lemon Balm. Dandelion leaf, Stinging Nettle leaf and Parsley are aquaretics (potassium-sparing diuretics) which can also be effective as a symptomatic treatment for hypertension.

CARMINATIVE COMPOUND™

CONTAINS: Hydroalcoholic extracts of fresh Wild Yam root (Dioscorea villosa), Fennel seed (Foeniculum vulgare), fresh Peppermint herb (Mentha x piperita), fresh Chamomile flowers (Matricaria recutita) and Ginger root (Zingiber officinale).

INDICATIONS: This carminative formula relieves symptoms of nausea caused by upset stomach, motion sickness, morning sickness and diarrhea. Carminative Compound™ is also useful for colic, biliousness, borborygmus and flatulence. Taken with bitters and antispasmodics it may also be helpful in treating hiatal hernia. Other indications include menstrual nausea, GI dysbiosis, nausea associated with intestinal viruses, and hepatic colic.

ACTIVITY: Wild Yam is an effective herb for intestinal spasms and the resultant nausea. It is also effective for treating gallbladder spasms, hepatic colic and IBS. Peppermint and Ginger calm the mesenteric brain in the gut which reduces nausea, gas and borborygmus. Ginger is a powerful anti-emetic, anti-inflammatory, and antibacterial agent, used to treat chemotherapy or anesthesia-induced nausea. Fennel is rich in essential oils which relax the intestines and reduce gas production. Chamomile also relaxes the bowel, acts as a GI Tract anti-inflammatory, relieves nausea and inhibits Campylobactor jejuni, one of the most common causes of diarrhea.

CONTRAINDICATIONS: Use in small amounts during pregnancy.

SUGGESTED USE: 40-60 drops (2-3 ml) TID/QID while symptoms persist.

ADDITIONAL RECOMMENDATIONS: For morning sickness the use of B Complex vitamins, especially B6 or Ume Plum candy can improve symptoms.

ADDITIONAL USEFUL HERBS: Ginger tea, Black Horehound, and Artichoke leaf are all anti-emetics.

CLARITY COMPOUND™

CONTAINS: Hydroalcoholic extracts of Gotu Kola herb (Centella asiatica), Chinese Schisandra berry (Schisandra chinensis), Ginkgo leaf (Ginkgo biloba), Bacopa herb (Bacopa monnieri), Lemon Balm herb (Melissa officinalis), Rosemary herb (Rosmarinus officinale) and vegetable glycerin.

INDICATIONS: This formula combines Eastern and Western herbs long used as nootropics or tonics for the mind and memory. These herbs increase circulation to the brain, act as mild stimulants (without caffeine) and have antidepressant and anxiolytic effects. Specific indications include mild depression, premature senility, early stage Alzheimer's disease, mental fatigue, poor memory, anxiety, vasoconstrictive headaches and what in Traditional Chinese Medicine are known as deficient liver/kidney patterns with symptoms such as dizziness or tinnitus.

ACTIVITY: Gotu Kola and Bacopa has long been used in Ayurvedic medicine for enhancing clarity of thought. Both herbs have anxiolytic and nervine qualities and have been found in clinical trials to improve memory, cognitive performance, relieve anxiety, and depression (Morgan & Stevens, 2010, Calabrese, et al., 2008). Ginkgo is used to treat a broad range of vascular insufficiency problems, but particularly conditions affecting the brain such as senility, mental fatigue, loss of hearing and decreased visual activity. Human studies of Ginkgo extracts have confirmed that it can slow the progression of Alzheimer's disease and dementia. (Rainer, et al., 2013, Ihl, et al., 2012). Schisandra is an adaptogen that helps people to feel both calm and focused. It was often used as a tea in Toaist Monasteries to enhance relaxation and produce a meditative state. Lemon Balm is a mild antidepressant especially useful for seasonal affected disorder (SAD), it also acts as a nervine, anxiolytic and nootropic. Rosemary also increases circulation to the brain and has long been used to improve memory. A human trial found that the herb (750 mg per day) enhanced cognitive function in the elderly (Pengelly et al., 2012).

CONTRAINDICATIONS: Vaso-dilative migraines.

SUGGESTED USE: 40-80 drops (2-4 ml) TID as needed.

ADDITIONAL USEFUL HERBS: Damiana, Cola Nut or Lavender all enhance cognitive function. Other adaptogens can also enhance cognitive function especially Red Ginseng, Holy Basil, Eleuthero, Rhodiola and Reishi.

DAILY ADAPT™

CONTAINS: Hydroalcoholic extracts of Eleuthero root (Eleutherococcus senticosus), fresh Oat milky seed (Avena sativa), Schisandra berry (Schisandra chinensis), fresh Gotu Kola herb (Centella asiatica), Rhodiola root (Rhodiola rosea), fresh American Ginseng root (Panax quinquefolius) and vegetable glycerin.

INDICATIONS: This formula is designed to enhance HPA Axis and SAS (Sympatho-adrenal system) function, which influence and help regulate endocrine, nervous system and immune function. Careful formulation has created a balanced adaptogenic formula that is energizing without being overstimulating for most people. It is appropriate for the stress-filled lives most of us seem to be living. Daily Adapt™ improves stamina, mental clarity and work performance. It also helps to maintain vitality, immune function and physical performance and can be used for adult ADHD, brain fog, for treating CFID's, fibromyalgia, deficient depression and elevated cortisol levels.

ACTIVITY: The herbs in this formula are adaptogens (Eleuthero, Schisandra, Rhodiola, American Ginseng), nervines (Fresh Oat), or nootropics (Gotu Kola). They strengthen and normalize adrenal, hypothalamus and pituitary function. In healthy people these herbs act as cumulative tonics. In chronic stress conditions the effect is much more pronounced, and a noticeable difference may be felt within a few days. Adaptogens have been found to act something like a "stress vaccine", helping the body to respond more quickly and appropriately to chronic stress. They not only reduce excess cortisol levels, but they also stimulate heat shock proteins and forkhead proteins which prevent mitochondrial dysfunction which inhibits ATP production in our cells.

CONTRAINDICATIONS: Pregnancy.

SUGGESTED USE: 40-60 drops (2-3 ml) TID; long-term use is indicated.

ADDITIONAL RECOMMENDATIONS: Stress reduction techniques can be useful and adequate sleep is essential. A low glycemic index/load diet can be useful as are probiotics, magnesium , L-theanine and B Complex vitamins.

ADDITIONAL USEFUL HERBS: Other adaptogens may be used with this formula including Codonopsis, Holy Basil, Seven Precious Mushrooms™ or Ashwagandha. Nervine herbs such as Skullcap, Chamomile, Lemon Balm, Linden flower or Hawthorn may also be useful for relieving the effects of excessive stress.

ECHINACEA/GOLDENSEAL COMPOUND™

CONTAINS: Hydroalcoholic extracts of Goldenseal root (Hydrastis canadensis), fresh Echinacea purpurea flower and Echinacea purpurea root.

INDICATIONS: This formula is used to treat acute bacterial and viral infections, especially of the sinuses and respiratory tract, i.e. bronchitis, ear infections, influenza, sinusitis, strep throat, laryngitis and colds. It can also be used for bladder and urinary tract infections such as cystitis and urethritis.

ACTIVITY: Echinacea stimulates macrophage activity as well as production of T-4 cells and interferon. It contains hyaluronidase inhibitors which are believed to prevent viruses from infecting new cells thus inhibiting viral infections. Echinacea also enhances lymphatic circulation and acts as an alterative. Echinacea purpurea cones (flowers) contain high levels of the mouth-tingling isobutylamides. These important compounds contain the active constituents that stimulate immune response, promotes circulation and are anti-inflammatory. Goldenseal is a powerful broad spectrum antibacterial agent, especially useful for infections of mucous membranes, (upper respiratory tract, mouth, sinuses, throat) and urinary tract. It's primary constituent Berberine, has been shown to have in vivo antiviral activity against influenza virus (Wu, et al., 2011) as well as cytomegalovirus and herpes.

CONTRAINDICATIONS: Use with caution during pregnancy as Goldenseal may stimulate uterine contractions (theoretical).

SUGGESTED USE: 20-30 drops (1-1.5 ml) 3-5 times per day in acute situations. *Not for long-term use.*

ADDITIONAL RECOMMENDATIONS: Include foods rich in immune potentiating carotenoids and increase intake of Vitamin C, and sublingual zinc.

ADDITIONAL USEFUL HERBS: All of the following herbs are traditionally used to treat viral or bacterial infections; Astragalus/Echinacea Compound™, Garlic, Elecampane, Myrrh, Ultimate Echinacea Compound™, Isatis, Thyme, Andrographis, Usnea, Elderflower, Japanese Honeysuckle, Houttuynia, Sage, White Sage, Spilanthes, and Yarrow.

ELI JONES' COMPOUND SYRUP OF SCROPHULARIA

CONTAINS: Figwort fresh herb (Scrophularia nodosa), Yellow Dock fresh root (Rumex crispus), Poke fresh root (Phytolacca americana), Burdock Seed (Arctium lappa), Corydalis yanhusuo rhizome (C. yanhusuo), Juniper berry (Juniperus communis), water extract of Mayapple root (Podophyllum peltatum), Guaiac wood (Guaiacum officinale), Prickly Ash bark (Zanthoxylum clavaherculis), Peppermint essential oil in a Black Cherry sucanat syrup.

INDICATIONS: This powerful alterative formula has been used for over a hundred years to enhance elimination of metabolic waste via the liver, bowel, lymph, kidney and skin. The great Eclectic physician Eli Jones, MD created and used this Formula for treating a wide variety of cancers as well as arthritis and chronic skin conditions.

ACTIVITY: Figwort is an alterative that enhances lymphatic and kidney function. In laboratory studies Scrophularia down regulated NF-Kβ, caspase-3 and other cell cycle regulators and oncogenes. Poke is a strong alterative that promotes bowel, kidney and lymphatic activity. It has a long history of use for treating cancer, lymphatic stagnation, chronic skin conditions and arthritis. Yellow Dock root is a bitter tonic, aperient and cholagogue; the Eclectics felt it was specific for treating cachexia caused by cancer. Chinese Corydalis replaces its endangered native American relative Turkey Corn (Dicentra canadensis). It is used for cancer pain and enhances liver and gallbladder function. Mayapple contains cytotoxic compounds which have been used to treat a number of cancers, including testicular cancer. The water extract avoids the highly toxic resins which are also strongly cathartic. Eli Jones MD, J. M. Scudder MD and Sebastian Kneipp all used Juniper berry to stimulate kidney function, digestion and as an antidyscratic herb. In laboratory studies this herb and its constituents have been shown to inhibit a wide range of cancers. Prickly Ash enhances circulation, digestive function, relieves nerve pain and promotes absorption of the entire formula. It too has been found to have chemopreventive and antitumor activity in in vitro studies. Finally, Guaiac is anti-inflammatory and a bitter tonic, also used to prevent or treat cachexia.

CONTRAINDICATIONS: Use only under practitioner supervision. This Formula does not replace orthodox therapies for serious illnesses. Discontinue if this product causes diarrhea or gastric upset. Avoid use in pregnancy or lactation.

SUGGESTED USE: 90 drops (4.5 ml), take 3 times per day in juice or water.

ADDITIONAL RECOMMENDATIONS: Eliminate refined sugars and carbohydrates from the diet. Make sure that there are adequate levels of vitamins D, K, A and C. The nutritional supplements IP-6 (inositol hexaphosphate) and modified citrus pectin have both been shown to inhibit metastasis and promote cancer cell apoptosis.

ADDITIONAL USEFUL HERBS: Chaga, Seven Precious Mushrooms™, Immune Adapt™, Turmeric, Milk Thistle, Scudder's Alterative, and Alterative Compound™ have all been used to treat chronic degenerative diseases including cancer.

EMOTIONAL RELIEF™

CONTAINS: Hydroalcoholic extracts of St. John's wort flowering tops (Hypericum perforatum), fresh Lemon Balm herb (Melissa officinalis), Mimosa bark (Albizia julibrissin), fresh Black Cohosh root (Actaea racemosa), fresh Night Blooming Cereus stem (Selenicereus pteranthus, S. grandiflorus), fresh Holy Basil herb (Ocimum tenuiflorum), and Lavender flowers (Lavendula angustifolia).

INDICATIONS: This formula is useful for mild to moderate depression. It can be used for seasonal affective disorder (SAD), situational or "stagnant" depression, old-age depression, and hormonal depression.

ACTIVITY: St. John's wort has been shown to be as effective as SSRI's and SNRI's for mild to moderate depression (Singer et al., 2011 Bratstrom, 2009). I use it for hepatic or GI based depression, for people with a sour attitude, biliousness, and GI dysfunction. Used with Lemon Balm it can be effective for treating seasonal affective disorder (SAD). Lemon Balm is a mild mood elevator, anxiolytic and nervine. Mimosa bark is the most effective mood elevator I have ever utilized, helping to relieve grief, chronic emotional pain, and sadness. Animal studies also indicate that Mimosa has antidepressant and anxiolytic activity. Black Cohosh and Night Blooming Cereus are indicated for "gloom and doom" or for menopausal depression. Night Blooming Cereus is also used for old-age depression and "cardiac" depression. Holy Basil acts as a mood elevator, mild adaptogen, and it enhances mental clarity. Lavender is used for stagnant depression which is situational depression that becomes chronic. It also enhances sleep quality and improves focus and concentration and in a human trial when given with a pharmaceutical antidepressant it enhanced the efficacy of the drug. (Akhondzadeh, et al., 2003)

CONTRAINDICATIONS: Do not use during pregnancy or with severe, suicidal depression or bi-polar depression. Use with caution while on prescription antidepressant medication. Do not use this product while taking any prescription drugs without the advice of your prescribing physician. Avoid excessive exposure to UV irradiation (e.g. sunlight, tanning) when using this product.

SUGGESTED USE: 30-40 drops (1.5-2 ml) TID/QID. It can take four to six weeks to reach full therapeutic effect.

ADDITIONAL RECOMMENDATIONS: For SAD increase exposure to sunlight or use a light box. Bach flower remedies can also be useful for some types of depression. The supplement SAMe is an effective antidepressant and can work in as little as two weeks. In can be taken with Emotional Relief™ to enhance activity and efficacy. Talk therapy, spending time in nature and lifestyle changes can offer significant benefits as well.

ADDITIONAL USEFUL HERBS: For weepy, "can't stop crying" types of depression especially in pale, asthenic women increase the Night Blooming Cereus and use small doses of Pulsatilla. Other herbs used for "stagnant depression" include Rosemary, Rose Petals and Damiana. For andropausal depression in men, use the formula Gentle-Man™. Adaptogens, especially Rhodiola, Asian Ginseng, Eleuthero, and Schisandra, can also enhance the efficacy of depression protocols.

ENERGY ADAPT™

CONTAINS: Hydroalcoholic extracts of Gotu Kola (Centella asiatica), Maca root (Lepidium meyenii or L. peruvianum), Red Ginseng (Panax ginseng), Rhodiola (Rhodiola rosea), Holy Basil (Ocimum tenuiflorum), Mimosa bark (Albizia julibrissin) and Rosemary (Rosamarinus officinalis)

INDICATIONS: This adaptogenic formula combines stimulating adaptogens (Red Ginseng, Rhodiola, Holy Basil), nootropics (Gotu Kola, Rosemary), nutritive tonics (Maca) and antidepressant (Mimosa bark, Rosemary, Holy Basil) herbs. It is appropriate for people who feel a lack of energy, fatigue, brain fog or mild depression. Energy Adapt™ can be used as part of a protocol to treat chronic fatigue syndrome, fibromyalgia or exhaustion due to chronic illness.

ACTIVITY: Stimulating adaptogens such as Red Ginseng, Rhodiola and Holy Basil enhance HPA axis and SAS function. Adaptogens have also been shown to help prevent cortisol-induced mitochondrial dysfunction, up-regulate neuropeptide Y and re-regulate endocrine, nervous system and immune function. Red Ginseng, Gotu Kola, Rhodiola, Holy Basil, Rosemary and Mimosa bark also improve mood, enhance cerebral circulation and are used to relieve depression and/or anxiety. Maca is a nutritive tonic which supports the effects of the adaptogenic herbs and along with Red Ginseng and Rhodiola supports healthy male and female sexual functioning. In addition many of the these herbs have anti-inflammatory (Gotu Kola, Red Ginseng, Rhodiola, Holy Basil, Rosemary, and Mimosa bark), neuroprotective (Rosemary, Gotu Kola, Red Ginseng and Rhodiola) and blood sugar lowering (Red Ginseng, Holy Basil) effects.

CONTRAINDICATIONS: Do not use if you have bipolar disorder or are easily overstimulated. This formula should not be taken before bedtime.

SUGGESTED USE: 50-70 drops (2.5-3.5 ml) in juice or water. Take 2-3 times per day. Shake well before using..

ADDITIONAL RECOMMENDATIONS: Drink green tea, get adequate sleep, eat a healthy diet, eliminating simple carbohydrates, exercise to tolerance.

ADDITIONAL USEFUL HERBS: Other nootropics such as Bacopa, White Peony, Lavender, Ginkgo can be used if needed.

FIT ADAPT™

CONTAINS: Hydroalcoholic extracts of Eleuthero root (Eleutherococcus senticosus), Chinese Schisandra berry (Schisandra chinensis), Hawthorn fruit, leaf and flower (Crataegus spp.), Reishi mushroom and mycelium (Ganoderma spp.), Sarsaparilla root (Smilax regelii), Ashwagandha root (Withania somnifera), Turmeric rhizome (Curcuma longa), Cordyceps mycelium and/or mushroom (Cordyceps Ophiocordyceps sinensis (a.k.a. Cordyceps sinensis) or Cordyceps militaris) and vegetable glycerin.

INDICATIONS: This formula is designed to be used along with a training program, a healthy diet and dietary supplements to enhance physical performance and improve recovery from strenuous workouts and training regimens.

ACTIVITY: The formula combines adaptogens, anti-inflammatory agents and nutritive tonics to strengthen cardiovascular, endocrine, nervous system and immune function. It will increase energy, help athletes recover more quickly from rigorous workouts and enhance focus and concentration. This formula has been used by world champion athletes to enhance their performance and contains no ingredients that are banned for professional athletes. Hawthorn is rich in flavonoids which strengthen the heart and circulatory system, thus increasing endurance and blood flow. Reishi, Eleuthero, Schisandra, Ashwagandha, and Cordyceps are adaptogens which help to support the HPA axis and SAS (sympatho-adrenal system). Recent research on adaptogens shows that they not only reduce the stress hormone cortisol but also inhibit mitochondrial dysfunction caused elevated nitric oxide (Panossian et al., 2009). By stimulating heat shock proteins, as well as forkhead proteins, adaptogens act similar to a vaccine, priming the body's ability to cope with physical or emotional stressors. In human studies both Ashwagandha and Schisandra have been shown to improve physical performance and endurance (Sandhu, et al., 2010, Panossian & Wikman, 2009). Sarsaparilla and Turmeric have anti-inflammatory activity as do Ashwagandha, Hawthorn, and Cordyceps, all of which help to prevent tissue damage and enhance tissue repair. Many of these herbs (Reishi, Ashwagandha, Schisandra and Hawthorn) also relieve anxiety and promote improved focus and concentration.

CONTRAINDICATIONS: Do not use if you have a mushroom allergy.

SUGGESTED USE: 60-80 drops (3-4 ml) TID/QID while training or to enhance athletic performance.

ADDITIONAL RECOMMENDATIONS: Eat a diet with good quality protein, complex carbohydrates, nuts, seeds, fresh fruits and vegetables. Nutrient dense foods such as Chlorella or Spirulina, and the supplements CO-Q-10, and L-carnitine can also enhance oxygenation of tissues and cardiac function.

ADDITIONAL USEFUL HERBS: Other adaptogens or tonic herbs such as Red Ginseng, American Ginseng, Shatavari, Prince Seng, Gotu Kola or Chinese Peony can also enhance athletic performance. Anti-inflammatory herbs such as Solomon's Seal, Muscle/Joint Tonic™, Hawthorn Solid Extract™, Pomegranate-Goji Berry Solid Extract™ or Blueberry Solid Extract™, Rosehips, Amla fruit, Teasel root, Turmeric, Bupleurum, Devil's Claw or Yucca can be used to prevent or treat sore overworked muscles and sports injuries.

FOCUS FORMULA™

CONTAINS: Hydroalcoholic extracts of dried Hawthorn fruit, leaf and flower (Crataegus spp.), Lemon Balm herb (Melissa officinalis), fresh Oat milky seed (Avena sativa), Bacopa herb (Bacopa monnieri), Ginkgo leaf (Ginkgo biloba), Skullcap herb (Scutellaria lateriflora), and vegetable glycerin.

INDICATIONS: This is a gentle, yet useful formula for children or adults with attention deficit hyperactive disorder (ADHD). It is also indicated for anxiety, irritability, poor memory or concentration and restless sleep. For many people, it can be "an herbal alternative to prescription drugs."

ACTIVITY: Fresh Oat, Lemon Balm and Skullcap are "nerve tonics" (nervines) that nourish and calm the nervous system. Fresh Oat helps to re-establish an emotional balance in people who are emotionally labile and hyperreactive. Lemon Balm enhances cognitive function, improves sleep quality and helps relieve anxiety. Skullcap is especially useful for people who develop muscle spasms, tremors or tics when under stress. It is also effective for calming emotional outbursts and anger. Hawthorn strengthens the heart and circulatory system and calms the *Shen* (Mind/Consciousness). It is one of the primary herbs I use for stress-induced agitation or irritability. Ginkgo increases vascular circulation, improving memory and concentration. Bacopa has significant anxiolytic, nootropic and nervine qualities, (Calabrese, et al., 2008) and is used to relieve irritability, impaired memory and anxiety.

CONTRAINDICATIONS: None.

SUGGESTED USE: Adults: 60-100 drops (3-5 ml) TID Children: 10-20 drops (.5-1 ml) BID/QID taken in warm milk or Chamomile/Lemon Balm tea.

ADDITIONAL RECOMMENDATIONS: Reduce your child's consumption of refined sugars, artificial colors, preservatives and flavorings. Decrease exposure to TV's, computer screens, fluorescent lighting and video games, all of which can cause excessive neuroexcitment.

ADDITIONAL USEFUL HERBS: Adding Chamomile tea unsweetened or mixed 1/2 and 1/2 with apple juice can be calming. Adding Hawthorn Solid Extract™ may also be a helpful adjunctive therapy for ADHD.

FULL MOON - WOMEN'S ANTI-SPASMODIC COMPOUND™

CONTAINS: Hydroalcoholic extracts of fresh Black Haw bark (Viburnum prunifolium), Cyperus root (Cyperus rotundus), Roman Chamomile flowers (Chamaemelum nobile), fresh Wild Yam root (Dioscorea villosa), Jamaica Dogwood bark (Piscidia piscipula), Corydalis yanhusuo rhizome (Corydalis yanhusuo). and vegetable glycerin.

INDICATIONS: This compound is an effective antispasmodic formula primarily useful for mild to severe menstrual cramps (dysmenorrhea). It can also be effective for acute muscle spasms, back pain, torticollis (wry neck), bladder spasms, IBS, pain caused by uterine fibroids or endometriosis, hepatic colic, gallbladder spasms (with celandine) hiccoughs and bruxism. This formula combined with Carminative Compound™ can also be use to relieve the nausea caused by severe menstrual cramps.

ACTIVITY: This formula combines herbs that are effective antispasmodics (Black Haw, Roman Chamomile, Wild Yam) and analgesics (Cyperus, Corydalis, and Jamaica Dogwood) to relieve spasms and pain especially dysmenorrhea. In addition, many of the secondary effects associated with menstrual cramps such as nausea, lower back pain and diarrhea can be relieved with the use of this formula. Black Haw has a long history of use for menstrual pain, but is also useful for intercostal, uterine or testicular pain. Roman Chamomile has anti-inflammatory activity, as well as being a bitter tonic, carminative and antispasmodic. Wild Yam is indicated for dysmenorrhea with nausea, Hepatic colic, IBS, gallbladder spasms and abdominal pain. Cyperus or Mu Xiong is very useful for treating dysmenorrhea with nausea, gastric, uterine or intestinal pain. Corydalis and Jamaica Dogwood are powerful analgesics used instead of NSAIDS for systemic pain relief.

CONTRAINDICATIONS: Pregnancy and breastfeeding. Persons on prescription pain relievers or muscle relaxants should use caution as it is possible that concurrent use of this formula could cause additive effects.

SUGGESTED USE: 30-50 drops (1.5-2.5 ml) QID while symptoms persist. *Not intended for long-term or daily use.*

ADDITIONAL RECOMMENDATIONS: Increase dietary or supplementary magnesium intake (250 mg taken twice per day). For restless leg syndrome use Full Moon - Women's Anti-Spasmodic Compound™ with magnesium and iron (if serum levels are low).

ADDITIONAL USEFUL HERBS: For spasms: Cramp Bark, Motherwort, Skullcap, Blue Vervain, Kudzu, or J. Kloss Anti-Spasmodic Compound may be helpful. For pain: Aspirea Compound™ or Indian Pipe can be added to Full Moon - Women's Anti-Spasmodic Compound™.

GENTLELAX™

CONTAINS: Hydroalcoholic extracts of Butternut root bark (Juglans cinera), aged Buckthorn bark (Frangula alnus), Culver's Root root (Veronicastrum virginicum), fresh Dandelion root (Taraxacum officinale), Ginger rhizome (Zingiber officinale) and vegetable glycerin.

INDICATIONS: This formula works via the liver and gallbladder to enhance bile production and excretion. Improving bile flow gently stimulates intestinal peristalsis and can ease acute constipation and soften stools. It is not intended for chronic, long-term bowel problems. Improving the diet (soluble fiber, whole grains, legumes, raw fruits and vegetables) and increased water consumption are more appropriate treatment for chronic constipation. Gentlelax™ will give overnight relief of constipation without cramping. Specific indications include hard or clay colored stools, and stress or travel-related constipation.

ACTIVITY: Butternut bark is the mildest of the stimulant laxatives. It can be used long term without causing bowel dependence. Aged Buckthorn is a much stronger stimulant laxative and only occasional use is appropriate. Culver's Root is a cholagogue, increasing bile secretion and excretion, which promotes bowel function. Dandelion root is a bitter tonic and aperient which gently enhances bowel activity and digestive function . Ginger helps prevent intestinal cramping that can be caused by Buckthorn and it enhances digestion and relieves flatulence, bloating and nausea.

CONTRAINDICATIONS: Pregnancy, lactation, IBD, diarrhea or IBS-D. Long term use can lead to bowel dependency.

NOTICE: This formula contains Buckthorn. Do not use if you have or developed diarrhea, loose stools, or abdominal pain because Buckthorn may worsen these conditions and be harmful to your health. Consult your physician if you have frequent diarrhea or if you are pregnant, nursing, taking medication, or have a medical condition.

SUGGESTED USE: 20-30 drops (1-1.5 ml) BID as needed.

ADDITIONAL RECOMMENDATIONS: Take mild laxatives such as prune juice, figs soaked in black cherry juice and increase soluble fiber in the diet including oatmeal, seaweed, barley, carrots, bananas, beans, psyllium, chia or flax seed. Adequate water consumption is important, as is the use of probiotics which can be highly beneficial. Eliminating refined carbohydrates and replacing them with whole grains is also a good idea, as is avoiding unhealthy fats and processed foods.

ADDITIONAL USEFUL HERBS: Slippery Elm acts as a bulk laxative and Original Bitters™ enhances digestion, absorption and elimination.

GINKGO/HORSECHESTNUT COMPOUND™

CONTAINS: Hydroalcoholic extracts of fresh Collinsonia whole plant (Collinsonia canadensis), autumn-gathered Ginkgo leaf (Ginkgo biloba), fresh Gotu Kola herb (Centella asiatica), Hawthorn fruit, leaf and flower (Crataegus spp.), Lycium fruit (Lycium barbarum), Cinnamon bark (Cinnamomum verum), fresh Horse Chestnut seed (Aesculus hippocastanum) and vegetable glycerin.

INDICATIONS: This formula is a tonic to the entire circulatory system, it will increase circulation and enhance venous integrity. It is indicated for impaired peripheral circulation with cold hands and feet, Raynaud's disease, peripheral neuropathy, arteriosclerosis, Buerger's disease (thromboangiitis obliterans) chronic venous insufficiency, intermittent claudication and impotence caused by impaired circulation. It is particularly useful for varicosities such as hemorrhoids and varicose veins.

ACTIVITY: Aromatic Collinsonia is a vascular tonic rich in flavonoids which exert a strengthening effect on weak or hypotonic blood vessels. Ginkgo increases circulation especially to extremities. Ginkgo also contains anti-inflammatory compounds and a fresh extract improved microcirculation and antioxidant status in elderly patients (Suter, et al., 2011). Hawthorn and Lycium fruits are rich sources of flavonoids which strengthen the arteries, veins and capillaries, and inhibit arteriosclerosis. Both herbs have a long history of use for promoting circulation and inhibiting inflammation. Cinnamon is a warming herb used for stimulating micro-circulation and reducing insulin resistance, which promotes arteriosclerosis. Gotu Kola has anti-inflammatory activity and has a long history of use for treating varicose veins, hemorrhoids, lymphadenitis, chronic venous insufficiency (Chong & Aziz, 2013) and for decubitus ulcers/bedsores (orally and topically). Horse Chestnut is a classic remedy used in Europe for varicose veins and hemorrhoids. It is a powerful vaso-tonic used to treat chronic venous insufficiency with edema (Pittler & Ernst, 2012), as well as varicose veins, intermittent claudication and Buerger's disease.

CONTRAINDICATIONS: Pregnancy, constipation.

SUGGESTED USE: 30-40 drops (1.5-2 ml) BID/TID; long-term use is indicated.

ADDITIONAL RECOMMENDATIONS: Increase flavonoid-rich foods such as blueberries, grapes, elderberries, cherries, rosehips, green tea, buckwheat, barley powder, or take flavonoid-rich supplements. Spicy and pungent herbs such as ginger, garlic, cinnamon or cayenne in the diet enhance circulation. Dry skin brushing, weekly saunas, massage and hydrotherapy may also be useful for improving circulation.

ADDITIONAL USEFUL HERBS: Hawthorn Solid Extract™, Blueberry Solid Extract™ and Pomegranate/Goji Berry Solid Extract™ all are excellent sources of OPCs (oligomeric procyanidins) which help stabilize vascular integrity.

GRIEF RELIEF™

CONTAINS: Hydroalcoholic extracts of Hawthorn fruit, flower, and leaf (Crataegus spp.), Mimosa bark (Albizia julibrissin), Rose petals (Rosa spp.) and vegetable glycerin.

INDICATIONS: This is a formula that I have used in my clinical practice for many years to help to start the healing process for people who are grieving or suffering melancholia, or emotional trauma. While these herbs are no replacement for therapy, they seem to help people who are "stuck" in their pain. I feel it is especially useful for people suffering from broken hearts, stagnant depression (chronic situational depression), unresolved grief, and even some types of posttraumatic stress disorder.

ACTIVITY: Mimosa bark is an antidepressant and profound mood elevator used in TCM for depression, anxiety, and insomnia. It has been found to have both antidepressant and anxiolytic activity in animal studies. Roses have long been associated with emotional healing. In Banckes' Herbal published in 1525, just smelling roses is said to "comfort the brain and the heart and quickeneth the spirit". Li Shizhen, in his classic Bencao Gangmu, says roses "drive away melancholia". The modern tradition of giving fragrant roses to a loved one, comes from not only their beauty, but their healing fragrance. Hawthorn is commonly thought of as a cardiac remedy, but in my experience it also helps the emotional heart as well. Researchers have found that the heart not only pumps blood, but has receptors for many hormones and neuropeptides. The long held belief that the heart is also the "seat of emotions' turns out to have an actual physiological basis. I use Hawthorn for anxiety-induced palpitations or angina pain, ADD/ADHD, and as a calming nervine.

CONTRAINDICATIONS: Use cautiously with antidepressant medications and during pregnancy. Do not use if you have bipolar disorder.

SUGGESTED USE: 40-45 drops (2-2.25 ml) TID.

ADDITIONAL RECOMMENDATIONS: Stress reduction techniques including meditation, yoga, hypnosis and Tai Qi can be of benefit. Working with a good grief counselor or therapist is essential.

ADDITIONAL USEFUL HERBS: Many herbs including fresh Oat, Emotional Relief™, Rosemary, Damiana, Bacopa, Chinese Polygala, Motherwort, Blue Vervain, Pulsatilla, Serenity Compound™, Tension Relief™, St. John's wort, Night Blooming Cereus, Lavender, and Holy Basil can help relieve either anxiety or depression.

HEALTHY HEART COMPOUND™

CONTAINS: Hydroalcoholic extracts of Hawthorn fruit, leaf and flower (Crataegus spp.), Chinese Salvia root (Salvia miltiorrhiza), Night Blooming Cereus stem (Selenicereus pteranthus, S. grandiflorus), Astragalus root (Astragalus membranaceus), Corydalis yanhusuo rhizome (Corydalis yanhusuo), Dong Quai root (Angelica sinensis) and vegetable glycerin.

INDICATIONS: This formula acts as a mild but effective heart and circulatory tonic. The herbs in this formula can enhance cardiac function, improve oxygenation of the heart muscle, as well as promoting systemic circulation. Healthy Heart Compound can be useful as part of a protocol for treating angina, mild to moderate congestive heart failure, palpitations and arrhythmias.

ACTIVITY: This formula combines several cardiotonic herbs to enhance heart function. Hawthorn is a time tested trophorestorative to the heart and circulatory system. It has mild positively inotropic and negatively chronotropic effects. In clinical trials in people with mild to moderate congestive heart failure it has improved exercise tolerance, quality of life and cardiac function, as well as reducing fatigue and dyspnea (Eggeling, et al., 2011; Degenring, et al., 2003; Tauchert 2002; Zapfe jun 2001; Rietbrock, et al., 2001). Dan Shen, Dong Quai and Corydalis yanhusuo have a long history of use in China for treating blood stasis with pain. This would include conditions such as angina, thromboangitis obliterans, intermittant claudication and congestive heart failure. Night Blooming Cereus was introduced into medical use by the Eclectic physicians who found it was an excellent cardiac tonic for stress-, exercise- or nicotine-induced arrhythmias and palpitations as well as mitral valve prolapse. Astragalus and Dong Quai are commonly used in Chinese medicine (along with Dan Shen and Corydalis yanhusuo) to enhance cardiac function, especially left ventricular ejection fraction, as well as dilating the coronary arteries (Young, et al. 2012 & 2010). CONTRAINDICATIONS: It may potentiate prescription cardiac medications. Avoid concurrent use with blood thinning or antiplatelet medications. If treating CHF, arrhythmias and people recovering from myocardial infarctions, the use of this product should be discussed with a person's cardiologist.

SUGGESTED USE: Take 40-60 drops (2-3 ml) in juice or water 3 times per day. It is safe for older people and long term use is indicated. Talk to your physician before using this product, especially if you are taking prescription medications for heart problems or if you have a serious heart condition.

ADDITIONAL RECOMMENDATIONS: Maintain a healthy diet by including deep sea fish, dark green leafy vegetables, fresh fruits and berries, whole grains, nuts/seeds and legumes. Avoid processed foods (white flour or rice, sugar and other high glycemic index/load foods, salt and trans-fats). Nutritional supplements such as L-carnitine, fish oils, Vitamin E, Co-Q10, magnesium, L-Arginine, B Complex vitamins and carotenoids may be useful to enhance cardiac function.

ADDITIONAL USEFUL HERBS: Add Garlic and other alliums to the diet. Safflower/ Hong Hua, Arjuna bark and Tienqi Ginseng all offer additional cardiovascular benefits.

HEALTHY KID'S COMPOUND™

CONTAINS: Glycerin extracts of Echinacea root (E. angustifolia), Elderberry (Sambucus nigra var. canadensis), Lemon Balm herb (Melissa officinalis) and orange extract.

INDICATIONS: This formula is indicated for acute onset of viral or bacterial conditions such as colds, influenza, otitis media, sinus infections and mild upper respiratory tract infections. It can also be used for intestinal viruses, chicken pox, measles, German measles and Fifth disease.

ACTIVITY: Echinacea is a safe and gentle first line defense against common viral infections. Although there are conflicting studies, the better studies show that Echinacea has the ability to increase immune response and can prevent or reduce the severity and duration of colds and influenza. (Jawad, et al., 2012) Contrary to what some books state, Echinacea does not lose effectiveness if taken more than 7-14 days. Lemon Balm is a pleasant tasting member of the mint family that has a long history of use for treating colds, stomach virus and respiratory tract infections. It is rich in volatile oils as well as rosmarinic and caffeic acids which are powerful antioxidants and viral inhibitors. Several human trials have shown that Elderberry is a safe and effective treatment for viral infections. (Zakay-Rones, et al., 2004 & 1995) The sweet fruity berries inhibit viral replication and shorten the duration of colds, influenza and upper respiratory infections.

CONTRAINDICATIONS: For serious viral or bacterial infections consult a physician.

SUGGESTED USE: 20-30 drops (1-1.5 ml) QID.

ADDITIONAL RECOMMENDATIONS: Add dietary sources of vitamin C and antiviral flavonoids such as amla fruit, citrus, blueberries, rosehips and other berries. Also include dietary sources of anti-inflammatory carotenoids such as sweet potatoes, pumpkins, winter squash, red and yellow peppers, beets, dried apricots or carrots. Garlic has pronounced antibacterial and antiviral activity, as do spices such as thyme, oregano and sage. Zinc lozenges have also been found to shorten recovery time from colds. Regular use of probiotics has been found to help reduce the incidence of upper respiratory tract infections.

ADDITIONAL USEFUL HERBS: For children, a tea of peppermint and elder-flower is a traditional remedy for treating colds and influenza. elderberry syrups can also be of benefit.

HEALTHY SKIN TONIC™

CONTAINS: Hydroalcoholic extracts of Sarsaparilla root (Smilax regelii), Yellow Dock root (Rumex crispus), Burdock seed (Arctium lappa), Horsetail herb (Equisetum arvense), Red Alder bark (Alnus rubra) and vegetable glycerin.

INDICATIONS: This formula nourishes the skin and has anti-inflammatory and antibacterial activity. It promotes healthy liver, bowel and kidney function, which is the foundation of healthy skin. The herbs are rich in minerals, especially silica which is essential for beautiful skin. The specific indications for this for-mula include acne, dry or irritated skin, rosacea (orally and topically), psoriasis, eczema, seborrhea and inflammations of the sebaceous glands.

ACTIVITY: Sarsaparilla binds endotoxins in the gut enhancing their excretion. It also reduces inflammation of the skin and connective tissue and is used for skin that is red and feels hot. Red Alder bark enhances liver and bowel function, it is most prominently used for acne, boils, and acne rosacea. Alnus is antibacterial and anti-inflammatory and is indicated for large red pimples (comedones) on the back, neck or buttocks. Recent research confirms the traditional belief that gut health (intestinal microbiome/gut/skin axis) has a pronounced effect on the health of the skin (Arck, et al., 2010). This helps explain why herbs that strongly affect gut health (sarsaparilla, yellow dock, red alder bark) are so effective for skin conditions. Horsetail is rich in silica (silicic acid) which strengthens the skin, bone, hair and nails. Horsetail is effective for treating skin that feels like paper, tears easily and has lost its normal elasticity. Burdock seed is used for dry, itchy, scaly or crusty skin conditions; while Yellow Dock is useful for oozing, weepy skin problems, it also promotes liver and bowel function.

CONTRAINDICATIONS: Pregnancy and lactation.

SUGGESTED USE: 30-40 drops (1.5-2 ml) TID for at least two months. If using this product topically, dilute in water before using it on the skin and avoid the eyes.

ADDITIONAL RECOMMENDATIONS: Increase intake of B vitamins, omega 3 fatty acids (fish oil) and zinc; decrease the amount of saturated and hydrogenated fats, and fried foods in the diet. Probiotics and prebiotics can also help treat inflammatory skin conditions.

ADDITIONAL USEFUL HERBS: Topical creams or lotions with Aloe, Comfrey, Calendula, Plantain or Chickweed may provide temporary relief. Internally Stinging Nettle, Butternut bark, Oregon Grape root or Figwort may also be useful for certain skin conditions. Gotu Kola is helpful for inflammatory skin conditions that are red or hot.

HERB-CAL™ (Herbal Calcium)

CONTAINS: Vinegar extract of organic eggshells, and hydroalcoholic extracts of fresh Oat milky seed (Avena sativa), Horsetail herb (Equisetum arvense), Stinging Nettle leaf (Urtica dioica), fresh Chamomile flowers (Matricaria recutita) and Alfalfa herb (Medicago sativa)

INDICATIONS: Herb-Cal™ can be used as a daily calcium and mineral supplement and for conditions such as osteoporosis, osteoarthritis, muscle cramps, and weak tooth enamel. It may also help speed healing of bone fractures.

ACTIVITY: This is a unique formula combining a vinegar extract of organic eggshells (calcium acetate) with herbs rich in calcium and other minerals. While this formula contains small quantities of calcium compared to other calcium supplements, the calcium in it is highly assimilable. Horsetail is a rich source of silicic acid, an important co-factor for calcium absorption. Horsetail also enhances the maturation of osteoblasts in the bones. Nettles and Alfalfa contain calcium, iron, boron, magnesium, potassium and other important minerals, as well as Vitamin K-2. All of which are essential for calcium absorption. Chamomile flowers and fresh oats are also mineral rich and Chamomile has been found in laboratory studies to stimulate osteoblast differentiation and mineralization of bone (Kassi, et al., 2004). Vinegar used in the eggshell extract helps increase gastric acidity which is necessary for absorption of all nutrients. Contrary to popular belief excessive stomach acid is relatively uncommon (especially in people over 40) and a lack of stomach acid (achlorhydria) is a much more common issue.

CONTRAINDICATIONS: None.

SUGGESTED USE: As a daily food supplement 30-40 drops (1.5-2 ml) TID in cases of serious deficiency 40-60 drops (2-3 ml) TID.

ADDITIONAL RECOMMENDATIONS: Include calcium-rich foods such as carrots, hulled sesame seeds, tahini, broccoli, almonds, dark green leafy vegetables, oats, yogurt, sardines and seaweed in the diet. Calcium absorption is dependent on adequate gastric hydrochloric acid and bile secretion as well as Vitamins D and K, potassium, magnesium and boron. Excess phosphorus and saturated fats may inhibit calcium absorption. Calcium supplements, especially calcium citrate or chelate can help supplement dietary calcium sources if needed.

ADDITIONAL USEFUL HERBS: OsteoHerb™, Sichuan Teasel, Processed Rehmannia, Amla, Dandelion leaf, Epimedium and Kudzu have all been shown to enhance bone density.

HERBAL RELIEF BOTANICAL THROAT SPRAY™

CONTAINS: Hydroalcoholic extracts of fresh Echinacea angustifolia root, Goldenseal root (Hydrastis canadensis), Licorice root (Glycyrrhiza glabra), Sage herb (Salvia officinalis), Cinnamon bark (Cinnamomum verum), fresh Collinsonia whole plant, (Collinsonia canadensis), Myrrh gum resin (Commiphora molmol), Osha root (Ligusticum porteri), Propolis resin, essential oils of Cinnamon, Lemon and Peppermint, and vegetable glycerin.

INDICATIONS: Herbal Relief Botanical Throat Spray™ provides topical relief for sore, painful throats, laryngitis, pharyngitis and thrush. It can also be useful for the scratchy, irritated throat associated with the early onset of colds or influenza, to help inhibit the progression of the illness.

ACTIVITY: This formula combines antibacterial, antiviral, anti-inflammatory, demulcent and analgesic herbs for quick and effective relief of sore throat symptoms. The volatile oils and resins found in Sage, Cinnamon, Propolis, Myrrh and Osha, as well as the three essential oils (Cinnamon, Lemon and Peppermint), reduce throat pain. They also inhibit the growth of many common bacteria, viruses and yeasts (thrush). Licorice soothes irritated tissue and relieves dry coughs. Collinsonia is specific for "minister's throat," which is a chronic low grade irritation of the vocal cords. Goldenseal is antibacterial, antiviral and is appropriate for red or painful mucous membranes of the throat, mouth or tongue. Echinacea's isobutylamides anesthetize the throat while stimulating local phagocytosis. Osha and Sage are broad spectrum antimicrobials that also relieve pain and inflammation.

CONTRAINDICATIONS: Avoid use in children under 4 years old and pregnant or lactating women.

SUGGESTED USE: 1-2 sprays every 1/2 to 2 hours throughout the day.

ADDITIONAL RECOMMENDATIONS: Traditional remedies for sore throats include lemon and honey in water and gargling with salt water.

ADDITIONAL HERBAL RECOMMENDATIONS: A tea made from Slippery Elm or Marshmallow can be soothing for dry ticklish coughs and throat pain. Other herbs that clear "damp heat" such as Isatis, Andrographis, Japanese Honeysuckle, Figwort or Usnea can also help to treat sore throats.

IMMUNE ADAPT™ (Fu Zheng Capsules)

CONTAINS: Powdered extracts of Astragalus root (Astragalus membranaceus), Eleuthero root (Eleutherococcus senticosis), Reishi mushroom (Ganoderma lucidum), Schisandra berry (Schisandra chinensis), Chinese Licorice root (Glycyrrhiza uralensis), Ligustrum berry (Ligustrum lucidum), and Maitake mushroom (Grifola frondosa) in a vegetable-based capsule.

INDICATIONS: In Traditional Chinese Medicine Fu Zheng Pei Ben therapy is used to restore energy and balance to the body so that it is better equipped to deal with chronic diseases, physical or emotional stress or the debilitating effects of the conventional Western cancer treatments (Mingji, et al., 1992). Immune Adapt™ is a Fu Zheng formula that strengthens the Chinese kidney, spleen and lung and thus tonifies the Qi, Blood and Jing. The term Fu Zheng Pei Ben translates as "supports the normal, strengthens resistance". From a Western perspective, Fu Zheng herbs enhance immune potential, improve digestion and support endocrine function. This formula is very useful as an adjunct therapy to reduce the side effects and enhance efficacy of chemotherapy and radiation treatments for cancer and can also be used for immune deficiency conditions such as HIV/AIDS, fibromyalgia, chronic fatigue immune deficiency syndrome (CFIDS) and chronic persistent Lyme disease. This formula also contains immune amphoteric herbs which can help re-regulate a disordered immune system, and so can also be useful for treating autoimmune disease and allergies.

ACTIVITY: One of the common side effects of Western cancer treatments is a reduction of white blood cells. This makes the body more susceptible to opportunistic infection and can interfere with conventional therapy. If white blood cell counts are too low, chemotherapy treatments must be suspended until the levels rise again, thus prolonging the treatment cycle. Clinical trials have shown that the herbs in Immune Adapt™, taken concurrently with chemotherapy, stabilize white blood cell counts and reduce gastro-intestinal, liver or kidney damage caused by chemotherapy. Maitake activates macrophages and T cells, enhances the cytotoxicity of natural killer (NK) cells by stimulating interleukin-12 (IL-12) production and, when used in conjunction with chemotherapy, enhances immune-competent cell activities when compared to chemotherapy alone. Many chemotherapeutic agents can cause kidney damage. Astragalus and Licorice have been shown to lower blood urea nitrogen (BUN) and creatinine (Cr) levels, thus reducing the incidence of drug-induced nephrotoxicity. Astragalus has been shown in human clinical trial to enhance immune function, extend life expectancy and improve quality of life in patients with lung cancer (Upton, 1999a). Studies have demonstrated that Astragalus stimulates macrophage and natural killer cell activity and balances abnormal Th1/Th2 cytokine levels. Reishi mushroom is an immune amphoteric, mild adaptogen and nervine. It induces apoptosis, inhibits cell proliferation and suppresses cell migration of prostate cancer cells by modulating MAPK and Akt cellular signaling and inhibiting transcription factors, thus possibly inhibiting some of the early events in angiogenesis. Eleuthero is an adaptogen and immune amphoteric. It inhibits the cyclooxygenase (COX) enzyme and lipid peroxidation, both of which are elevated in inflamed or cancerous cells. Schisandra is an adaptogen that helps strengthen the whole body by fortifying mitochondrial antioxidant status and up-regulating gene expression related to detoxification. It is also particularly useful as a hepatoprotective agent. It also has been used to reduce multidrug resistance of cancer cells, thus allowing conventional cancer treatments to be more effective. Ligustrum (Nu Zhen Zi) has been shown in animal studies to inhibit lipopolysaccharide-induced tumor necrosis factor alpha (TNF-α) production, increase the activity of endogenous antioxidant enzymes and it also helps prevent chemotherapy-induced leukopenia.

CONTRAINDICATIONS: Chronic diarrhea, gas and abdominal bloating may be exacerbated by this formula. Adding pungent and fragrant herbs such as citrus and ginger can alleviate this problem. Do not use if you have a mushroom allergy.

SUGGESTED USE: Take 2 capsules BID/TID. For chronic conditions, this formula should be taken continuously for an extended period of time.

ADDITIONAL RECOMMENDATIONS: Good nutrition is essential to restoring health when recovering from any illness. A low glycemic index/load diet helps to lower cortisol levels and inhibits insulin resistance, both of which promote cancer growth. The flavonoid quercitin, which is found in capers, apples, onions, red grapes, citrus fruits and broccoli, has been shown to inhibit cancers with estrogen binding sites by 50-80%. Genistein, an isoflavone which is present in high concentrations in soy, legumes and parsley, helps inhibit estrogen- and testosterone-dependent cancers. Modified citrus pectin (MCP) and IP-6 (inositol hexaphosphate) have been shown to inhibit cancer metastasis and promote apoptosis.

ADDITIONAL USEFUL HERBS: For immune depletion Seven Precious Mushrooms™, Rhodiola, Chaga, Codonopsis or Cordyceps can also be utilized. Traditional alterative formulas such as Alterative Compound™, Eli Jones Compound Syrup of Scrophularia and Scudders Alterative may be appropriate as a part of a cancer protocol. For auto-immune disorders Turmeric, Sarsaparilla, Chinese Salvia, Huang Qin, Unprocessed Rehmannia, Ashwagandha, Maitake, Cats Claw, Gotu Kola can offer additional benefits.

IMMUNE ADAPT™ (Fu Zheng Compound)

CONTAINS: Hydroalcoholic extracts of Codonopsis root (Codonopsis lanceolata), Eleuthero root (Eleutherococcus senticosus), Reishi mushroom and mycelium (Ganoderma spp.), Schisandra fruit (Schisandra chinensis), Astragalus root (Astragalus membranaceus), Bai-Zhu Atractylodes root (Atractylodes macrocephala), Licorice root (Glycyrrhiza glabra), Ligustrum berry (Ligustrum lucidum), and vegetable glycerin.

INDICATIONS: In traditional Chinese Fu Zheng Pei Ben therapy strives to restore the vital energy and balance to the body so that it is better equipped to deal with chronic diseases, physiological or emotional stress or the debilitating effects of the conventional Western cancer treatments (Mingji et al., 1992). This formula strengthens the Chinese kidney, spleen and lung and thus tonifies the Qi, Blood and Jing. The term Fu Zheng Pei Ben translates as "supports the normal, strengthens resistance". From a Western perspective, Fu Zheng enhances the immune reservoir, improves digestion and supports endocrine function. This formula is very useful as an adjunct therapy to reduce the side effects of chemotherapy and radiation treatments for cancer and can also be used for immune deficiency conditions such as HIV/AIDS, fibromyalgia, chronic fatigue immune deficiency syndrome (CFIDS) and chronic persistent Lyme disease. It also contains immune amphoteric herbs which help re-regulate a disordered immune system making it useful for treating autoimmune disease and allergies.

ACTIVITY: One of the common side effects of Western cancer treatments is a reduction of white blood cells. This makes the body more susceptible to opportunistic infection and can interfere with conventional therapy. If white blood cell counts are too low, chemotherapy treatments must be suspended until the levels rise again, thus prolonging the treatment cycle. Clinical trials have shown that the herbs in Immune Adapt™, taken concurrently with chemotherapy, stabilize white blood cell counts and reduce gastrointestinal and general toxicity symptoms. Codonopsis positively affects lymphocyte proliferation and interleukin-2 (IL-2) response rate and protects against the immunoglobulin M (IgM) suppressing effects of radiation therapy. Many chemotherapeutic agents can cause kidney damage. Astragalus, Bai-Zhu Atractylodes, Codonopsis and Licorice have been shown to lower blood urea nitrogen (BUN) and creatinine (Cr) levels, thus reducing the incidence of drug-induced nephrotoxicity. Reishi mushroom is an immune amphoteric, mild adaptogen and nervine. It induces apoptosis, inhibits cell proliferation and suppresses cell migration of prostate cancer cells by modulating MAPK and Akt cellular signaling and inhibiting transcription factors, thus inhibiting some of the early events in angiogenesis. Eleuthero is an adaptogen and immune amphoteric. It inhibits the cyclooxygenase (COX) enzyme and lipid peroxidation, both of which are elevated in inflamed and cancerous cells. Schisandra is a calming adaptogen that helps strengthen the whole body by fortifying mitochondrial antioxidant status and up-regulating gene expression related to detoxification. It is also particularly useful as a hepatoprotective agent. It also has been used to reduce multidrug resistance of cancer cells, thus allowing conventional cancer treatments to be more effective. Ligustrum (Nu Zhen Zi) has been shown in animal studies to inhibit lipopolysaccharide-induced tumor necrosis factor alpha production, regulate lipid metabolism, increase the activity of antioxidant enzymes and it helps prevents chemotherapy-induced leukopena.

CONTRAINDICATIONS: It may exacerbate damp spleen conditions (chronic diarrhea, gas and abdominal bloating). If it is necessary to use this formula with these problems, add pungent or fragrant herbs such as Citrus peel or Ginger. Do not use if you have a mushroom allergy.

SUGGESTED USE: 60-100 drops (3-5 ml) QID. For chronic conditions this formula should be taken continuously for an extended period of time.

ADDITIONAL USEFUL HERBS: For immune depletion Seven Precious Mushrooms™, Rhodiola, Cordyceps, Chaga or Maitake can be added. Traditional alterative formulas such as the Alterative Compound™, Scudders Alterative or Eli Jones Compound Syrup of Scrophularia may be appropriate as part of a cancer protocol. For auto-immune disorders Turmeric, Sarsaparilla, Chinese Salvia, Huang Qin, Ashwagandha, Maitake, Cordyceps, Gotu Kola, Unprocessed Rehmannia, or Cat's Claw can offer additional benefits.

IMMUNE BALANCE COMPOUND™

CONTAINS: Hydroalcoholic extracts of Reishi mushroom and mycelium (Ganoderma spp.), fresh Turmeric rhizome (Curcuma longa), Huang Qin root (Scutellaria baicalensis), Ashwagandha root (Withania somnifera), Licorice root (Glycyrrhiza glabra), and Unprocessed Rehmannia root (Rehmannia glutinosa).

INDICATIONS: This formula is indicated for auto-immune conditions such as rheumatoid arthritis (RA), ankylosing spondylitis, Grave's disease, polymyositis, scleroderma, Sjogren's Syndrome, psoriatic arthritis, Crohn's disease/IBD,

Hashimoto's Thyroiditis, psoriasis, idiopathic thrombocytopenic purpura, mixed connective tissue disease, vasculitis, antiphospholipid syndrome, lupus/SLE and other immune-mediated diseases. It can also be useful for treating pollen and animal dander allergies.

ACTIVITY: This formula contains herbs that are immune amphoterics (Reishi, Licorice, and Ashwagandha) and immunoregulators (Turmeric, Huang Qin, Unprocessed Rehmannia). Immune amphoterics normalize immune function and can be used in either hypo-active or hyper-immune conditions which includes immune depletion, auto-immune conditions and Atopy/allergies. Immune amphoterics strengthen and nourish the immune system helping it to regain its normal self-regulatory function. Immunoregulatory herbs reduce inflammatory Cytokines (Interleukins), leukotrienes and prostaglandin production, thus modifying inflammation and the resultant immune activation. Some research suggests they may also inhibit immune complex deposition. These herbs also inhibit histamine release and stabilize mast cells, which down-regulates allergic response. Turmeric has been shown in human and animal models to help relieve RA, psoriasis, IBD and MS (Bright, 2007). Huang Qin clears damp heat (inflammation) and in animal studies it strongly inhibited COX-2, NF Kappa β, TNF-α and inflammatory interleukins (Kim, et al., 2009). Unprocessed Rehmannia is used in TCM to cool the blood and clear heat. I use it in formulas to treat both allergies and auto-immune conditions.

CONTRAINDICATIONS: Not for use in pregnancy unless otherwise directed by a qualified expert. Do not use if you have a mushroom allergy.

SUGGESTED USE: 40-60 drops (2-3 ml) TID/QID.

ADDITIONAL RECOMMENDATIONS: Auto-immune diseases can have multiple possible triggers including chronic low grade infections (gum disease, chronic sinusitis, UTI's), genetic factors, hormonal causes (women have more autoimmune diseases than men) and gut permeability with concurrent food sensitivities. Understanding underlying factors and resolving them can significantly increase efficacy of treatment protocol.

ADDITIONAL USEFUL HERBS: For Sjogren's Syndrome add fish oil and yin tonics. For hay fever (allergic rhinitis) add Sinus Support Compound™. For psoriatic arthritis add Gotu Kola and Sarsaparilla. For rheumatoid arthritis, add Cat's Claw, Devil's Claw, Sarsaparilla or Gum Guggul.

INSIGHT COMPOUND™

CONTAINS: Blueberry juice concentrate (Vaccinium spp.), hydroalcoholic extracts of Ginkgo leaf (Ginkgo biloba), Lycium fruit (Lycium barbarum), Chrysanthemum flowers (Dendranthema x grandiflorum) and vegetable glycerin.

INDICATIONS: This is a flavonoid rich formula that strengthens capillary integrity especially in the eyes. It is useful for enhancing vision and preventing degenerative eye disease. Regular use of these herbs has been shown to improve night vision and slow the progression of wet macular degeneration, hemorrhagic retinopathy and retinitis pigmentosa. This formula can also be used as a support for glaucoma and to help prevent diabetic retinopathy, cataracts and age-related macular degeneration (AMD). This formula also promotes endothelial function and strengthens the veins, capillaries and arteries. Regular use may help inhibit arteriosclerosis, prevent or treat varicose veins and reduce capillary leakage.

ACTIVITY: Flavonoids, especially anthocyanosides, are important nutrients for the blood vessels and small capillaries. These herbs are rich sources of these phytochemicals and they enhance microcirculation, especially to the eyes, and act as anti-inflammatories reducing oxidative damage to eye tissue. Ginkgo and Blueberry (which is chemically similar to Bilberry) have been extensively researched and found to strengthen, protect and heal damage to the eyes and vision. Lycium fruit/Goji berry and Chrysanthemum flowers are used in Traditional Chinese Medicine for a variety of eye problems, including poor vision, painful eyes, excessive tearing and floaters. They also improve retinal circulation and help prevent age-related macular degeneration (AMD). In a human trial Lycium fruit enhanced the antioxidant status in the eyes and inhibited progression of AMD (Bucheli, et al., 2011). In an animal study it prevented the loss of retinal ganglion cells due to glaucoma (Chan, et al., 2007)

CONTRAINDICATIONS: None.

SUGGESTED USE: 30-40 drops (1.5-2 ml) TID.

ADDITIONAL RECOMMENDATIONS: Include foods rich in carotenoids (especially Lutein) such as carrots, sweet potatoes, yellow squash, dried apricots, red peppers, beets, dark green leafy vegetables, especially spinach, dulse, cayenne pepper, tomatoes/tomato paste, and pumpkin. Antioxidant nutrients including lutein, lycopene, vitamin E, vitamin C, selenium and zinc have been found to inhibit age-related macular degeneration. Flavonoid rich foods and supplements such as green tea, grape seed extract, blueberries, grape juice, pomegranate, dark chocolate, red wine and pine tree bark extracts are also beneficial for protecting against sun or age-related eye damage.

ADDITIONAL USEFUL HERBS: Solid extracts of Blueberry, Elderberry, Pomegranate/Goji berry, and/or Hawthorn are rich in anti-inflammatory and antioxidant flavonoids which protect the eyes and enhance circulation. Triphala, Amla fruit, Turmeric, Rose hips and Calendula also contain flavonoids or carotenoids and have a long history of use for preventing or treating eye problems.

INTESTINAL CALMPOUND™

CONTAINS: Hydroalcoholic extracts of fresh Catnip flowering tops (Nepeta cataria), fresh Chamomile flowers (Matricaria recutita), Kudzu root (P. montana), Sarsaparilla root (Smilax regelii), fresh Turmeric rhizome (Curcuma longa), Wild Yam root (Dioscorea villosa), fresh Cyperus root (Cyperus rotundus), Yarrow flowering tops (Achillea millefolium) and vegetable glycerin.

INDICATIONS: This formula is useful for a wide range of bowel disorders including spastic colon/IBS, diverticulitis, leaky gut syndrome, Celiac disease, (to heal damage caused by gluten consumption), IBD/Crohn's disease and ileitis. It can also be useful as an adjunctive treatment for liver/gallbladder colic and painful flatulence.

ACTIVITY: The herbs in this formula reduce spasms and cramping of the gastro-intestinal tract and act as intestinal anti-inflammatories. Yarrow is anti-inflammatory and helps control bleeding and diarrhea caused by IBS-D or inflammatory bowel diseases (IBD). Turmeric is a powerful anti-inflammatory to the mucosa of the small and large intestines. It can help heal GI inflammation caused by IBS, IBD, ileitis, Crohn's Disease or Celiac. Wild Yam has a long history of use by native peoples, as well as the Eclectic and Physiomedical physicians. It is specific for bilious colic, IBS and gas pain. Catnip is used for stress-induced spasms of the large intestine, it relieves flatulence and abdominal bloating and it inhibits biofilm production by Heliobacter pylori. Sarsaparilla has anti-inflammatory activity, helps heal red, inflamed GI tract tissue and binds with endotoxins enhancing their excretion. Chamomile is a carminative, GI anti-inflammatory and mild antispasmodic useful for gas pain, diarrhea and IBS symptoms. Kudzu (Ge Gen) and Cyperus (Xiang Fu) are used in Traditional Chinese Medicine (TCM) for treating a number of bowel disorders. Kudzu is soothing to the GI tract and helps promote a healthy intestinal epithelial barrier. It also has antispasmodic effects. Cyperus is a strong GI antispasmodic, analgesic and anti-inflammatory. It is often used to treat intestinal colic, IBS, or functional abdominal pain syndrome (FAPS).

CONTRAINDICATIONS: People with inflammatory bowel disease (IBD) should always consult with a gastroenterologist, before attempting self-treatment. Pregnant women should seek medical advice before using this formula.

SUGGESTED USE: 50-75 drops (2.5-3.75 ml) QID while symptoms persist. For chronic conditions long term treatment is recommended.

ADDITIONAL RECOMMENDATIONS: Reduce stress and eliminate food allergens from diet especially dairy or wheat. Probiotics and prebiotics, as well as live fermented foods have been shown to improve bowel flora and relieve many GI symptoms.

ADDITIONAL USEFUL HERBS: Take Slippery Elm or Marshmallow tea (decoction) 3 times per day between meals. Essential oil of Peppermint in enteric coated capsules has been found to reduce symptoms in people suffering from IBS. For Crohn's disease/IBD add Immune Balance Compound™, Reishi, Turmeric, Licorice, Maitake, or Huang Qin to reduce auto-immune response. For IBD with bleeding, Reckless Blood Tonic™, Shepherd's Purse or Yarrow may be helpful.

IRON EXTRACT™

CONTAINS: Beet succus (Beta vulgaris), and hydroalcoholic extracts of Alfalfa herb (Medicago sativa), fresh Parsley leaf and root (Petroselinum crispum), Stinging Nettle leaf (Urtica dioica), Yellow Dock root (Rumex crispus), , Ashwagandha root (Withania somnifera), fresh Watercress herb (Rorippa nasturtium-aquatica), Blackstrap Molasses and vegetable glycerin.

INDICATIONS: Specific indications for this formula include iron or folate-deficient anemia with low hematocrit/hemoglobin and ferritin levels. Women who are tired, with heavy menstrual bleeding, feel cold all the time, have pale fingernails and tongue and bluish scleras often respond well to this formula.

ACTIVITY: ACTIVITY: This formula combines the fresh juice of organic beets and iron rich blackstrap molasses with mineral rich herbs such as Nettles, Parsley,

Watercress, Ashwagandha and Alfalfa. Yellow Dock also seems to increase the liver's ability to store iron. Alfalfa, Parsley and Stinging Nettle are rich sources of folate which is also necessary to treat some types of anemia. In a clinical study of girls with low Folate and Iron levels, Alfalfa was as effective as supplemental Iron and Folic Acid, even though it contains much less of these nutrients (Vyas, et al., 2009). This illustrates the bioavailability of the nutrients in these herbs. Some of these herbs contain Vitamin C which is needed for proper iron absorption. This formula will not cause stomach upset or constipation as many iron supplements do.

CONTRAINDICATIONS: Hemochromatosis or hemosiderosis.

SUGGESTED USE: As a daily food supplement 40-50 drops (2-2.5 ml) TID.

ADDITIONAL RECOMMENDATIONS: Include dark green leafy vegetables, beets, raisins, artichokes, sea vegetables, spirulina and sources of heme iron (organically raised red meats) in the diet. The use of cast iron cookware can improve iron levels. Taking Vitamin C with iron enhances its absorption. Smoking interferes with iron absorption and women who are vegan/vegetarian are more likely to develop anemia, so they should take supplemental iron.

ADDITIONAL USEFUL HERBS: Processed Rehmannia, Dandelion leaf, and Artichoke leaf all contain iron or folate.

J. KLOSS ANTISPASMODIC COMPOUND

CONTAINS: Hydroalcoholic extracts of fresh Black Cohosh root (Actaea racemosa), Myrrh gum resin (Commiphora molmol), fresh Skullcap herb (Scutellaria lateriflora), fresh Skunk Cabbage root (Symplocarpus foetidus), Lobelia herb in flower and seed (Lobelia inflata), Cayenne pepper (Capsicum annum) and apple cider vinegar.

INDICATIONS: Jethro Kloss' classic antispasmodic formula is indicated for most types of cramps as well as spasms of the lungs, uterus or muscles of the back, neck, and legs. It is useful for treating torticollis, back spasms, menstrual cramps, spasmodic headaches, coughs, spasmodic asthma, trigeminal neuralgia, TMJ pain, facial tics and the spasticity associated with Tourette's syndrome or Tardive dyskinesia. It can also be of use for some cases of restless leg syndrome.

ACTIVITY: Black Cohosh, Skullcap, Skunk Cabbage, and Lobelia are active anti-spasmodics, with a long history of use by the Thomsonians, Eclectics and Physiomedicalists. Black Cohosh relieves muscle spasms, back pain, testicular cramps, dysmenorrhea, and spasmodic coughs. Skullcap is indicated for stress-induced tics or spasms and can help control tremors caused by Parkinson's disease. Skunk Cabbage is powerful spasmolytic used for asthma, back pain and torticollis. Lobelia has a long history of use for spasmodic coughs, asthma, angina pain, headaches and petit mal seizures Myrrh and Cayenne are used to increase absorption of the other herbs in the formula and promote circulation.

CONTRAINDICATIONS: Pregnancy and lactation. It may potentiate antispasmodic or sedative medication. Consult a healthcare professional before use if you have or have had liver problems, frequently use alcoholic beverages, or take any medications.

SUGGESTED USE: 5-20 drops (.25-1 ml) TID only as symptoms persist.

ADDITIONAL RECOMMENDATIONS: Increase calcium and magnesium intake.

ADDITIONAL USEFUL HERBS: For GI spasms - Cyperus, Catnip, Chamomile, Valerian or Hops are useful. For muscle spasms - Blue Vervain, Black Haw, Kudzu or Kava can offer additional benefits. For respiratory spasms - Lung Relief Antispasmodic™, Khella, Wild Cherry bark or Licorice can be effective adjunctive therapies.

KIDNEY RELIEF COMPOUND™

CONTAINS: Hydroalcoholic extracts of Celery seed (Apium graveolens), Parsley whole plant (Petroselinum crispum), Buchu leaf (Agathosma betulina), Corn silk (Zea mays) and Pipsissewa herb (Chimaphila umbellata).

INDICATIONS: Kidney Relief Compound™ has two primary uses; it enhances uric acid excretion and it is an antiseptic diuretic. It is appropriate for treating gout and gouty arthritis, as well as relieving edema, cystitis, urethritis and PMS water retention.

ACTIVITY: Celery seed and Parsley are very effective for enhancing excretion of uric acid. Both are diuretics (Kreydiyyeh and Usta, 2002) and have anti-inflammatory activity. In several animal studies Celery seed protected against hyperuricemia and kidney damage (Tong, et al., 2008, Mohamed and Al-Okbi 2008). Buchu and Pipsissewa are antiseptic diuretics used for treating urinary tract infections. Both also have a long history of use for treating gout and gouty arthritis. Corn silk is a soothing diuretic (Maksimović et al., 2004) long used in folk medicine for relieving gout.

CONTRAINDICATIONS: Avoid concurrent use with cardiac glycosides (Digoxin, Lanoxin) as this product may increase potassium loss, thus increasing the risk of arrhythmias. Do not use with lithium as diuretics can increase lithium's toxicity.

SUGGESTED USE: 60-80 drops (3-4 ml) TID in juice or water.

ADDITIONAL RECOMMENDATIONS: People with gout or gouty arthritis should eat a diet that limits fish, meat, poultry, alcohol (especially beer) and high-fructose corn syrup. Increase consumption of low-fat dairy products, vegetables, fresh fruits (especially black cherries) and water intake.

ADDITIONAL USEFUL HERBS: Hibiscus tea has also been found to enhance uric acid excretion (Prasongwatana et al., 2008) and Goldenrod, Cleavers and Stinging Nettle leaf have all been used to enhance diuresis and purine excretion.

KIDNEY SUPPORT COMPOUND™

CONTAINS: Hydroalcoholic extracts of Stinging Nettle seed (Urtica dioica), Astragalus root (Astragalus membranaceus), Processed Rehmannia root (Rehmannia glutinosa), Stinging Nettle leaf (Urtica dioica) and Cordyceps mycelium and/or mushroom (Cordyceps Ophiocordyceps sinensis (a.k.a. Cordyceps sinensis) or Cordyceps militaris).

INDICATIONS: This formula is indicated for chronic kidney disease with degeneration. I use it for mild to moderate loss of kidney function associated with chronic nephritis, glomerulonephritis, idiopathic primary renal hematuric/ proteinuric syndrome (Bergers's disease) and nephrotoxic disorders.

ACTIVITY: Stinging Nettle leaf is well-known as a gentle, potassium-sparing diuretic. It is a tonic to the kidney because it is rich in anti-inflammatory carotenoids and minerals and it relieves kidney pain. Stinging Nettle seed is a powerful trophorestorative to the kidney. The use of Stinging Nettle seed is recorded in early English herbals and modern clinical use has shown the validity of this herb for mild to moderate degenerative kidney disease (Treasure, 2003). It contains neophroprotective lectins and is our most powerful nephroprotective herb. Astragalus is nephroprotective preventing antibiotic-induced kidney disease, lithotripsy-induced kidney damage and improving kidney function in people with idiopathic membranous nephropathy (Ahmed, et al., 2007). Processed Rehmannia is used in Traditional Chinese Medicine as a kidney yin tonic. It is prescribed for lower back pain, frequent urination, hypertension and tinnitus. Cordyceps is an important tonic remedy in China. It tonifies both the kidney yin and yang, as well as the endocrine and immune systems. Human studies show it is nephroprotective and helps prevent medication-induced kidney damage. (Zhang, et al., 2011, Li, et al., 2009)

CONTRAINDICATIONS: There is no clinical data to support or contraindicate the formula's use in the case of severe kidney disease and patients undergoing dialysis. Until further research is done, it is advisable to avoid use under these circumstances.

SUGGESTED USE: 30-60 drops (1.5-3 ml) TID.

ADDITIONAL RECOMMENDATIONS: Dietary restrictions of sodium, potassium, phosphorus and protein may be advised by a physician. Kidney disorders may be associated with abnormalities of calcium, vitamin E and phosphorus metabolism.

ADDITIONAL USEFUL HERBS: To protect against nephrotoxic medications add Milk Thistle. For degenerative kidney disease other "kidney restoratives" such as the European herb Parsley Piert, Chinese Dogwood fruit, Chinese Salvia, Astragalus, and small amounts of Rhubarb root can be added.

KID'S CALMPOUND GLYCERITE™

CONTAINS: Glycerin extracts of Catnip flowering tops (Nepeta cataria), Chamomile flowers (Matricaria recutita), fresh Oat milky seed (Avena sativa) and Skullcap herb (Scutellaria lateriflora).

INDICATIONS: This is a general nervine/sedative formula useful in mild to moderate cases of insomnia, restlessness, anxiety, irritability, hyperactivity and bad dreams. The herbs also have antispasmodic and mild analgesic (pain relieving) activity which makes them useful for stress-induced stomach or headaches, bruxism, hyperactivity and muscle spasms.

ACTIVITY: Skullcap is an excellent nervine and antispasmodic, it is indicated for stress-induced fidgeting, nervous tics and emotional outbursts. Oat is highly nourishing and rejuvenating to the nervous system, so it helps children who are under stress and feeling anxious or irritable. Catnip and Chamomile are gentle nervines especially useful for people who internalize emotions in the gut. This can cause stress-induced gastric and intestinal disturbances. Both Skullcap and Chamomile have been shown to relieve anxiety in human clinical trials (Wolfson & Hoffman 2003, Amsterdam, et al., 2009).

CONTRAINDICATIONS: Severe Ragweed allergies.

SUGGESTED USE: For insomnia 15-30 drops (.75-1.5 ml) in the evening (ideally in Chamomile tea) while symptoms persist. For general anxiety or irritability 10-20 drops (.5-1 ml) TID.

ADDITIONAL RECOMMENDATIONS: Increase intake of B vitamins, calcium, magnesium and DHA-rich omega 3 fatty acids. Reduce exposure to television, video games and fluorescent lighting which are overstimulating. Reduce refined sugars, artificial colors, preservatives and beverages such as cola that contain caffeine or artificial sweeteners such as aspartame.

ADDITIONAL USEFUL HERBS: Some pleasant tasting and calming teas include Linden flower, Longan fruit and Lemon Balm.

KID'S TUMMY RELIEF™

CONTAINS: Glycerin extracts of Catnip flowering tops (Nepeta cataria), Chamomile flowers (Matricaria recutita), Ginger rhizome (Zingiber officinale), Lemon Balm herb (Melissa officinalis), Dandelion root (Taraxacum officinale), vegetable glycerin and Peppermint Essential Oil.

INDICATIONS: This carminative formula relieves symptoms of upset stomach, nausea and flatulence caused by stress, intestinal viruses, overeating, motion sickness and diarrhea. It is useful for colic, biliousness, borborygmus and painful gas. Other indications include intestinal dysbiosis, medication-induced nausea, vomiting and acid stomach.

ACTIVITY: Ginger enhances digestion and helps relieve nausea, gas and borborygmus. In clinical trials Ginger was effective in relieving nausea in children undergoing chemotherapy (Pillai, et al., 2011), as well as motion sickness (Lien, et al., 2003) and post-operative nausea. Chamomile relieves bowel spasms and due to its aromatic volatile oils, it helps reduce flatulence. It is also anti-inflammatory to the GI tract and inhibits Campylobacter pylori, a major cause of diarrhea. Catnip is especially effective for gastro-intestinal tract symptoms including stress-induced stomach aches, diarrhea, constipation and abdominal bloating. Lemon Balm helps relieve gas and excess stomach acid. Peppermint oil has been clinically shown to reduce intestinal spasms and dyspepsia. Dandelion root is an aperient, bitter tonic and cholagogue. It enhances digestion especially of fats and helps promote normal bowel function.

CONTRAINDICATIONS: None.

SUGGESTED USE: 15-30 drops (.75-1.5 ml) 3 times per day in juice or water or as needed.

ADDITIONAL RECOMMENDATIONS: Avoid greasy fried foods and fast foods. Eat a light nourishing diet. Children's probiotic formulas are very useful especially if antibiotic use has disrupted the normal bowel flora.

ADDITIONAL USEFUL HERBS: Fennel, Cinnamon, Spearmint, Linden flower teas are also useful for stomach aches, nausea and diarrhea.

LUNG RELIEF ANTISPASMODIC™

CONTAINS: Hydroalcoholic extracts of Wild Cherry bark (Prunus virginiana), Licorice root (Glycyrrhiza glabra), Mullein leaf (Verbascum thapsus), Lobelia herb in flower and seed (Lobelia inflata), Wild Lettuce herb (Lactuca virosa), Khella seed (Ammi visnaga), vegetable glycerin and Apple Cider vinegar.

INDICATIONS: This formula is effective for respiratory conditions with spasmodic or ticklish coughs and intercostal or back pain from constant coughing. It can also be used as part of a treatment protocol for mild to moderate asthma, or COPD. In addition it can be used to treat the spasmodic coughs of pertussis, measles, respiratory syncytial virus (RSV), bronchitis, and some types of pneumonia.

ACTIVITY: This formula contains herbs that are antispasmodic (Wild Cherry bark, Licorice, Khella, Wild Lettuce), anti-inflammatory (Licorice, Mullein), and analgesic (Wild Cherry bark, Lobelia, and Wild Lettuce). Khella relaxes the smooth muscle of the bronchi, and is especially useful for bronchial asthma. Lobelia stops bronchospasm in pertussis and asthma. Licorice effectively suppresses dry ticklish coughs such as smoker's cough. It also has antiviral, demulcent (yin tonic) and expectorant properties. Licorice, Lobelia and Mullein are expectorants and can help expel sticky, hard-to-expectorate mucus that can trigger spasmodic coughs.

CONTRAINDICATIONS: Pregnancy.

SUGGESTED USE: 30-40 drops (1.5-2 ml) up to 6 times per day.

ADDITIONAL RECOMMENDATIONS: Dry air can exacerbate dry spasmodic coughs. A good humidifier can help increase humidity in our homes especially during the dry winter months. Magnesium deficiency can increase spasm, inducing respiratory spasms and a lack of omega 3 fatty acids (fish oil) can promote inflammation and airway hyperactivity. Allergens including dust mites, particulates, animal dander and pollen can also cause inflammation and asthma.

ADDITIONAL USEFUL HERBS: For allergy-induced respiratory problems use Immune Balance Compound™, Amla, or Blueberry or Pomegranate/Goji berry as well as other sources of anti-inflammatory polyphenolic compounds.

LUNG RELIEF COLD/DAMP™

CONTAINS: Hydroalcoholic extracts of Thyme herb (Thymus vulgaris), Yerba Santa leaf (Eriodictyon californicum), Orange peel (Citrus aurantium), Ginger rhizome (Zingiberis officinalis) and Osha root (Ligusticum porterii).

INDICATIONS: Use this formula for respiratory conditions associated with excessive mucus or fluid in the lungs, and sinuses, including walking pneumonia, chronic bronchitis (cold/damp), head colds, and allergic rhinitis. In a cold/damp condition, the mucus is profuse and clear or white in color. The person feels cold, may have chills, with dull pain upon coughing, a pale, wet tongue, a slow pulse, and they crave warmth. Other symptoms which indicate a cold/damp condition include fatigue, cloudy thinking, edema or profuse clear urination, dyspnea, wheezing, postnasal drip, or a runny nose.

ACTIVITY: These herbs are warming antibacterials and antivirals. They have anti-inflammatory, antioxidant, expectorant, and circulation enhancing effects.

Osha is an excellent antihistamine for allergic rhinitis, and Orange Peel, Ginger, and Yerba Santa help stabilize mast cells and reduce histamine production and nasal secretions. Thyme, Yerba Santa and Osha are bronchodilators and expectorants, they help expel mucus, and promote freer breathing. In combination, these herbs will dry up excessive secretions, promote expectoration, and help prevent or treat respiratory infections caused by bacteria or viruses.

CONTRAINDICATIONS: Pregnancy and cold/dry, hot/dry or hot/damp respiratory tract conditions.

SUGGESTED USE: 40-60 drops (2-3 ml) QID.

ADDITIONAL RECOMMENDATIONS: Steam inhalations with 1-3 drops of warming essential oils (Marjoram, Cinnamon or Oregano e.o.) in a kettle of boiling water can help relieve cold/damp lung conditions.

LUNG RELIEF COLD/DRY™

CONTAINS: Hydroalcoholic extracts of Spikenard root (Aralia racemosa), Licorice root (Glycyrrhiza glabra), Prince Seng root (Pseudostellaria heterophylla), Astragalus root (Astragalus membranaceus) and Chinese Asparagus root (Asparagus cochinchinensis).

INDICATIONS: This formula is indicated for respiratory conditions associated with dry coughs with little or no mucus (if there is mucus, it is sticky, clear, or white), chills, wheezing, and a dry mouth. From a TCM perspective this would be considered a deficient yin syndrome, often occurring as an aftermath of an acute respiratory infection. The original condition (hot bronchitis, hot/damp pneumonia) has consumed the lung *yin* and left the tissue dry, depleted, and irritated. Cold/dry lung conditions can also be caused by breathing excessively dry air, especially in the winter.

ACTIVITY: The herbs in this formula are nourishing *yin* tonics, which moisten the mucous membranes and respiratory tract. They enhance normal mucus production, strengthen the lungs and the *wei qi* (protective qi). Licorice, Prince Seng, Astragalus, and Chinese Asparagus are immune tonics and they promote macrophage activity, as well as reducing inflammation. Prince Seng and Licorice are also Qi tonics helping to relieve fatigue and debility that occurs after pneumonia. Spikenard is a warming and moistening expectorant which helps to eliminate dry, sticky mucus.

CONTRAINDICATIONS: Pregnancy and cold/damp, hot/damp or hot/dry respiratory tract conditions.

SUGGESTED USE: 50-60 drops (2.5-3 ml) TID.

ADDITIONAL RECOMMENDATIONS: Dry air can exacerbate dry spasmodic or ticklish coughs. A good humidifier can help increase humidity in our homes especially during the dry winter months.

LUNG RELIEF HOT/DAMP™

CONTAINS: Hydroalcoholic extracts of Japanese Honeysuckle flower (Lonicera japonica), Ground Ivy herb (Glechoma hederacea), Pleurisy root (Asclepias tuberosa), Huang Qin root (Scutellaria baicalensis) and White Sage leaf (Salvia apiana).

INDICATIONS: Use this formula for respiratory conditions associated with inflammatory pneumonia, bronchitis, lung abscesses, sinusitis, tonsillitis, sore throat, and hemoptysis with excessive mucus. In hot/damp conditions, the sputum is yellow, green, or bloody. The patient may also have a fever (with sweating), red inflamed tonsils, a red tongue with a thick yellow moss (lingual coating), and a rapid slippery pulse. Other signs indicating a hot/damp condition include a sharp, tearing pain upon coughing, a strong desire for cool temperatures, painful ear infections, irritability, and dark, scalding urine.

ACTIVITY: The herbs in this formula are all strongly antibacterial, and antiviral, they reduce excessive secretions, are anti-inflammatory, and clear damp heat. Pleurisy root is especially useful for conditions where "it hurts to breathe". It was used by Native Americans, the Thomosonians, Eclectics and Physiomedicalists for treating pleurisy, bronchitis and pneumonia. White Sage is rich in essential oils which numb inflamed nerve endings, helping to reduce throat pain. It is also effective for reducing excess mucus production. Ground Ivy enhances expectoration of mucus and is used to treat bronchitis and pneumonia. Honeysuckle flowers and Huang Qin are especially indicated for respiratory conditions with fever, coughing blood, yellow mucus and headaches. As a gargle, this formula is very effective for tonsillitis, sore throat, and uvulitis.

CONTRAINDICATIONS: Pregnancy, and hot/dry, cold/damp or cold/dry respiratory tract conditions. Avoid use in young children.

SUGGESTED USE: 40-60 drops (2-3 ml) QID.

ADDITIONAL RECOMMENDATIONS: Steam inhalations with 1-3 drops of cooling essential oils (Eucalyptus, Peppermint or Tea Tree) in 16 oz boiling water can help relieve hot/damp lung conditions.

LUNG RELIEF HOT/DRY™

CONTAINS: Hydroalcoholic extracts of Chinese Asparagus root (Asparagus cochinchinensis), Horehound flowering tops (Marrubium vulgare), Platycodon root (Platycodon grandiflorum), Red Clover blossom (Trifolium pratense) and Elecampane root (Inula helenium).

INDICATIONS: This formula is indicated for respiratory conditions associated with inflammatory bronchitis, pertussis, and asthma, with little or no sputum (if there is mucus, it is difficult to expectorate and usually is yellow, green, or bloody). The patient may also have a fever (with little or no sweating), dry mouth, a dry, irritative cough, a red, furred tongue, and red, dry, glistening tonsils.

ACTIVITY: Chinese Asparagus (or Tian Men Dong) is a yin tonic used for dry, irritated or inflamed mucous membrane tissue. It is frequently used in formulas for dry coughs, dry mouth and hot/dry bronchitis or asthma. Elecampane is a powerful antibacterial/antiviral agent that soothes irritated mucous membranes. Platycodon is used in TCM for a wide variety of respiratory problems because it is a non-irritating expectorant and anti-inflammatory. It is frequently used to treat asthma, bronchitis, laryngitis, spasmodic coughs and some painful throats. Red Clover and Horehound are mild tonic expectorants that moisten the pulmonary tissue and reduce inflammation. The Eclectics felt Red Clover was especially effective for ticklish coughs caused by measles or adult pertussis. All of the herbs in this formula have a mild demulcent effect on the mucous membranes and sooth irritated tissue in the lungs via a reflex action.

CONTRAINDICATIONS: Cold/damp, cold/dry, hot/damp respiratory tract conditions.

SUGGESTED USE: 60-80 drops (3-4 ml) TID/QID.

ADDITIONAL RECOMMENDATIONS: Dry air can exacerbate hot/dry coughs. A good humidifier can help increase humidity in our homes especially during the dry winter months.

MEN'S ADAPT™

CONTAINS: Hydroalcoholic extracts of Ashwagandha root (Withania somniferum), Cynomorium stem (Cynomorium songaricum), Maca root (Lepedium meyenii), Red Ginseng root (Panax ginseng), Epimedium herb (Epimedium grandiflorum) and vegetable glycerin.

INDICATIONS: This is a general tonic for the male reproductive system. It strengthens endocrine function and helps normalize hormonal balance. Indications include low testosterone levels, male infertility caused by a low sperm count or poor sperm motility, lack of libido, impotence, deficient kidney yang patterns (characterized by chronic low back pain, erectile dysfunction, fatigue and weak ankles or knees) and mild benign prostatic hyperplasia.

ACTIVITY: Ashwagandha and Red Ginseng are adaptogens that normalize endocrine, nervous system and immune functions. Both herbs have reputations for strengthening male reproductive function especially in tired, overworked and stressed-out men. In human studies Red Ginseng enhanced erectile function, thus supporting its traditional usage (de Andrade, et al., 2007, Hong, et al., 2002). In another clinical trial Ashwagandha enhanced sperm counts and motility and improved serum testosterone levels (Ahmad, et al., 2010). Suo Yang is used in TCM for lack of libido and erectile dysfunction, as is Epidmedium (Horny Goat Weed or Yin Yang Huo). In animal studies Epimedium increased sexual functioning in aged test subjects. Maca is a nutritive tonic that supports healthy male sexual functioning.

CONTRAINDICATIONS: Prostate inflammation, prostatitis or priapism.

SUGGESTED USE: 40-60 drops (2-3 ml) TID for at least 3 months for chronic conditions.

ADDITIONAL RECOMMENDATIONS: Include nutrients that are essential to healthy male reproductive function such as zinc, vitamin E and fish oils as well as foods rich in these nutrients including pumpkin seeds, sardines and sesame seeds.

ADDITIONAL USEFUL HERBS: Morinda root, Cistanche/Rou Cong Rong and Cordyceps have all been used to enhance male reproduction function.

MEN'S MIDLIFE TONIC™

CONTAINS: Oat milky seed (Avena sativa), Ashwagandha root (Withania somnifera), Black Cohosh root (Actaea racemosa), Mimosa bark (Albizia julibrissin),

Saw Palmetto berry (Serenoa repens), Pulsatilla herb (Pulsatilla vulgaris) and orange flavoring.

INDICATIONS: Men's Midlife Tonic™ is used to help relieve the emotional instability, irritability and grouchiness that can occur as men go through Andropause. Andropause describes the period in men's lives, usually from age 50-65, where serum testosterone levels drop, cortisol levels rise, and men facing major life changes (especially retirement and aging issues) often find themselves feeling isolated, overwhelmed, anxious, angry, impatient, disillusioned or depressed. Other symptoms of andropause can include lethargy, lack of energy, decreased libido, difficulty concentrating, insomnia and osteoporosis.

ACTIVITY: Milky oat is one of the great nerve trophorestoratives. It gently helps to restore emotional balance. It is useful for anxiety, depression or irritability. Animal studies show that milky Oat can improve stress response, enhance learning and decrease social avoidance behaviors (Schellekens, et al., 2009). Ashwagandha is a calming adaptogen that also enhances testosterone levels and libido. In a human clinical trial, it enhanced sperm quality in infertile men (Ahmad, et al., 2010). Withania has also shown the ability to reduce the effects of chronic stress and alleviate depression and anxiety. Black Cohosh is effective for treating hormonal depression, which includes andropausal depression in men. Mimosa bark or He Huan Pi (Collective Happiness Bark) is one of the most effective mood elevators known. It can be used for depression, chronic grief and "broken hearts". Saw Palmetto is mostly known for its beneficial effects on the prostate gland. It not only reduces symptoms of BPH, it also helps relieve "Grumpy Old Man Syndrome", which is exacerbated by increasing levels of dihydrotestosterone (DHT). Saw Palmetto can inhibit conversion of testosterone to DHT by inhibiting 5-alpha reductase. Pulsatilla is used in very small amounts for hormonal depression, anxiety, irritability, moodiness and "fly off the handle" anger.

CONTRAINDICATIONS: Not for use by pregnant women. Consult a healthcare professional before use if you have or have had liver problems, frequently use alcoholic beverages, or take any medications. Do not use if you have bipolar disorder.

SUGGESTED USE: 60-80 drops (3-4 ml) two times per day in juice or water.

ADDITIONAL RECOMMENDATIONS: Increase exercise and lose weight, as obesity and insulin resistance can worsen andropausal symptoms. Regular exercise has also been shown to enhance testosterone levels. Avoid isolating oneself and find new creative and social outlets. Avoid excessive alcohol consumption and eat a low glycemic index/load diet. Healthy foods include fresh vegetables and fruits, deep sea fish, lean organic meats, legumes, nuts, seeds, whole grains and olive oil. Fish oils (omega 3 fatty acids) and adequate nutrients, especially B Complex vitamins, Vitamins D and E, minerals such as zinc, selenium, chromium and magnesium, are all essential (and often lacking) for healthy aging.

ADDITIONAL USEFUL HERBS: Tension Relief™ is useful if anxiety is also a significant problem. Red Ginseng, Epimedium, Cordyceps, Cynomorium, Rhodiola and Maca can also enhance male reproductive function and mood.

MEN'S PROSTATE TONIC™

CONTAINS: Hydroalcoholic extracts of Saw Palmetto berry (Serenoa repens), White Sage herb (Salvia apiana), whole fresh Collinsonia plant (Collinsonia canadensis), Stinging Nettle root (Urtica dioica) and vegetable glycerin.

INDICATIONS: This formula has been of benefit to men suffering from lower urinary tract symptoms (LUTS) when other treatments have failed. It is indicated for benign prostatic hypertrophy (BPH), urinary frequency as well as inflammation of the vas deferens or spermatic cord. This formula is more effective than Saw Palmetto alone, in reducing prostatic swelling, nocturia and incomplete emptying of the bladder.

ACTIVITY: White Sage helps to shrink a swollen prostate gland while also having anti-inflammatory, antibacterial and antioxidant activity. Saw Palmetto and Stinging Nettle root act as mild 5-alpha reductase inhibitors. They also inhibit prolactin, aromatase, phospholipase A2, and estrogen receptors in prostate tissue. This reduces inflammation, inhibits the growth of prostate tissue, and relieves BPH symptoms. Collinsonia was used by the Eclectic physicians to reduce venous congestion in the prostate and inhibit urinary dribbling and prostatic inflammation.

CONTRAINDICATIONS: None.

SUGGESTED USE: 40-60 drops (2-3 ml) TID for at least 4-6 months.

ADDITIONAL RECOMMENDATIONS: Increase dietary zinc intake by eating pumpkin seeds, oysters or bee pollen or take a Zinc supplement (30 mg per day). The amino acids glycine, alanine and glutamic acid have been found to reduce BPH symptoms as has beta-sitosterol. Alternating hot/cold sitz baths, and pelvic floor exercises can also be of benefit. Regular beer drinking can increase excretion of Zinc and worsen BPH symptoms.

ADDITIONAL USEFUL HERBS: Pygeum bark, Corn silk, Cleavers, Couch Grass and Pipsissewa have all been used to reduce symptoms of BPH.

METABOLIC SUPPORT™

CONTAINS: Hydroalcoholic extracts of Bitter Melon fruit (Mormordica charantia), Cinnamon bark (Cinnamomum verum), Fenugreek seed (Trigonella foenumgraecum), Olive leaf (Olea europaea), Artichoke leaf (Cynara scolymus), Holy Basil herb (Ocimum tenuiflorum), Lycium fruit (Lycium barbarum)

INDICATIONS: This formula helps reduce insulin resistance and the resultant metabolic syndrome (METS). Metabolic syndrome has a wide range of sequeli including increased deposition of belly fat (obesity also can cause metabolic syndrome), increased inflammation, unhealthy blood lipids, elevation of blood pressure, impaired sleep, decreased immune and digestive functions, increased cell growth (cancer, skin tags, BPH, Fibroids) and risk of cardiovascular and neurodegenerative disease.

ACTIVITY: Most of the herbs in this formula have been traditionally used to treat obesity and type II Diabetes (T2D). Not all herbs that treat T2D are appropriate for treating metabolic syndrome (METS). Each of the herbs in Metabolic Support™ have been shown to help improve glycemic control, inhibit insulin resistance, reduce inflammation and the other issues associated with METS. In clinical studies Bitter Melon decreased insulin resistance, waist circumference, LDL/VLDL cholesterol and triglycerides in patients with METS (Tsai, et al., 2012). Cinnamon enhances the beta cells ability to utilize insulin and inhibits Metabolic Syndrome, as well as conditions associated with METS such as PCOS and NAFLD (Kort & Lobo, 2014; Askari, et al., 2014). Fenugreek seed has long been used to treat type II Diabetes (T2D) and in a human study inhibited METS and helped to prevent its progression to T2D (Gaddam, et al., 2015). Olive leaf is widely touted for its antibacterial and antiviral activity. There is no human or animal research confirming this belief, but there is a traditional of use and human studies showing it can increase insulin sensitivity (de Bock, et al., 2013) while also reducing blood pressure (Perrinjaquet-Moccetti, et al., 2008; Somova et al., 2003) and improve endothelial function (Lockyer, et al., 2017). Artichoke leaf was given to people with METS, it reduced blood sugar levels, HbA1c and homeostatic metabolic assessment (HOMA). In addition, it has been shown to reduce LDL/VLDL cholesterol levels (Rondanelli, et al., 2013). Holy Basil or tulsi is a mild adaptogen, carminative, nootropic, immune amphoteric, anxiolytic and antidepressant. In several human studies it has been shown to reduce insulin resistance, blood sugar, LDL/VLDL cholesterol, triglycerides, BMT, Liver enzymes and uric acid levels (Satapathy, et al., 2017; Jamshidi & Cohen, 2017; Devra, et al., 2012). Gou Qi Zi or Goji Berries have become popular as a "superfood" They are rich in anti-inflammatory carotenoids and flavonoids. Regular use can inhibit atherosclerosis, protect against hyperglycemic-induced capillary, nerve, eye, or kidney damage. It also modestly decreases blood sugar levels as well as triglycerides, and LDL cholesterol levels (Luo, et al., 2004).

CONTRAINDICATIONS: Monitor blood sugar levels carefully when using in combination with blood sugar lowering medications. Do not use during pregnancy unless otherwise directed by a qualified expert.

SUGGESTED USE: 60-80 drops (3-4 mL) TID

MUSCLE/JOINT TONIC™

CONTAINS: Hydroalcoholic extracts of Sarsaparilla root (Smilax regelii), fresh Turmeric rhizome (Curcuma longa), Devil's Claw tuber (Harpagophytum procumbens), Bupleurum root (Bupleurum falcatum), Ginger rhizome (Zingiber officinale), Willow bark (Salix spp.), Sichuan Teasel root (Dipsacus japonicus) and vegetable glycerin.

INDICATIONS: This is a general anti-inflammatory formula useful for treating muscle and joint inflammation associated with osteoarthritis, back and neck pain, bursitis, rheumatoid arthritis, muscle stiffness and trauma injuries. Combined with carminative herbs, it can also be a useful part of a protocol for irritable bowel syndrome.

ACTIVITY: Most of the herbs in this formula have systemic anti-inflammatory activity. Sarsaparilla, Turmeric, Ginger, Japanese Teasel, Devil's Claw, and Bupleurum all reduce inflammation, inhibit histamine release and the production of inflammatory prostaglandins. By using different plants with differing modes of action this unique formula produces a synergistic effect in the body. Ginger and Turmeric act as a mild COX-2 inhibitors, without unduly disrupting COX-1 enzymes like aspirin does, or causing heart problems like pharmaceutical COX-2 inhibitors. In a human trial, Ginger had significant benefits for reducing symptoms of osteoarthritis of the knee (Altman & Marcussen, 2001), and numerous animal studies show that turmeric can inhibit inflammation and reduce symptoms of osteo- and rheumatoid arthritis. Willow bark has mild aspirin-like activity, but does not irritate the GI tract or irreversibly inhibit platelets as does aspirin. Several human trials show it has modest benefits for musculoskeletal pain and osteoarthritis (Schmid, et al., 2001, Chrabasik, et al., 2000). Ginger inhibits inflammatory prostaglandins, as well as downregulating leukotriene synthesis. Devil's Claw has been found to relieve arthritis in multiple human trials. (Warnock, et al., 2007, Göbel, et al., 2001)

SUGGESTED USE: 60-80 drops (3-4 ml) TID/QID in acute situations. For chronic inflammation use 30-40 drops (1.5-2 ml) TID for at least 1 month.

CONTRAINDICATIONS: Not for use in pregnancy unless otherwise directed by a qualified expert.

ADDITIONAL USEFUL HERBS: For osteoarthritis add Burdock/Red Root Compound™, or anti-inflammatory herbs. For fibromyalgia add Black Cohosh, Kava, Ashwagandha or Chinese Peony. For rheumatoid arthritis add Ashwagandha, Immune Balance Compound™, Feverfew, Maitake, Reishi, Huang Qin or Chinese Salvia.

OLD WORLD BITTERS™

CONTAINS: Hydroalcoholic extracts of Blessed Thistle herb (Cnicus benedictus), Elderflower flowers (Sambucus nigra ssp. canadensis, S. nigra), Linden flower and leaf (Tilia sp.), Roman Chamomile flowers (Chamaemelum nobile), Gentian root (Gentiana lutea), Hops strobiles (Humulus lupulus), Fenugreek seed (Trigonella foenum-graecum)

INDICATIONS: This formula stimulates the entire process of digestion, absorption and elimination by increasing production of gastric hydrochloric acid as well as liver, pancreatic and small intestine digestive enzymes and juices. By stimulating bile production this formula also enhances fat metabolism and acts as a natural aperient/laxative. Indications include achlorhydria/hypochlorhydia, malabsorption, chronic gas, belching, indigestion and abdominal bloating. Old World Bitters™ is a useful adjunct for any protocol addressing GI dysbiosis or food sensitivities caused by leaky gut syndrome. Many chronic conditions such as arthritis, auto-immune disorders, skin conditions, etc. will benefit from enhancing digestive and liver/gallbladder function.

ACTIVITY: This "old world" bitters formula contains herbs long used in Europe to promote healthy digestion, absorption and elimination. It combines cooling bitters such as Blessed Thistle, Gentian and Hops with warming flowers (Elderflower and Roman Chamomile) and seeds (Fenugreek). With a "hoppy" taste, this formula improves secretion of gastric HCL, small intestine and pancreatic juices and bile secretion and bile excretion. This allows for a greater ability to absorb the "grain Qi" (nutrients), reduce rebellious Qi (heartburn, belching) and promote liver and gallbladder function.

CONTRAINDICATIONS: Do not use if you have hyperchlorhydria. Use cautiously if you have gastric ulcers, gastritis or GERD.

SUGGESTED USE: 15-30 drops (.75-1.5 ml) taken 10-15 minutes before meals. Shake well before using.

Sprayer suggested use: 1-2 sprays on the tongue 10-15 minutes before meals. Shake well before using.

ADDITIONAL RECOMMENDATIONS: Eat slowly, chew thoroughly and eat simple meals. Avoid drinking large amounts of cold liquids with meals. Relax at meals; do not eat while standing up, watching TV or when you are upset.

ADDITIONAL USEFUL HERBS: For flatulence add Fennel, Ginger, Lavender or Carminative Compound™. Plant enzymes or Papaya tablets may help improve protein digestion.

ORIGINAL BITTERS™

CONTAINS: Hydroalcoholic extracts of fresh Dandelion root (Taraxacum officinale), fresh and dried Artichoke leaf (Cynara scolymus), Gentian root (Gentiana lutea), fresh Peppermint herb (Mentha x piperita), Angelica root (Angelica archangelica) and Orange Peel (Citrus spp.).

INDICATIONS: This formula stimulates the entire process of digestion, absorption and elimination by increasing production of gastric hydrochloric acid as well as liver, pancreatic and small intestine digestive enzymes and juices. By stimulating bile production this formula also enhances fat metabolism and acts as a natural aperient/laxative. Indications include achlorhydria/hypochlorhydia, malabsorption, chronic gas, belching, indigestion and abdominal bloating. Original Bitters™ is a useful adjunct for any protocol addressing GI dysbiosis or food sensitivities caused by leaky gut syndrome. Many chronic conditions such as arthritis, auto-immune disorders, skin conditions, etc. will benefit from enhancing digestive and liver/gallbladder function.

ACTIVITY: Dandelion, Gentian and Artichoke are bitter tonics which stimulate the digestive function of the stomach, liver and pancreas which in turn increase absorption of nutrients via the small intestine. Peppermint is a classic carminative for enhancing digestion and preventing gas or bloating. Angelica and Orange Peel are warming bitters which not only enhance digestive functions but make this a balanced formula that can be used on a long term daily basis. Taking only cooling bitters (Gentian or Artichoke) can over a period of time inhibit digestive function unless paired with warming bitters.

CONTRAINDICATIONS: Gastric ulcers, gastritis, hyperchlorhydria.

SUGGESTED USE: 15-30 drops (.75-1.5 ml) taken 10-15 minutes before meals. Continue for at least 2 months for chronic digestive problems.

ADDITIONAL RECOMMENDATIONS: Eat slowly, chew thoroughly and eat simple meals. Avoid drinking large amounts of cold liquids with meals. Relax at meals; do not eat while standing up, watching TV or when you are upset.

ADDITIONAL USEFUL HERBS: For flatulence add Fennel, Ginger, Lavender or Carminative Compound™. Plant enzymes or Papaya tablets may help improve protein digestion.

OSTEO HERB™

CONTAINS: Stinging Nettle leaf (Urtica dioica), Horsetail herb (Equisetum arvense), Alfalfa herb (Medicago sativa), Dandelion leaf (Taraxacum officinale), Oat straw (Avena sativa) and Black Pepper (Piper nigrum).

INDICATIONS: This formula helps to remineralize weak, brittle bones. It is indicated for osteoporosis, degeneration of the jaw, hip, vertebrae or other osseous tissue and slowly healing bone fractures. It is a useful supportive therapy for osteoarthritis and also strengthens the hair, nails, teeth and skin.

ACTIVITY: The herbs in this formula are rich sources of absorbable minerals including calcium, magnesium, potassium and silica, plus numerous trace elements including boron. Silica has been shown to be a co-factor in calcium absorption, increasing bone density and strength. Horsetail contains silica and has long been used for strengthening bones, hair, skin and nails; it also stimulates the maturation of osteoblasts. Mineral rich Oat straw and Stinging Nettle are also traditionally used for strengthening the bones, skin and fingernails. Alfalfa is rich in vitamins and minerals, as is Dandelion leaf. Both contain vitamin K, which is essential for healthy bones. Black pepper enhances digestion and absorption of the herbs in this formula.

CONTRAINDICATIONS: If you are pregnant or lactating consult your physician before taking this product.

SUGGESTED USE: 2 capsules BID/TID with meals.

ADDITIONAL RECOMMENDATIONS: The following foods are rich in absorbable calcium: dark green leafy vegetables, cabbage, broccoli, yogurt, carrots, sesame seeds, canned Alaskan salmon and sardines. Magnesium, silica, potassium, boron, vitamins D and K and essential fatty acids are necessary for calcium metabolism. Excess saturated fats, sodium, phosphorus (carbonated drinks) and lead are calcium antagonists.

ADDITIONAL USEFUL HERBS: Teasel root, Drynaria root, Kudzu and Processed Rehmannia have shown the ability to increase bone density. Include mineral-rich herbs/foods such as spirulina, parsley and seaweeds (dulse, nori, kombu and hijiki) in the diet.

PANCREAID™

CONTAINS: Hydroalcoholic extracts of Bitter Melon (Mormordica charantia), Gymnema herb (Gymnema slyvestre), Cinnamon bark (Cinnamomum verum), Fenugreek seed (Trigonella foenum-graecum), Gentian root (Gentiana lutea), Kudzu (P. montana), Yellow Root (Xanthoriza simplicissima) and vegetable glycerin.

INDICATIONS: This formula enhances pancreatic function, supporting the beta cells' ability to maintain healthy blood sugar levels. It is indicated for borderline to mild cases of type II diabetes; it can also be used as a pancreatic tonic or bitter tonic for impaired digestion and assimilation.

ACTIVITY: Gymnema, Bitter Melon and Fenugreek have been used throughout the world for treating Type II diabetes. Human clinical trials with Gymnema show that it can lower blood sugar levels and HbA1c, as well as reduce hunger and fatigue in people with diabetes (Kumar, et al., 2010, Baskaran, et al., 1990). Mormordica has been found to effective for treating NIDDM, especially in people with obesity and unhealthy blood lipids (Tayyab, et al., 2016, Ahmad, et al., 1999). It works by reducing insulin resistance and improving cellular uptake of glucose (Lo, et al., 2013). In a human clinical study Fenugreek seed was shown to decrease fasting blood glucose, hemoglobin A1c, serum insulin and triglycerides (Rafraf, et al., 2014). In another study it improved glycemic control and decreased insulin resistance (Gupta, et al., 2001). Cinnamon has been found to lower blood sugar levels in diabetics (Lu, et al., 2012, Akilen, et al., 2010) as well as hemoglobin A1c and blood pressure. It also reduced insulin resistance in people with metabolic syndrome (Ziegenfuss, et al., 2006). Bitters like Gentian root have traditionally been used to normalize blood sugar levels, to reduce insulin resistance and improve digestion.

CONTRAINDICATIONS: In people with insulin-dependent diabetes use only under a doctor's supervision. Use cautiously in people with metabolic syndrome as it is unclear whether Gymnema is appropiate for this condition.

SUGGESTED USE: 30-40 drops (1.5-2 ml) TID for at least 4 months.

ADDITIONAL RECOMMENDATIONS: Include bitters, bean pod tea, prickly pear, complex carbohydrates and soluble fiber in the diet. The nutrients chromium, selenium, and zinc are essential for healthy blood sugar metabolism, as are omega-3 fatty acids. Eliminate refined carbohydrates, sugars (sucrose, fructose, high-fructose corn syrup, honey, maple or agave syrup) and low quality fats (hydrogenated and partially hydrogenated fats, fried foods). Regular exercise can reduce insulin resistance and blood sugar levels.

ADDITIONAL USEFUL HERBS: Holy Basil, Hibiscus or Chinese Yam lower blood sugar levels and may also be helpful. In addition, nervines and calming adaptogens can reduce the effects of chronic stress and help to lower elevated cortisol levels which promote insulin resistance.

PHYTOCALM™

CONTAINS: Hydroalcoholic extracts of fresh Skullcap herb (Scutellaria lateriflora), fresh Oat milky seed (Avena sativa), fresh Hops strobiles (Humulus lupulus), fresh Passionflower herb (Passiflora incarnata), fresh Valerian root (Valeriana officinale), fresh California Poppy whole plant (Eschscholzia californica) and vegetable glycerin.

INDICATIONS: This is a nervine/sedative formula that is useful in mild to moderate cases of insomnia, restlessness, anxiety, tension, and stress-induced headaches. Phytocalm also has antispasmodic and mild analgesic activity. It can be useful for muscle spasms, tension headaches, trigeminal neuralgia and back pain, as well as modestly inhibiting tremors associated with Parkinson's disease or essential tremors.

ACTIVITY: Skullcap is an excellent nervine, anxiolytic (Wolfson and Hoffmann,

2003) and antispasmodic used for stress-induced tics, muscle spasms and tight or painful muscles. Oat is highly nourishing and a trophorestorative to the nerves. It helps mitigate withdrawal symptoms (nicotine, caffeine or opiates) and is especially useful for emotionally labile, easily over-excited people. Hops, Valerian and California Poppy are well-known sedatives and analgesics, used for pain or stress-induced insomnia, as well as bruxism and tension headaches. Several human clinical studies show that combinations of Hops and Valerian help to relieve insomnia and improve sleep quality (Dimpfel & Suto, 2008, Koetter, et al., 2007, Morin, et al., 2005). Passionflower is a nervine/sedative that is specifically indicated for circular thinking (repetitive thoughts) that keeps someone from falling asleep. It promotes better sleep quality (Ngan & Conduit, 2011) and is also indicated for occipital headaches and generalized anxiety disorder.

CONTRAINDICATIONS: Use of excessive or very large quantities may cause drowsiness and temporarily impair motor skills (driving, etc.).

SUGGESTED USE: For insomnia 60-80 drops (3-4 ml) in the evening (ideally in Chamomile tea) while symptoms persist. For general anxiety or withdrawal symptoms 40-60 drops (2-3 ml) TID/QID.

ADDITIONAL RECOMMENDATIONS: Increase your intake of B vitamins, calcium and magnesium. Stress reduction techniques such as meditation, yoga, Tai Chi or biofeedback may be helpful and good sleep hygiene is essential (regular sleep patterns, avoiding stimulants and stimulating activity).

ADDITIONAL USEFUL HERBS: Corydalis can be added for pain-induced insomnia. Kava or Gambir spines can be added for muscular tension or anxiety. Bacopa, Polygala or Tension Relief™ can also be used for anxiety.

PHYTODENT™

CONTAINS: Hydroalcoholic extracts of Spilanthes herb (Spilanthes spp.), Witch Hazel leaf (Hamamelis virginiana), Myrrh gum resin (Commiphora molmol), Calendula flower (Calendula officinalis), Goldenseal root (Hydrastis canadensis), Thyme herb (Thymus officinalis), and Essential Oils of Peppermint and Cinnamon.

INDICATIONS: Phytodent is used to prevent and treat periodontal diseases such as gingivitis. It kills the bacteria that cause both tooth decay and gum disease and helps reduce plaque formation which contributes to receding gums and tooth loss. Studies on antibacterial mouthwashes conclude that daily oral use is an effective adjunct to flossing for preventing gum disease (Stoeken, et al., 2007).

ACTIVITY: Diluted in water and used as a mouthwash, the herbs in Phytodent™ have been shown to inhibit bacterial, viral and fungal growth (Goldenseal, Myrrh, Calendula, Thyme and Cinnamon essential oil), act as an astringent and anti-inflammatory (Witch Hazel, Calendula), stimulate saliva flow (Spilanthes) and help prevent plaque and biofilm formation. It can also be applied directly on infections in the mouth or canker sores. (The undiluted tincture can sting or irritate the mucous membrane tissue.) This formula also helps stop bleeding of gums, bad breath (halitosis) and can be used as a gargle for sore throats and tonsillitis.

CONTRAINDICATIONS: None.

SUGGESTED USE: Use daily as a mouthwash - 15-20 drops (.75-1 ml) in 1-2 ounces of water.

ADDITIONAL RECOMMENDATIONS: Increase vitamin C and flavonoids in the diet. Practice regular good oral hygiene - regular brushing of teeth, flossing, gum massage, or the use of chewing sticks. Use along with OsteoHerb™, calcium ascorbate, and vitamins D and K to prevent bone loss.

RECKLESS BLOOD TONIC™

CONTAINS: Hydroalcoholic extracts of Bugleweed flowering tops (Lycopus virginicus), fresh Shepherd's Purse herb (Capsella bursa-pastoris), Yarrow flowers (Achillea millefolium), Cinnamon bark (Cinnamomum verum), Witch Hazel leaf (Hamamelis virginiana) and vegetable glycerin.

INDICATIONS: This formula is indicated for capillary or passive bleeding, including menorrhagia, polymenorrhagia, nosebleeds, hemoptysis, blood in the urine, dysfunctional uterine bleeding, bleeding gums, inflammatory bowel disorders with blood in the stool and mild to moderate gastric or duodenal ulcers with bleeding.

ACTIVITY: Each of the herbs in this formula act as styptics and antihemorrhagic agents. Yarrow's reputation for staunching blood flow goes back to the Greek myth of Achilles; supposedly if he had Yarrow, his wounds would have been staunched. This aromatic herb can be used for nosebleeds, heavy menstrual bleeding and to control bleeding gums. Fresh Shepherd's Purse contains acetylcholine which is a vasoconstrictor and vitamin K is necessary for normal blood clotting. It too has a long history of use for menorrhagia dysfunctional uterine bleeding and hematuria. Cinnamon bark is a styptic which helps control capillary bleeding and was used by the Eclectic physicians for excessive gynecological, urological or respiratory tract bleeding. Bugleweed was used by the Eclectic physicians especially for coughing blood (hemoptysis) as well as bleeding from the stomach, bowel, bladder or kidneys. Witch Hazel is used orally as well as topically to enhance capillary and venous integrity, and control gastric, hemorrhoidal or uterine bleeding.

CONTRAINDICATIONS: Pregnancy; do not use with blood thinning or antiplatelet medication.

SUGGESTED USE: 30-40 drops (1.5-2 ml) taken as needed to control bleeding.

ADDITIONAL RECOMMENDATIONS: To strengthen vascular integrity use dietary sources of flavonoids such as blueberries, cherries, blackberries, green tea, grape juice, red wine, dark chocolate or beets. To increase platelet activity, increase dietary consumption of dark green leafy vegetables, which are rich in vitamin K-1.

ADDITIONAL USEFUL HERBS: Take Blueberry Solid Extract™, Hawthorn Solid Extract™ or Pomegranate/Goji Berry Solid Extract™ to help promote capillary integrity.

REPLENISH COMPOUND™

CONTAINS: Hydroalcoholic extracts of fresh Oat milky seed (Avena sativa), Shatavari root (Asparagus racemosus), Dong Quai root (Angelica sinensis), fresh White Pond Lily root (Nymphaea odorata), Licorice root (Glycyrrhiza glabra) and vegetable glycerin.

INDICATIONS: This is an oral formula to enhance vaginal lubrication in peri-menopausal and menopausal women. It can be used for mild to moderate vaginal dryness. It also acts as a general yin tonic, benefitting dry mouth, dry coughs, and deficient stomach yin.

ACTIVITY: These herbs are yin tonics which increase moisture and secretions of the mucous membrane tissue. Licorice is an adaptogen, a yin tonic and it nourishes the adrenal glands which continue to secrete sex hormones after menopause. Shatavari is a rasayana or Ayurvedic rejuvenative remedy, as well as an adaptogen and yin tonic. It is believed to help keep women young and sexually active. Dong Quai is a blood tonic and it enhances uterine circulation. It is used in many Chinese formulas for gynecological problems including menopausal symptomatology. Animal research suggests that it can promote cornification of the vaginal epithelium, the outer layer of tissue that becomes atrophic in menopausal women (Circosta, et al., 2006). White Pond Lily is a little-known but useful tonic to the uterus and vaginal mucous membranes. Fresh Oat is a traditional nerve tonic used for sexual neurasthenia and as a demulcent to mucous membranes.

CONTRAINDICATIONS: Use cautiously in patients with hypertension.

SUGGESTED USE: 40-60 drops (2-3 ml) TID while symptoms persist.

ADDITIONAL RECOMMENDATIONS: Add vitamin E (mixed tocopherols with tocotrienols) and omega 3 fatty acids (preferably fish oils) to diet. Vaginal lubricants with Aloe and Vitamin E or Comfrey/Calendula Ointment™ may be applied topically for temporary relief of dryness. In severe cases natural progesterone creams are very useful. Pelvic floor exercises can be helpful, as they stimulate the pubococcygeal muscles and increase pelvic circulation.

ADDITIONAL USEFUL HERBS: Chaste Tree berry, Processed Rehmannia or Women's Transition Compound™ may also be of benefit due to their ability to relieve hormonal imbalances.

RESPIRATORY CALMPOUND™

CONTAINS: Hydroalcoholic extracts of autumn-gathered Ginkgo leaf (Ginkgo biloba), Khella seed (Ammi visnaga), Reishi mushroom and mycelium (Ganoderma spp.), Schisandra berry (Schisandra chinensis), Licorice root (Glycyrrhiza glabra), Lobelia herb in flower and seed (Lobelia inflata), vegetable glycerin and Apple Cider vinegar.

INDICATIONS: This formula is designed to help control asthma, especially stress or allergy-induced asthma. It is also useful for diminished airway syndrome, spasmodic coughing and allergies which affect breathing.

ACTIVITY: Reishi, Schisandra and Licorice are immune amphoterics which inhibit allergic response in the respiratory system. They are also adaptogens which help regulate stress hormones (Cortisol and Epinephrine/Adrenaline) and reduce inflammation. Schisandra has a long history of use in Chinese medicine for asthma with wheezing (kidneys not grasping the lung Qi). Ginkgo inhibits platelet aggregating factor (PAF), a chemical which increases inflammation and promotes asthma attacks. In a human trial a liquid Ginkgo extract significantly reduced airway hyperactivity (Li, et al., 1997). In an animal study Ginkgo was also effective in alleviating respiratory inflammation (Babayigit, et al., 2009). Lobelia and Khella are antispasmodic to the lungs and have a long history of use for treating asthma, spasmodic coughs and COPD.

CONTRAINDICATIONS: Pregnancy and lactation. Do not use if you have a mushroom allergy.

SUGGESTED USE: 40-60 drops (2-3 ml) TID/QID.

ADDITIONAL RECOMMENDATIONS: Asthma often has allergy and stress components. For allergic asthma avoid as much as possible exposure to chlorinated pools and showers, animal dander, dust mites, cockroaches, heavily polluted air (especially particulates), cigarette smoke and foods containing sulfites. Food allergies (dairy and wheat allergies being the most common) may contribute to asthma as well. Avoiding these foods may be helpful. Increasing consumption of beneficial foods containing anti-inflammatory carotenoids (sweet potatoes, winter squashes, yellow or red sweet peppers, apricots, carrots, beets, pumpkin, etc.) is a good idea. Also important are nutrients that have antioxidant and anti-inflammatory activity such as vitamin A, B Complex, C, E and selenium, as well as magnesium, quercitin, bromelain and omega-3 fatty acids, especially those found in fish oils.

ADDITIONAL USEFUL HERBS: Mullein leaf tea (strain through cheese cloth or a coffee filter), Elecampane and Thyme are respiratory expectorants and can help expel excessive mucus. For dry asthma use *yin* tonics such as Chinese Asparagus root or Prince Seng.

SCUDDER'S ALTERATIVE

CONTAINS: Figwort fresh herb (Scrophularia nodosa), Red Alder bark (Alnus rubra), Yellow Dock fresh root (Rumex crispus), Corydalis Yanhusuo rhizome (C. yanhusuo), Black Cherry sucanat syrup and water extract of Mayapple root (Podophyllum peltatum)

INDICATIONS: This Formula was developed by the renowned Eclectic physician, John M. Scudder, MD. He used it to treat chronic diseases including arthritis, skin conditions (eczema, psoriasis), cancer and autoimmune disease.

ACTIVITY: Alterative herbs enhance normal eliminatory function via the liver, bowel, lungs, lymph, kidneys and skin. Figwort has antibacterial, diuretic and anti-inflammatory activity. It stimulates lymphatic circulation and is used for lymphadenitis, cellulitis and cystic breast disease. Red Alder bark enhances liver and bowel function and is frequently used for chronic skin conditions such as acne, acne rosacea and eczema. Yellow Dock also promotes liver and bowel function; it was used by the Eclectics for treating cachexia, chronic skin conditions and hepatic torpor. In laboratory studies Rumex has been found to promote apoptosis in leukemia cells, and have antibacterial and antioxidant activity. The endangered Turkey Corn (Dicentra canadensis) is replaced by its close relative, Chinese Corydalis. Both herbs are used to stimulate liver and gallbladder function and to relieve cancer pain. In Chinese medicine Corydalis is used to relieve blood stagnation which causes pain. In animal and laboratory studies this herb inhibits cancer growth, relieves inflammation and inhibits metastasis. Mayapple is used to promote liver and bowel activity. A special water extraction is used to eliminate the potentially toxic resins found in the rhizomes.

CONTRAINDICATIONS: Use only under the guidance of a trained practitioner.

SUGGESTED USE: 20-30 drops (1-1.5 ml) TID.

ADDITIONAL RECOMMENDATIONS: Dietary supplementation of anti-inflammatory and antioxidant carotenoids, as well as vitamins D, E and K can inhibit inflammatory cytokines which create an environment conducive to oxidative disease. Green Tea, Brassica family vegetables such as broccoli, kale, watercress or cauliflower, and Allium family vegetables such as garlic, ramps and onions may be beneficial as they also inhibit inflammation and have antimutagin and antitumor activity.

ADDITIONAL USEFUL HERBS: Scudder's Alterative can be used as part of a protocol with other alterative formulas such as Eli Jones Compound Syrup of Scrophularia, Burdock/Red Root Compound™, or Alterative Compound™. It can also be combined with immune supportive Formulas such as Seven Precious Mushrooms™ or Immune Adapt™.

SERENITY COMPOUND™

CONTAINS: Hydroalcoholic extracts of Eleuthero root (Eleutherococcus senticosus), fresh Skullcap herb (Scutellaria lateriflora), fresh Chamomile flowers (Matricaria recutita), fresh Oat milky seed (Avena sativa), Linden flower (Tilia sp.) and vegetable glycerin.

INDICATIONS: This formula is used to help relieve daily stress and/or anxiety. It enhances HPA axis function and calms the nervous system, both of which are negatively affected by chronic stress. It can be effective for relieving symptoms such as anxiety, nervous headaches, stress-induced insomnia, bruxism and muscle pain. It can also be useful for stress related syndromes such as nervous palpitations, excessive vasovagal response, irritable bowel syndrome or back and neck pain. Serenity Compound™ will not cause drowsiness or worsen depression as prescription sedatives can.

ACTIVITY: Eleuthero is a mild non-stimulating adaptogen which strengthens the adrenal glands and endocrine system. Skullcap, Chamomile, Linden flower and fresh Oat are nervine tonics which are calming and help enhance relaxation. Linden flower also acts as a mild hypotensive agent and mood-elevator, while Skullcap relieves muscle spasms, anxiety (Wolfson and Hoffman, 2003), emotional outbursts and nervous tics. Fresh Oat is our greatest nervous system trophorestoravtive. It is especially beneficial for tired, overstressed people with labile emotions. Chamomile can relieve anxiety (Amsterdam, et al., 2009) as well as bruxism, stress-induced dyspepsia or IBS and bad dreams.

CONTRAINDICATIONS: None.

SUGGESTED USE: 40-60 drops (2-3 ml) TID/QID while symptoms persist.

ADDITIONAL RECOMMENDATIONS: Increase dietary or supplementary calcium, magnesium, and B Complex vitamins. Eat foods rich in calcium and magnesium such as oatmeal, chlorella, sea vegetables, carrots, beets and wild greens. The non-essential amino-acid L-theanine has also been shown to relieve stress and anxiety.

ADDITIONAL USEFUL HERBS: Calming adaptogens such as Reishi, Schisandra, Ashwagandha or Jiaogulan may be of additional benefit, as can other nervine herbs such as Passionflower, Lemon Balm, Motherwort or Blue Vervain.

SEVEN PRECIOUS MUSHROOMS™

CONTAINS: Hydroalcoholic extracts of Black Reishi fungus (Ganoderma sinense), Red Reishi fungus (Ganoderma lucidum), Reishi mycelium, Chaga fungus (Inonotus obliquus), Shiitake fungus (Lentinula edodes), Maitake fungus (Grifola frondosa) and Cordyceps mycelium and/or mushroom (Cordyceps Ophiocordyceps sinensis (a.k.a. Cordyceps sinensis) or Cordyceps militaris).

INDICATIONS: Mushrooms have a long history of use as tonic remedies in Chinese medicine. This formula contains powerful immunomodulating fungi that are used for immune deficiency conditions (cancer, CFIDS, chronic persistent Lyme disease), immune excess conditions (allergies and allergic asthma) and hypo/hyper conditions such as auto-immune diseases (multiple sclerosis, rheumatoid arthritis, scleroderma, lupus, etc.). In Traditional Chinese Medicine many of these mushrooms are used to strengthen the *Wei Qi* (protective Qi) which helps prevent colds, influenza and other infectious diseases. Cordyceps and Reishi are also adaptogens which help to enhance HPA axis and SAS function.

ACTIVITY: Mushrooms are a rich source of immune-stimulating high molecular weight polysaccharides. These compounds have been studied since the 1950s and have been found to increase the activity of the macrophages, T Lymphocytes and NK cells, which inhibit cancer, Hepatitis B virus, as well as bacteria and fungi. Other active compounds include triterpenes which have antitumor, anti-allergic hepatoprotective and hypotensive activity, Sterols (provitamin D) which are anti-inflammatory and Betalinic acid which has pronounced antitumor activity. Reishi, Maitake and Cordyceps are also immune amphoterics which nourish the immune system, allowing it to regain its normal regulatory control. Because of this activity this formula can be used for immune deficiency, autoimmune and allergic conditions.

CONTRAINDICATIONS: Mushroom allergies.

SUGGESTED USE: 1/2 tsp. (50 drops) (2.5 ml) TID/QID.

ADDITIONAL USEFUL HERBS: To stimulate *immune activity* - Astragalus/ Echinacea Compound™, Andrographis, Isatis, Ultimate Echinacea™, or Myrrh may be beneficial.

For auto-immune conditions - Immune Balance Compound™, Huang Qin, Chinese Salvia, Turmeric, Sarsaparilla, Cat's Claw, Licorice, Ashwagandha, Gotu Kola or Bupleurum may be useful.

SINUS SUPPORT COMPOUND™

CONTAINS: Hydroalcoholic extracts of fresh Echinacea root and flower (Echinacea purpurea), Eyebright herb (Euphrasia spp.), Horseradish root (Armoracia rusticana), Kudzu root (P. montana), Osha root (Ligusticum porteri), Bayberry root bark (Morella cerifera) Collinsonia whole plant (Collinsonia canadensis) and vegetable glycerin.

INDICATIONS: This formula is useful for treating acute symptoms of head colds, seasonal hay fever (allergic rhinitis) and other pollen allergies, sinusitis and animal hair/dander allergies. Specific indications include itchy, scratchy red eyes, sinus congestion, excessive clear or white mucous production, frequent sneezing, upper respiratory tract congestion and post nasal drip.

ACTIVITY: Echinacea root and flowers reduce mucous membrane inflammation in the upper respiratory tract, help prevent secondary infections and have mild antihistamine activity. Bayberry bark reduces excess sinus secretions and acts as an anti-inflammatory agent. Eyebright soothes itchy, scratchy red eyes, and stabilizes the mast cells, reducing histamine response. Horseradish acts as a decongestant and bronchodilator and opens clogged sinuses and breathing passages. Kudzu (Ge Gen in chinese) has antihistamine activity, reducing sinus congestion and helping to control allergic rhinitis. Osha is also a decongestant as well as an effective antibacterial/antiviral agent. The Eclectic physicians recommended Collinsonia for muscous memebranes that were boggy, atonic and with a tendency to oversecrete mucous. The "aromatic Collinsonia" (made from the entire fresh herb - root, leaf & flower) has anti-inflammatory activity, it stabilizes mast cells, prevented degranulation and inhibits histamine release.

CONTRAINDICATIONS: Heat symptoms such as dry, red, inflamed sinuses, yellow sticky mucus or dry eyes. Pregnancy.

SUGGESTED USE: 20-40 drops (1-2 ml) TID/QID while symptoms persist.

ADDITIONAL RECOMMENDATIONS: Eliminate possible allergens from the diet especially dairy products or wheat. Increase dietary flavonoid sources which are anti-inflammatory such as green tea, blueberries, red grapes, cherries, rose hips, buckwheat and amla fruit. The supplements Quercitin and Bromelain may also be helpful to reduce inflammation as can flavonoid rich Blueberry, Hawthorn or Pomegranate/Goji Berry Solid Extracts™.

ADDITIONAL USEFUL HERBS: There are two types of herbs that can inhibit allergic response. Immunoregulators such as Sarsaparilla, Turmeric, Huang Qin, Unprocessed Rehmannia, Gotu Kola, Bupleurum or Chinese Salvia are anti-inflammatory and stabilize mast cells inhibiting histamine and other inflammatory cytokines. Immune amphoterics such as Schisandra, Cat's Claw, Eleuthero, Licorice, Ashwagandha, Astragalus and American or Red Ginseng help to re-regulate a disordered immune system, allowing it to regain its normal self-regulatory functions.

SMOKER'S RESQ™

CONTAINS: Hydroalcoholic extracts of fresh Oat milky seed (Avena sativa), fresh Skullcap herb (Scutellaria lateriflora), fresh Plantain herb (Plantago major), Licorice root (Glycyrrhiza glabra), Lobelia herb in flower and seed (Lobelia inflata) and apple cider vinegar.

INDICATIONS: This formula helps reduce cravings and symptoms of withdrawal from tobacco. It should be used to assist the person who needs additional support to stop smoking cigarettes, cigars or chewing tobacco.

ACTIVITY: Oat and Skullcap are strengthening nervines which calm jangled nerves and reduce anxiety (Wolfson and Hoffman, 2003). Fresh Oat has a reputation for reducing withdrawal cravings for tobacco, opium and coffee. It is a gentle but effective trophorestorative to the nervous system, helping to relieve anxiety, irritability and labile emotions. Plantain is utilized in the homeopathic materia medica for helping to relieve nicotine addiction (Boericke, 1976). Licorice makes tobacco distasteful and is an expectorant and adaptogen. Adaptogens are useful during drug withdrawal as they help relieve HPA axis hyperactivity and an exaggerated stress response, both of which promote greater need for smoking (McKee, et al., 2011) and interfere with smoking cessation. Lobelia contains the alkaloid lobeline which inhibits the nicotinic acid receptors release of dopamine and helps to reduce tobacco cravings (Dwoskin and Crooks, 2002).

CONTRAINDICATIONS: Pregnancy and lactation.

SUGGESTED USE: 20-25 drops (1-1.25 ml) TID/QID while symptoms persist.

ADDITIONAL RECOMMENDATIONS: Increase B vitamins in the diet. Acupuncture or hypnosis may also help some people to quit smoking.

ADDITIONAL USEFUL HERBS: Nervine herbs such as Passionflower, Chamomile, Linden flower or Lemon Balm may be very helpful, especially in tea. Calming adaptogens such as Reishi, Schisandra or Ashwagandha can help to inhibit the stress response and promote a feeling of well being.

SPICED BITTERS™

CONTAINS: Hydroalcoholic extracts of dried Artichoke leaf (Cynara scolymus), Fenugreek seed (Trigonella foenum-graecum), Gentian root (Gentiana lutea), Cinnamon bark (Cinnamomum verum), Ginger rhizome (Zingiber officinale), Orange Peel (Citrus spp.) and Cardamom seed (Elettaria cardamomum)

INDICATIONS: This formula stimulates the entire process of digestion, absorption and elimination by increasing production of gastric hydrochloric acid as well as liver, pancreatic and small intestine digestive enzymes and juices. By stimulating bile production this formula also enhances fat metabolism and acts as a natural aperient/laxative. Indications include achlorhydria/hypochlorhydia, malabsorption, chronic gas, belching, indigestion and abdominal bloating. Spiced Bitters™ is a useful adjunct for any protocol addressing GI dysbiosis or food sensitivities caused by leaky gut syndrome. Many chronic conditions such as arthritis, auto-immune disorders, skin conditions, etc. will benefit from enhancing digestive and liver/gallbladder function.

ACTIVITY: This blend of traditional bitters (Gentian root, Artichoke leaf) with aromatic spices creates a wonderful "chai-like" formula to enhance digestion, absorption and elimination. Cooling bitters like Gentian and Artichoke are effective for increasing gastric HCL production, the release of small intestine and pancreatic juices, as well as bile secretion from the liver and bile excretion from the gallbladder. Cooling bitters initially enhance digestion, but when used by themselves over time they "damp down stomach fire". This means they eventually diminish digestive ability. There are two ways to create a sustainable "bitters formula", by adding warming bitters (see Original Bitters, Old World Bitters, Bitter Roots) or by adding warming spices. The addition of Ginger, Cinnamon, Orange Peel, and Cardamon allows this formula to be used before every meal for extended periods of time without losing efficacy and helping improve digestion.

CONTRAINDICATIONS: Do not use if you have hyperchlorhydria. Use cautiously if you have gastric ulcers, gastritis, or GERD.

SUGGESTED USE: 15-30 drops (.75-1.5 ml) taken 10-15 minutes before meals. Shake well before using.

Sprayer suggested use: 1-2 sprays on the tongue 10-15 minutes before meals. Shake well before using.

ADDITIONAL RECOMMENDATIONS: Eat slowly, chew thoroughly and eat simple meals. Avoid drinking large amounts of cold liquids with meals. Relax at meals; do not eat while standing up, watching TV or when you are upset.

ADDITIONAL USEFUL HERBS: For flatulence add Fennel, Ginger, Lavender or Carminative Compound™. Plant enzymes or Papaya tablets may help improve protein digestion.

SPIROLYD COMPOUND™*

CONTAINS: Hydroalcoholic extracts of Sarsaparilla root (Smilax regelii), Andrographis herb (A. paniculata), Cat's Claw/Una de Gato (Uncaria tomentosa) or Una de Gato, Guaiacum wood (G. officinale) and Prickly Ash bark (Zanthoxylum clava-herculis).

INDICATIONS: This formula is an experimental protocol for treating antibiotic-resistant Lyme disease. It can be used with antibiotics or after patients have completed oral and intravenous regimens without success.

ACTIVITY: There is little data or research on the use of herbs for Lyme disease. The concept of this formula started by looking at herbs that were used (and are believed to have been effective) for treating another spirochete Treponema pallidium, the cause of syphilis. In the 1700's - 1800's, wealthy men with Syphilis would go to the Caribbean for treatment of this disease. The treatment consisted of drinking large amounts of Sarsaparilla and Guaiac, while laboring in the hot sun and sleeping in a sweat bath. Reports from this time suggest the therapy may have actually worked. Preferring to avoid the hard work and discomfort of the treatment, many opted to just take the herbs, which was less effective and this treatment was mostly forgotten. These two herbs are the foundation for Spirolyd, along with the elevation of body temperature. In a Chinese study (of dubious quality) a related species of Smilax was effective for treating acute and chronic syphilis (Bensky et al., 2004). Sarsaparilla also binds endotoxins in the gut, increasing their elimination and is an anti-inflammatory, useful for Lyme arthralgia. Guaiac has antibacterial activity and is also strongly anti-inflammatory. Andrographis is used in Traditional Chinese Medicine and Ayurvedic traditions to clear blood heat or infections. It has antibacterial activity, as well as antiviral, antimalarial, anti-inflammatory, hepatoprotective, antitumor and gastroprotective effects. Cat's Claw also has significant anti-inflammatory activity and is used to clear "blood heat" (infections). Anecdotal reports of this herb reduced Lyme symptoms are common and it can relieve the pain associated with Lyme arthralgia. Prickly Ash has antibacterial activity; it enhances circulation, relieves pain and improve absorption of the other herbs in this formula.

CONTRAINDICATIONS: Pregnancy, breastfeeding, and as a first option in treating Lyme disease. This formula does not replace the need for antibiotics in treating Lyme disease and must be used under the supervision of a physician.

SUGGESTED USE: 60-80 drops (3-4 mL) TID. Take Spirolyd Compound™ alone for 10 days; stop for 5 days. Take Spirolyd Compound™ and Spirolyd Support™ for 10 days; stop for 5 days. Take Spirolyd Compound™ alone for 10 days; stop for 5 days. Repeat pattern throughout treatment.

ADDITIONAL RECOMMENDATIONS: This formula is designed to be used along with heat therapy to elevate body temperature. Saunas, hot tubs, hot baths and steam rooms are most effective to elevate the core body temperature to 101.5 - 102 degrees Fahrenheit for 15 minutes once per day. If saunas, hot tubs or steam baths are not available, hot baths combined with taking a diaphoretic tea (Yarrow, Elder Flower, Ginger) can be substituted. It is essential that patients rehydrate as they will increase fluid and electrolyte loss. This part of the therapy should be monitored by a physician, especially in the young, the elderly, or the infirm. Patients with hypertension or heart disease should avoid heat therapy. Neither the herbal formula nor the heat therapy has been clinically effective when used without the other part of the treatment protocol. For best results use both Spirolyd Compound™ and Spirolyd Support™ along with heat therapy.

SPIROLYD SUPPORT™*

CONTAINS: Hydroalcoholic extracts of Houttuynia leaf (Houttuynia cordata), Sichuan Teasel root (Dipsacus japonicus), Isatis root (Isatis tinctoria), Sweet Annie (Artemesia annua) and Lomatium root (Lomatium dissectum).

INDICATIONS: This formula is an experimental protocol for treating antibiotic resistant Lyme disease. It can be used with antibiotics or after patients have completed oral and intravenous regimens without success.

ACTIVITY: This formula is used to clear blood heat (infection) and to support the original Spirolyd Compound™. It is used to enhance overall activity and prevent the Lyme spirochette from becoming resistant to the treatment. Houttuynia/ Yu Xing Cao and Isatis root/Ban Lan Gen are used in Traditional Chinese Medicine to clear blood heat (infections). They have antibacterial, antiviral and anti-inflammatory activity. Sichuan Teasel is used to help relieve Lyme arthralgia symptoms; it is strongly anti-inflammatory. Contrary to reports on many websites it does not "cure" Lyme disease. Lomatium is a powerful antibacterial and antiviral herb, which can mildly elevate body temperature inducing a low-grade fever. While this may sound problematic, it can actually enhance the efficacy of the therapy. Sweet Annie has a long history of use in China and Southeast Asia for treating malaria and protozoal infections, including the common Lyme

Disease co-infection Babesia. It is also used for deficiency heat and blood heat symptoms such as painful bones (steaming bone syndrome), headache, low grade fever or purpuric rashes.

CONTRAINDICATIONS: Pregnancy, breastfeeding, or as a first option in treating Lyme disease. If a rash develops, discontinue this formula. This formula does not replace the need for antibiotics and must be used under the supervision of a physician.

SUGGESTED USE: 40-80 drops (2-4 ml) TID. Take 3 times per day with Spirolyd Compound™ for 10 days; stop both products for 5 days. Continue with use of Spirolyd Compound™ alone as directed for 2 cycles. Take with Spirolyd Compound™ for 10 days; stop both products for 5 days. Repeat entire pattern throughout treatment.

ADDITIONAL RECOMMENDATIONS: See Spirolyd Compound™.

TENSION RELIEF™

CONTAINS: Hydroalcoholic extracts of Motherwort herb (Leonurus cardiaca), Bacopa herb (Bacopa monnieri), Blue Vervain fresh herb (Verbena hastata), fresh Oat milky seed (Avena sativa), and Polygala root (Polygala tenuifolia).

INDICATIONS: Occasional feelings of anxiety are the body's normal response to stressful situations and these sensations are usually brief and relatively mild. Some people, however, experience anxiety on a more constant basis, and it may manifest itself in a number of ways such as constant worry, irritability, insomnia, headaches and social anxiety. In addition to emotional stress, anxiety takes a physical toll on our bodies in the form of elevated blood pressure and increased production of the stress hormone cortisol. Chronically elevated cortisol levels are linked to obesity, metabolic syndrome, insomnia, hypertension, PCOS, BPH, immune depletion and increased risk of cancer, heart disease, diabetes and arteriosclerosis. Tension Relief™ contains herbs that relieve the effects of both mental and physical stress so that we feel calmer and better able to handle the challenges of our busy stress-filled lives.

ACTIVITY: The Eclectic physicians in the latter 19th and early 20th century prescribed Blue Vervain, Milky Oat and Motherwort as nerve tonics to treat various nervous afflictions such as "hysteria" (premenstrual syndrome or menopausal anxiety), spasms (tension headaches, nervous tics or muscle tension) and nervous exhaustion. Bacopa and Polygala have a long history of use as anxiolytics in Ayurvedic and Traditional Chinese Medicine (TCM). Bacopa has also been shown in clinical studies to enhance cognitive function, while relieving irritability, depression and anxiety (Calabrese, et al., 2008). Motherwort is a calming nervine used for stress-induced palpitations and for mild hypertension. This action may be due to the alkaloid leonurine, which is a mild vasodilator. In TCM, Polygala is used to calm disturbed shen. Symptoms of disturbed shen include restlessness, anxiety, irritability, insomnia and bad dreams. The saponins contained in the root exhibit dopamine and serotonin receptor antagonist properties. Preclinical tests have shown that Polygala exerts protective effects against neuronal death and can also reduce insomnia, possibly by acting on the proliferation and outgrowth of neuronal cells. Oat milky seed is a nervous system trophorestorative and has a long history of use for treating chronic stress and anxiety. The alkaloidal constituents in the Oat, some of which are present only at the milky stage, have mild sedative effects. Oat tincture has been used successfully in clinical practice to curb nicotine and drug withdrawal symptoms. In animal studies Blue Vervain exerted cytoprotective effects on the central nervous system, which supports its historical use as an anxiolytic, nervine and sedative.

CONTRAINDICATIONS: Do not use during pregnancy unless you are under a clinician's care.

SUGGESTED USE: 60-80 drops (3-4 ml) TID/QID in juice or water.

ADDITIONAL RECOMMENDATIONS: Get adequate sleep, exercise regularly, cut down or eliminate caffeine, alcohol, and nicotine. Increase dietary intake of calcium and magnesium, as well as B Complex vitamins and probiotics (research shows probiotics can have anxiolytic activity).

ADDITIONAL USEFUL HERBS: Nervines such as Scullcap, Chamomile or Linden flower can help relieve tension and anxiety. Calming adaptogens including Ashwagandha, Reishi or Schisandra may also be of benefit.

THISTLES COMPOUND™

CONTAINS: Hydroalcoholic extracts of fresh Dandelion root (Taraxacum officinale), fresh Watercress herb (Rorippa nasturtium-aquatica), fresh Blessed Thistle herb (Cnicus benedictus), Milk Thistle seed (Silybum marianum), fresh Turmeric rhizome (Curcuma longa) and Oregon Grape root (Mahonia nervosa).

INDICATIONS: Thistles Compound™ is a balanced formula that helps to enhance liver function and liver health. It tonifies the liver, increasing hepatic glutathione levels and hepatocyte regeneration. It helps protect the liver from environmental toxins and gently stimulates bile production. It can be used to enhance recovery from hepatitis A, for mild cirrhosis, non-alcoholic fatty liver disease, biliary dyskinesia, biliousness, poor fat metabolism, and mild liver damage with elevated liver and biliary enzymes (SGOT/AST, SPGT/ALT, alkaline phosphatase, bilirubin, GGTP). Thistles Compound™ is also useful for digestive problems such as GI dysbiosis, chronic clay-colored stools with or without constipation and leaky gut syndrome.

ACTIVITY: Milk Thistle has pronounced hepatoprotective activity enhancing hepatocyte regeneration, hepatic glutathione levels and inhibiting damage caused by viruses, hepatotoxic medications or environmental pollutants (Abenavoli, et al., 2010). Many animal studies indicate that Turmeric (and its extract Curcumin) are also hepatoprotective. It has been shown to protect against acetaminophen, carbon tetrachloride and alcohol-induced liver damage, liver fibrosis, fatty liver disease and it inhibited liver damage caused by hepatitis B (Rivera-Espinosa & Muriel, 2009). Both herbs also have anti-inflammatory and anti-tumor activity and may help protect against cancer including liver cancer. Dandelion and Watercress are nutritive and tonifying to the liver. Dandelion root has also been shown in animal studies to have mild hepatoprotective activity. It helped to prevent alcohol, carbon tetrachloride and acetaminophen-induced liver damage.

Watercress also has powerful antioxidant activity, it enhances Phase II liver detoxification and it has antitumor activity (Rose, et al., 2000). Blessed Thistle and Oregon Grape are bitters that stimulate bile secretion and relieve hepatic torpor. The Chinese species of Mahonia has also been found in animal studies to protect against carbon tetrachloride-induced liver injury.

CONTRAINDICATIONS: Pregnancy.

SUGGESTED USE: 30-40 drops (1.5-2 ml) TID for an extended period of time. 3-6 months is recommended. Take in juice, water or warm tea.

ADDITIONAL RECOMMENDATIONS: Include bitters to stimulate liver and gallbladder function. Carotenoid rich foods can help inhibit hepatic inflammation (carrots, pumpkin, beets, watercress, dark green leafy vegetables, sweet potatoes, etc.). Eliminate fried foods, saturated fats, hydrogenated fats and alcoholic beverages from the diet.

ADDITIONAL USEFUL HERBS: Other useful herbs include hepatoprotective herbs such as Schisandra, Artichoke leaf and Licorice.

THYROID CALMPOUND™

CONTAINS: Hydroalcoholic extracts of fresh Motherwort herb (Leonurus cardiaca), fresh Bugleweed flowering tops (Lycopus virginicus) and fresh Lemon Balm herb (Melissa officinalis).

INDICATIONS: This formula can improve hyperthyroid conditions and the many symptoms associated with it, including nervousness, tachycardia, racing pulse, agitation and anxiety. For Grave's disease add immune amphoterics such as Reishi or Maitake mushroom to re-regulate the immune system and immunoregulators such as Turmeric or Huang Qin to down-regulate hyper-immune activity

ACTIVITY: The herbs in this formula are all members of the Laminaceae (mint) family and contain volatile oils which act as thyroxin inhibitors. They inhibit excess thyroid function and reduce the symptoms mentioned above. Bugleweed not only inhibits T-4 conversion to T-3, it also helps to prevent binding of Graves IgG to the TSH receptor (Winterhoff, et al., 1994, Auf'mkolk, et al., 1985). Motherwort is specific for hyperthyroid-induced palpitations and anxiety. Lemon Balm also decreases TSH binding and helps to relieve anxiety (Auf'mkolk, et al., 1985), sleeplessness and irritability.

CONTRAINDICATIONS: Hypothyroid conditions. Pregnant women should consult with a physician before using this product.

SUGGESTED USE: 30-40 drops (1.5-2 ml) TID.

ADDITIONAL RECOMMENDATIONS: Increase consumption of raw Cruciferaceae vegetables (broccoli, cauliflower, cabbage, brussels sprouts, pak choi, mustard greens, etc.) and unfermented soy foods because they act as mild thyroxin inhibitors. Avoid iodine sources such as seaweeds, milk, cheese, watercress, and iodine supplements.

ADDITIONAL USEFUL HERBS: Other members of the mint family such as Thyme, Holy Basil, Oregano, Self Heal and Peppermint tea also mildly inhibit thyroid function.

ULTIMATE ECHINACEA™

CONTAINS: Hydroalcoholic extracts of fresh Echinacea angustifolia root, fresh Echinacea purpurea root and flower, and fresh Echinacea pallida root.

INDICATIONS: This formula is useful to help prevent, treat and shorten the duration of acute viral and bacterial infections such as colds (Jawad, et al., 2012, Schoop, et al., 2006, Weber, et al., 2005), influenza (Lindenmuth and Lindenmuth, 2000), bronchitis, cellulitis, tonsillitis, laryngitis, cystitis, mastitis, sore throats, and sinus infections. Echinacea is specific in treatment of inner ear infections (otitis media) in adults and children and can be used topically for insect stings and bites.

ACTIVITY: Ultimate Echinacea is a superior Echinacea product rich in all the active constituents (isobutylamides/alkamides, echinacoside, polyacetylenes, polyenes, chicoric acid) naturally found in the fresh root, flower and seed of the three most commonly used species of Purple Coneflower. Echinacea is used to stimulate immune response; research has shown that it can increase activity in macrophages, NK and T-4 cells, as well as interferon and interleukin production.

CONTRAINDICATIONS: Avoid use if you have severe allergies to Asteraceae family plants such as Ragweed, Daisies, and Chrysanthemum.

SUGGESTED USE: For use in acute situations: 40-60 drops (2-3 ml) 4-6 times per day. If the condition does not resolve within 7 - 10 days, seek medical attention.

ADDITIONAL RECOMMENDATIONS: For colds and influenza increase vitamin C intake and take sublingual zinc tablets.

ADDITIONAL USEFUL HERBS: Other herbs used for bacterial and viral infections may be used concurrently with this formula including Echinacea/Goldenseal Compound™, Astragalus/Echinacea Compound™, Garlic, Elecampane, Herbal Relief Botanical Throat Spray™, Sage, Thyme, Andrographis and VX Immune Support™. Use Ultimate Echinacea™ with Eyebright for treating ear infections such as otitis media.

UTERINE TONIC™

CONTAINS: Hydroalcoholic extracts of Chaste Tree berry (Vitex agnus-castus), Dong Quai root (Angelica sinensis), Saw Palmetto berry (Serenoa repens), Chinese Peony root (Paeonia lactiflora), Shepherd's Purse whole plant (Capsella bursa-pastoris), Cinnamon bark (Cinnamomum verum), Cyperus root (Cyperus rotundus) and vegetable glycerin.

INDICATIONS: Uterine Tonic™ is used for impaired pelvic circulation with fibroids, ovarian cysts or pelvic fullness syndrome.

ACTIVITY: The formula combines traditional Chinese herbs with Western herbs to enhance its activity and efficacy. Chaste Tree works via the pituitary gland and HPA Axis lowering prolactin levels, which then affects FSH and estrogen levels. The result is to lower excess estrogen levels which stimulate the growth of fibroids and cysts. Dong Quai increases uterine circulation, increases liver and bowel excretion of hormones and builds the blood (*xue*). Saw Palmetto was used by the Eclectic physicians to slow fibroid growth and to relieve the symptoms of pelvic fullness syndrome. Chinese Peony nourishes the blood and is used in Chinese medicine for constrained liver Qi which causes fibroids and ovarian cysts, abnormal uterine bleeding and menstrual pain. Shepherd's Purse is used for passive bleeding including abnormal uterine bleeding, menorrhagia, nose-bleeds and post-partum bleeding. Eclectic physicians also stated that Shepherd's Purse was of benefit for non-malignant abdominal tumors (fibroids) in women. Cinnamon bark increases uterine and peripheral circulation and has long been used to reduce excessive bleeding. The fragrant herb Cyperus is used in TCM for stagnant liver *Qi* and to relieve gynecological pain. It is effective for relieving pain caused by fibroids or ovarian cysts, as well as menstrual pain, abdominal distention and nausea.

CONTRAINDICATIONS: Pregnancy or lactation.

SUGGESTED USE: 40-60 drops (2-3 ml) TID/QID. Long-term use is generally indicated.

ADDITIONAL RECOMMENDATIONS: Decrease exposure to dietary and exogenous estrogens by decreasing intake of commercial meats, eggs and dairy (use only organic animal products). Avoid exposure to xenoestrogens found in chlorinated water, pesticides, herbicides or by microwaving foods in plastic containers. Normalize bowel transit time by increasing intake of soluble fiber and bitters. This helps prevent the reabsorption of hormones via the bowel. Increase dietary consumption of isoflavones (phytoestrogens) by eating legumes, fermented soy products, carob, kudzu, peas, bean sprouts, and chickpeas, which weakly inhibit estrogen binding to its cellular receptors. A good whole foods diet rich in dark green leafy vegetables, whole grains, nuts, seeds and deep sea fish (avoid farm-raised fish) is also beneficial.

ADDITIONAL USEFUL HERBS: Women's Four Herb Tea (Si Wu Tang) with Cinnamon and Tree Peony added is used in TCM for treating uterine fibroids. For pain associated with ovarian cysts add Jamaica Dogwood.

UT COMPOUND™

CONTAINS: Hydroalcoholic extracts of Uva-Ursi leaf (Arctostaphylos uva-ursi), fresh Cleavers herb (Galium aparine), Hydrangea root (Hydrangea arbo-rescens), Corn Silk (Zea mays), fresh Agrimony herb (Agrimonia eupatorium), Oregon Grape root (Mahonia nervosa) and vegetable glycerin.

INDICATIONS: This formula can be effective in treating urinary tract infections such as cystitis, urethritis and mild to moderate nephritis. It can be used as part of a protocol for interstitial cystitis with the addition of immune amphoterics and urinary demulcents. UT Compound™ is also indicated for bladder spasms, inflammation of the vas deferens or spermatic cord and bacterial prostatitis.

ACTIVITY: Uva-Ursi contains arbutin, and Oregon Grape root contains ber-berine which are both effective urinary tract antiseptics. Both compounds have antibacterial activity against a wide range of pathogens. Agrimony, Cleavers and Cornsilk have mild antibacterial activity, but more importantly are effective urinary anti-inflammatories. Agrimony was used by the Eclectics for urinary frequency, mucous discharge from the urethra and kidney pain. In a human clinical trial it was shown to have significant anti-inflammatory activity (Ivanova, et al., 2013). Cleavers is specifically indicated for urinary tract pain and for inflammation and pain in the vas deferens or spermatic cord. Corn Silk in addition to its anti-inflammatory activity is a mild diuretic and has modest nephroprotective activity (Hasanudin, et al., 2012). Hydrangea is a urinary tract antispasmodic and analgesic used to relieve pain associated with the kidney, bladder and urethra.

CONTRAINDICATIONS: Pregnancy.

SUGGESTED USE: 40-60 drops (2-3 ml) TID/QID. Continue use for a few days after symptoms have resolved.

ADDITIONAL RECOMMENDATIONS: Any treatment for urinary tract infections is most effective when combined with dietary changes especially eliminating sugars from the diet (honey, white or brown sugar, maple syrup, fruit juices, etc.). Unsweetened Cranberry or Blueberry juice, Blueberry Solid Extract™ as well as Cranberry tablets taken at alternate times (separate ingestion by 2-3 hours) to UT Compound™ is useful to prevent adherence of bacteria to the bladder wall. The sugar D-Mannose also prevents urinary bacterial adhesion and allows normal urination to flush out pathogens such as E. Coli.

ADDITIONAL USEFUL HERBS: Urinary antiseptics such as Pipsissewa or Goldenrod can also be useful. Urinary analgesics such as Kava, anti-inflammatories including Marshmallow and Eryngo and immune amphoterics (Reishi or Maitake) can be added to treat interstitial cystitis.

VX IMMUNE SUPPORT™

CONTAINS: Hydroalcoholic extracts of Elderberry fruit (Sambucus canadensis, Sambucus nigra), fresh Hyssop herb (Hyssopus officinalis), Isatis root (Isatis tinctoria), Japanese Honeysuckle flowers (Lonicera japonica), fresh Lemon Balm herb (Melissa officinalis), Lomatium root (Lomatium dissectum), and St. John's wort flowering tops (Hypericum perforatum).

INDICATIONS: This formula has active antiviral and antibacterial properties appropriate in acute (influenza, colds, shingles, sore throat, tonsillitis) or chronic viral or bacterial infections (Herpes, HPV, CMV, EBV, Hepatitis B & C). It may help lessen the severity, duration and frequency of herpes outbreaks and warts.

ACTIVITY: This formula is a broad spectrum antimicrobial. St. John's wort has been found in laboratory and animal studies to be active against Streptococci, Staphylococci, Influenza virus and Gram positive bacteria (Xiuying, et al., 2012, Saddiqe, et al., 2010). Lomatium has shown in-vitro activity against CMV, EBV, Streptococcus pyogenes, E. coli, Pseudomonas aeruginosa, Proteus vulgaris, Diplococcus pneumoniae and Influenza virus. During the 1918 influenza epidemic, Lomatium is believed to have been effective for preventing infections and reducing the severity and duration of the illness in those who got ill. Hyssop is active against Herpes virus 1 and 2 as well as Influenza virus. It is a traditional remedy for colds, influenza, intestinal and respiratory viruses. Lemon Balm is active against Herpes virus (Mazzanti, et al., 2008) as well as some pathogenic bacteria such as Moraxella catarrhalis, Streptococcus pneumoniae and Haemophilus influenzae. Isatis root and leaf are active in in-vitro studies against influenza virus (Liu, et al., 2010), Shigella dysenteriae, Salmonella enteritidis, Streptococcus, Hepatitis virus, Haemophilus influenzae and Mumps. Isatis is used in Chinese medicine for clearing blood heat infections. It is frequently combined with Japanese Honeysuckle. Japanese Honeysuckle is a powerful antibacterial and antiviral agent used in TCM for treating pneumonia, UTI's, influenza, mastitis, dysentery and sore throats. Elderberry is very useful for treating colds, influenza, and other viral respiratory disorders (Zakay-Rones, et al., 2004). CONTRAINDICATIONS: Do not use during pregnancy or lactation. Discontinue use if skin rash develops. Do not use this product while taking any prescription drugs without the advice of your prescribing physician. Avoid excessive exposure to UV irradiation (e.g. sunlight, tanning) when using this product. SUGGESTED USE: 30-40 drops (1.5-2 ml) TID/QID. ADDITIONAL USEFUL HERBS: For colds or influenza, Chrysanthemum flower, Thyme, Andrographis and Yarrow can be useful.

WOMEN'S ADAPT™

CONTAINS: Hydroalcoholic extracts of processed Rehmannia root (Rehmannia glutinosa), Shatavari root (Asparagus racemosa), Damiana herb (Turnera diffusa), Red Ginseng root (Panax ginseng), Rose Petal flowers (Rosa gallica, Rosa damascena, Rosa centifolia)

INDICATIONS: This formula is designed to be used by women who are tired, fatigued, or have symptoms of blood or yin deficiency (anemia, vaginal dryness, dry skin, brain fog, weakness, hormonal imbalances, deficient insomnia, feel cold or depression). Adaptogens help re-regulate the HPA axis, SAS (sympathetic-adrenal system) and female reproductive systems.

ACTIVITY: This formula combines Adaptogenic herbs (Shatavari and Red Ginseng) with nutritive tonics such as processed Rehmannia and Rose Petals along with the antidepressant nervine Damiana. Shatavari is used in Ayurvedic medicine as a major rasayana or rejuvenative medicine. This herb has adapogenic (Krishnamurthy, et al 2013), anti-inflammatory, immune tonic, demulcent and antitussive activity. In India it is frequently used to promote fertility and libido, to reduce fatigue and reduce stress-induced oxidative damage. (Joshi, et al 2012). Red Ginseng is often thought of as a "men's" herb. This is totally untrue, in human clinical trials Panax was shown to inhibit llack of libido in post-menopausal women (Oh, et al 2010), it reduced menopausal symptoms and cardiovascular risk factors in women aged 45-60 (Kim, et al 2012). It improved chronic fatigue syndrome in women as well as men (Kim, et al 2013). It reduced menstrual irregularity, menstrual pain and constipation in young women (Yang, et al 2014) and it diminished residual depressive symptoms in women treated for major depressive disorder (Jeong, et al 2015). Processed Rehannia is a major blood (xue) tonic in Chinese medicine. It is an ingredient in the classic formula Women's Four Herb Tea used for amenorrhea, irregular menses, infertility, dysmenorrhea, and menopausal symptoms (vaginal dryness, brain fog). The herb also enhances bone density, lowers blood sugar levels and increases red blood cell counts. Damiana has a long held reputation for enhancing libido (in women and men) and it has carminative, antidepressant, nervine, anxiolytic and mild thyroid stimulating effects. Fragrant roses help restore the "emotional heart" and have antidepressant activity. They "calm the shen" and can be used to help resolve emotional trauma, "broken hearts", chronic grief and stagnant depression.

CONTRAINDICATIONS: None.

SUGGESTED USE: 60-80 drops (3-4 ml) in juice or water. Take 2-3 times per day. Shake well before using..

ADDITIONAL RECOMMENDATIONS: Get adequate sleep, avoid simple carbohydrates, exercise regularly.

ADDITIONAL USEFUL HERBS: Women's Calmpound™, Women's Transition™ or Women's Formula™ may be indicated for menopausal or menstrual issues.

WOMEN'S CALMPOUND™

CONTAINS: Hydroalcoholic extracts of Chaste Tree berry (Vitex agnus-castus), fresh Motherwort herb (Leonurus cardiaca), fresh Skullcap herb (Scutellaria lateriflora), fresh Blue Vervain flowering tops (Verbena hastata) and Pulsatilla (Pulsatilla vulgaris).

INDICATIONS: This formula is a combination of herbs known for reducing premenstrual tension and menopausal anxiety. It is effective for PMS-A (anxiety) with mood swings, anxiety attacks, headaches and emotional agitation. In menopause it helps with acute anxiety especially if associated with hot flashes, "skin-crawling" and palpitations.

ACTIVITY: Chaste tree effects pituitary and HPA Axis function, and binds to opiate receptors reducing irritability and anxiety. Motherwort and Blue Vervain are anxiolytic nervines indicated for PMS agitation, general anxiety, nervous tics and stress headaches. Skullcap is an effective muscle relaxant, nervine, and anti-anxiety agent. Pulsatilla has a long history of use by the Eclectic Physicans for treating menopausal anxiety, irritability, emotional instability and hormonal depression. Both Blue Vervain and Skullcap can relieve Petit Mal seizures, muscle spasms, "fly off the handle" anger and nervous tics that occur due to hormonal changes.

CONTRAINDICATIONS: Pregnancy.

SUGGESTED USE: 30-40 drops (1.5-2 ml) TID while symptoms persist. More may be taken in acute situations such as anxiety attacks (60-80 drops (3-4 ml) QID).

ADDITIONAL RECOMMENDATIONS: Increase B Complex vitamins, calcium, magnesium and probiotics.

ADDITIONAL USEFUL HERBS: Anxiolytic herbs including Tension Relief™, Passionflower, Kava, Bacopa, Lemon Balm, Polygala, Night Blooming Cereus or Chamomile tea may also be useful.

WOMEN'S FORMULA™

CONTAINS: Hydroalcoholic extracts of fresh Motherwort herb (Leonurus cardiaca), Raspberry leaf (Rubus idaeus), Processed Rehmannia root (Rehmannia glutinosa), Dong Quai root (Angelica sinensis), Ginger root (Zingiber officinale) and Chaste Tree berry (Vitex agnus-castus).

INDICATIONS: This formula is useful for balancing a woman's hormonal system during her child bearing years. Specific indications include premenstrual syndrome, irregular menses, amenorrhea, dysmenorrhea and pelvic fullness syndrome. It can also be useful for infertility associated with hormonal imbalance.

ACTIVITY: Chaste Tree normalizes the female reproductive function via the pituitary and HPA Axis. It reduces Prolactin levels which influences FSH and estrogen levels. It has also been found to bind the opiate receptors in the brain reducing irritability, pain and anxiety. Raspberry leaf strengthens uterine tonus and function reducing heavy menstrual bleeding. Motherwort relieves anxiety, nervousness and menstrual cramps. In clinical trials it has been shown to have sedative and hypotensive activity (Wojtyniak, et al., 2012). Dong Quai and Ginger increase uterine circulation. Dong Quai also enhances cardiac, bowel and liver function. Ginger acts as a systemic anti-inflammatory and improves digestion, antioxidant status and blood sugar/blood lipid metabolism (Li, et al., 2012). Processed Rehmannia builds the blood (*xue*), acts as a tonic to the kidney *yin* and female reproductive system.

CONTRAINDICATIONS: Pregnancy.

SUGGESTED USE: 30-40 drops (1.5-2 ml) TID for at least 3 menstrual cycles is recommended.

ADDITIONAL RECOMMENDATIONS: Increase intake of omega 3 fatty acids (Fish oil) as well as B Complex vitamins, vitamin E, calcium and magnesium.

ADDITIONAL USEFUL HERBS: For menstrual cramps Full Moon - Women's Anti-Spasmodic Compound™ or Cyperus may be helpful. Shatavari is a wonderful tonic for the female reproductive system.

WOMEN'S TRANSITION COMPOUND™

CONTAINS: Hydroalcoholic extracts of Chaste Tree berry (Vitex agnus-castus), fresh Black Cohosh root (Actaea racemosa), Dong Quai root (Angelica sinensis), Oat milky seed (Avena sativa), Shatavari root (Asparagus racemosa), fresh Night Blooming Cereus stem (Selenicereus pteranthus, S. grandiflorus) and Sage (Salvia officinalis).INDICATIONS: This is a useful formula for helping to normalize a woman's endocrine and reproductive systems, allowing for a healthy, symptom-free menopause. It is specifically useful for hot flashes, nightsweats, "skin crawling" and sleeplessness associated with menopause.

ACTIVITY: Chaste Tree is an excellent herb for women; it reduces elevated prolactin levels, thus positively affecting, estrogen and FSH levels. It works via the pituitary and HPA Axis, and has been found to bind to opiate receptors in the brain, reducing irritability, agitation and insomnia. Dong Quai and Black Cohosh have traditionally been used to treat menopausal discomforts including hot flashes, muscle pain and depression. Black Cohosh has been shown in numerous human trials to modestly reduce climateric symptoms such as hot flashes, night sweats, insomnia and anxiety (Molla, et al., 2009, Briese, et al., 2007, Bai, et al., 2007, Nappi, et al., 2005). In animal studies Dong Quai had estrogenic activity and it reduced serum LH levels (Circosta, et al., 2006). Dong Quai also enhances cardiac, bowel and liver function. Night Blooming Cereus helps relieve psychological symptoms of menopause including anxiety and depression. Milky Oat is one of our greatest nervine restoratives; it helps re-establish emotional balance, reducing anxiety, depression, irritablility and agitation. It also mildly promotes normal vaginal lubrication. Shatavari is a female reproductive system trophorestorative (i.e. food for the female reproductive system). It is a major rasayana (restorative remedy) in Ayurvedic Medicine. It is used to re-regulate female hormone balance, relieves vaginal dryness and has mild adaptogenic activity. Common garden Sage is not only a spice, it is a carminative, helps reduce menopausal sweating, and has nootropic and anti-inflammatory acitivity.

CONTRAINDICATIONS: Do not use during pregnancy.

SUGGESTED USE: 40-60 drops (2-3 ml) in juice or water. Take 3-4 times per day as needed. Shake well before using.

ADDITIONAL RECOMMENDATIONS: Include a diet rich in isoflavones and lignans (phyto-estrogens) like soy (miso, tempeh, tofu), beans (legumes), peas, lentils, flax seed, alfalfa sprouts, etc. Whole grains, nuts and seeds, and dark leafy vegetables are also beneficial. Important nutrients include vitamin E, omega 3 fatty acids (fish oil), B Complex vitamins especially folate, B6, and B12, as well as the essential minerals calcium, magnesium, chromium and zinc.

ADDITIONAL USEFUL HERBS: Osteoherb™ can enhance bone health and prevent osteopenia and osteoporosis. Replenish Compound™ can be added for vaginal dryness and Women's Calmpound™ for anxiety and depression.

DAVID WINSTON'S SOLID EXTRACTS

BLUEBERRY SOLID EXTRACT™

CONTAINS: Blueberry (Vaccinium spp.) fruit and Apple juice (Malas pumila).

INDICATIONS: Blueberries increase circulation to the capillaries of the eyes, which results in improved eyesight and reduced oxidation in these tissues. It is useful for helping to prevent diabetic retinopathy as well as treating night blindness. It can also inhibit the progression of age related macular degeneration (AMD) and cataracts. Blueberry is also beneficial for strengthening the capillaries, arteries and veins throughout the body. It can also be used for reducing capillary fragility and permeability in conditions such as varicose veins, spider veins and bruising easily (Bell, et al., 2006). Blueberries are antioxidant and anti-inflammatory, reducing inflammation and histamine release making it useful for treating allergies. Recent animal studies have shown that as little as 1/2 cup of blueberries per day can reduce symptoms of aging (memory loss, cognitive and motor impairment), protect against liver fibrosis, inhibit autoimmune encephalomyelitis and IBD, and may help to prevent cancer, heart disease and arthralgias. In human studies Blueberry enhanced the growth of healthy GI flora, inhibited adhesion of urinary pathogens, reduced blood pressure and insulin resistance (Basu & Lyons, 2011, Stull, et al., 2010).

ACTIVITY: Blueberries, like other Vaccinium species (Bilberry, Huckleberry, Cranberry) contain polyphenols such as proanthocyanidins (PCOs) which are potent anti-inflammatory agents. These berries have an ability to strongly inhibit pro-inflammatory cytokines which can cause tissue and cellular damage, cancer, as well as arteriosclerosis. They also inhibit histamine production, protect connective tissue, the eyes and the cardiovascular system.

CONTRAINDICATIONS: None.

SUGGESTED USE: 1/4 tsp. (2g) BID. (Which is equal to 1/2 ounce fresh berries per day.) This terrific tasting concentrate can be added to hot water to make tea, spread on bread or eaten off a spoon. Both children and adults will enjoy its taste and health benefits.

HAWTHORN SOLID EXTRACT™

CONTAINS: Hawthorn (Crataegus spp.) Blueberry fruit (Vaccinium spp.), Apple juice (Malus pumila) and glycerin.

INDICATIONS: Hawthorn Solid Extract™ provides the cardiac trophorestorative effects of hawthorn berries in a delicious tasting functional food. This fruit has been traditionally used in Europe to treat heart disease, coronary artery disease, hypertension, angina and hypercholesteremia. Recent research has shown that a diet rich in polyphenols decreases cardiovascular risk by inhibiting low density lipoprotein (LDL) oxidation, which is a primary event in atherosclerosis plaque formation (Bell & Gochenaur, 2006). Clinical trials using hawthorn in patients with and without prescription hypotensive agents showed a modest reduction in blood pressure as well as a decrease in clinical symptoms of fatigue, dyspnea and lack of vitality (Walker, et al., 2006, 2002). Hawthorn is also beneficial to patients with left ventricular systolic dysfunction and laboratory studies suggest that this may be due to improvement in the contractility of impaired myocardium (Rechciski & Kurpesa, 2005). A review of 9 different clinical trials designed to study the effect of hawthorn in patients with congestive heart failure concluded that "Crataegus is an effective and safe treatment for this indication". The positive effect of hawthorn on a wide range of cardiac and circulatory conditions demonstrates the ability of this medicinal fruit to deliver plaque-fighting capabilities and improve cardiac tonicity (Degenring, et al., 2003, Schmidt, et al., 1994). While many products increase blood circulation by elevating blood pressure, hawthorn is unique in that it increases circulation and simultaneously mildly lowers blood pressure.

ACTIVITY: Hawthorn fruit is a rich source of procyanidins oligomers (PCO's), which are anti-inflammatory polyphenols. The berries also contain other anti-inflammatory flavonoids such as Rutin, Quercetin, Catechin and triterpene acids such as Ursolic acid, Crateagolic acid, and Oleanolic acid. PCO's and other flavonoids help inhibit angiotensin-converting enzymes, causing vasodilation and hence, improve circulation and blood vessel integrity. The antioxidants in hawthorn reduce inflammation and stabilize cardiovascular tissue. Rutin and other flavonoids are thought to rebuild the collagen fibers in the outer layers of the blood vessels, which also strengthens them. Blueberries are also a rich source of PCO's and the addition of blueberry juice to the product adds to the cardiotonic effect of hawthorn as well as serving to enhance the berry flavor.

CONTRAINDICATIONS: Consult with a physician before using in patients with serious heart disease.

SUGGESTED USE: Take 1/4 to 1/2 tsp. (1.8-3.5g) BID mixed in tea, yogurt, smoothies or protein shakes.

POMEGRANATE-GOJI BERRY SOLID EXTRACT™

CONTAINS: Pomegranate juice (Punica granatum), Blueberry juice (Vaccinium spp.), Lycium fruit (Lycium barbarum), Blueberry fruit (Vaccinium spp.), Apple juice (Malus pumila) and glycerin.

INDICATIONS: Pomegranate-Goji Berry Solid Extract™ is a functional food that provides a rich source of carotenoids, minerals and flavonoids. Pomegranates are rich in ellagitannins which are polyphenols that have antioxidant and anti-inflammatory properties. Combined with the flavonoids in Goji berries (lycium) and anthocyanins in blueberries, this tasty spread provides a readily bioavailable source of antioxidants that have been shown to reduce the effects of oxidative stress involved in systemic inflammatory diseases, development and progression of prostate, gastric and skin cancer, deteriorating vision and mental decline.

ACTIVITY: Excessive oxidative stress and normal aging can switch on pro-inflammatory genes that trigger inflammatory cytokins and can result in the development of chronic degenerative disease. Recent research suggests that antioxidants do not actually quench "free radicals", but rather inhibit antioxidant responsive elements (AREs) on genes. So "antioxidant" compounds are actually acting more as anti-inflammatories than inhibiting reactive oxygen species (ROS) as previously believed (Finley, et al., 2011). Blueberry polyphenols can cross the blood brain barrier and localize in various regions of the brain that are important for learning and memory and therefore provide additional neuroprotective action. These findings are supported by human clinical trials that showed that ingestion of a Lycium product increased energy levels, mental acuity and reduced stress (Amagase and Nance, 2008). In a human clinical trial Lycium increased metabolic rate and reduced waist circumference (Amagase and Nance, 2011). The flavonoids found in both fruits accumulate in the eye, where they improve vascular integrity and increase capillary circulation which helps reduce oxidation in ocular tissues. The combination of Blueberry and Lycium fruit is beneficial for inhibiting the onset of glaucoma, macular degeneration and cataracts. Pomegranate's ellagitannins inhibit gene expression of androgen-synthesizing hormones and nuclear factor-kappaB (NF-kappaß), both of which are involved in tumor cell growth of recurrent prostate cancer. This inhibition of angiogenesis may be useful as a chemopreventative or chemotherapeutic agent, especially when combined with conventional treatment. The polyphenolics in pomegranate have also been shown to reduce oxidative DNA damage caused by UVA and UVB ultraviolet light exposure to skin. In human clinical trials Pomegranate juice was found to reduce blood pressure and endothelial dysfunction in people with hypertension (Asgary, et al., 2013) and it reduces oxidative stress and disease activity in people with rheumatoid arthritis (Balbir-Gurman, et al., 2011)

CONTRAINDICATIONS: Do not use this product if you have a nightshade sensitivity.

SUGGESTED USE: Take 1/4-1/3 tsp. BID/TID. This fruity spread can be used on toast or eaten directly off the spoon. It is also delicious when used as a fruit spread or a topping for cottage cheese or yogurt and in smoothies.

THERAPEUTIC PROTOCOLS

RESTORATIVE CLEANSING PROTOCOL

TWO WEEK RESTORATIVE ALTERATIVE CLEANSE PROGRAM

CONTAINS: Gentlelax™, Burdock/Red Root Compound™, Healthy Skin Tonic™, Thistles Compound™

INDICATIONS: Alteratives are herbs that enhance normal elimination via the major eliminatory organs (the liver, bowel, skin, kidneys, lymph and lung). This is a healthy and safe way of promoting excretion of metabolic wastes. Many alteratives also improve digestion and absorption of nutrients, circulation, cellular regeneration, immune function and they help to maintain a healthy weight. Periodic "spring cleaning" (it can be done any time of they year) helps to promote and enhance overall well being that comes from eating a healthy diet, getting adequate exercise and sleep and making good lifestyle choices.

ACTIVITY: Many of the herbs in these formulas, such as Red Alder bark, Yellow Dock, Culvers Root, Blessed Thistle, Turmeric and Oregon Grape root, are bitters which can improve digestion, absorption and elimination. Red Alder bark, Yellow Dock, Turmeric, and Culvers root are cholagogues which stimulate liver, gallbladder and bowel function. The herbs in Burdock/Red Root Compound™ enhance lymphatic circulation. Horsetail and Burdock seed stimulate kidney function and elimination of uric acid. Turmeric and Milk Thistle are hepatoprotective; they not only protect the liver, but help repair liver damage, enhance hepatic glutathione levels and stimulate Phase II hepatic detoxification.

CONTRAINDICATIONS: Pregnancy, lactation, Caution: Gentlelax™ contains the laxative herb, Buckthorn. Do not use if you have or develop diarrhea, loose stools or abdominal pain. Consult your physician if you have a medical condition or are taking any medication, but especially digoxin/lanoxin or lithium as it can increase potassium loss.

SUGGESTED USE:

Week 1 - Deep Cleanse and Detox for one week:

    Gentlelax™ - 20-30 drops (1-1.5 mL) once daily before bedtime to promote bowel and liver function.

    Burdock/Red Root Compound™ - 40 drops (2 mL) twice daily (before breakfast and before dinner) to promote liver and lymphatic function.

Week 2 - Rebalancing Cleanse and Detox for one week:

    Take the two formulas together before breakfast and before dinner.

    Healthy Skin Tonic™ - 40 drops (2 mL) twice daily to enhance skin, kidney, bowel and liver function, it also can bind endotoxins in the gut and promote their excretion.

    Thistles Compound™ - 40 drops (2 mL) twice daily to stimulate liver and gallbladder function and enhance hepatic glutathione levels and hepato-cyte repair.

ADDITIONAL RECOMMENDATIONS: Increase dietary intake of bulk fiber in diet. Sources of bulk fiber include oatmeal, brown rice, barley, psyllium seed, chia seed, flax seed, marshmallow, aloe gel, slippery elm and seaweeds. Eat at least 1-2 servings of fruits or vegetables at meals or for snacks. Drink 6 to 8 - 8 oz. glasses of water a day preferably with lemon or pomegranate juice added. Reduce or eliminate all saturated fats, fried foods, and trans fats from the diet. Add omega 3 fatty acids to the diet from wild caught fish or fish oil supplements. Limit meat intake during the cleanse - Follow the Asian "meat as a condiment" practice. Avoid or reduce alcohol consumption while doing this protocol.

SELECTED BOTANICAL MATERIA MEDICA - SPECIFIC INDICATIONS

The following section discusses "black letter symptoms" or specific indications for the therapeutic use of each given herb.

KEY TO ABBREVIATIONS
BID = two times per day
TID = three times per day
QID = four times per day

* = Use only with a practitioner's guidance

- *Preparation notes:* When it says to make tea and steep covered, this means to cover the teacup with a saucer or use a closed vessel. The herbs contain essential oils which can be lost with the steam. When you decoct an herb, you bring it to a boil, then turn the heat down to a very low simmer.

Agrimony *flowering tops (Agrimonia eupatora)* shows specific activity for the urinary tract, especially the bladder, urethra and ureters. It is used for inflammation, irritation and burning/scalding urine associated with cystitis, urethritis, and interstitial cystitis. I use it with Schisandra for bedwetting due to urinary irritation in children, as well as for treating urinary frequency in adults. It is also soothing to inflamed bile ducts, is a mild liver tonic and has significant antioxidant/anti-inflammatory activity .

Tea-1-2 tsp. of the dried herb to 8 oz. hot water, steep 15 minutes. Take 4 oz. 2-3 times per day.

Tincture - 20-40 drops (1-2 ml) TID.

Alfalfa *leaf (Medicago sativa)* is rich in minerals (calcium, iron, potassium, magnesium), vitamins (A, folate, C, D, E, & K) and trace elements that are easily absorbable. It also is a concentrated source of isoflavones (phytoestrogens) and has been used to prevent menopausal symptomology, osteoporosis, anemia, and to lower LDL cholesterol and triglyceride levels.

Tea - 1 tsp. of the dried herb to 8 oz. hot water, steep 1/2 hour. Take 4 oz. 3 times per day.

Tincture - 30-40 drops (1.5-2 ml) QID.

American Ginseng *fresh organically woods grown root (Panax quinquefolius)* is a nourishing adaptogen indicated in cases of chronic stress, fatigue, nervous exhaustion, jet lag, metabolic syndrome, chronic fatigue immune deficiency syndrome and nervous dyspepsia. American Ginseng will help normalize function of the HPA Axis and the endocrine, immune and nervous systems. It is an immune amphoteric and can be used for hyperimmune conditions (allergies, allergic asthma), autoimmune diseases (Sjörgrens Syndrome) and immune deficiency. In Chinese medicine the American species is used as a tonic remedy to strengthen the Chinese spleen and lung *Qi* and to speed recovery after pneumonia or bronchitis. Less stimulating than Asian Ginseng, this root is appropriate for

daily use by both sexes, including people in their 30's - 40's.
Tea - 1 tsp. of the dried root to 12 oz. water, decoct 20-30 minutes, steep 1 hour. Take 4 oz. 2-3 times per day.
Tincture - 40-60 drops (2-3 ml) TID.

Amla *fruit (Phyllanthus emblica, syn: Emblica officinalis)* is used in Ayurvedic medicine as a Rasayana or rejuvenative remedy. While older research described Amla as being rich in vitamin C, some newer research disputes these findings. Regardless of which research is accurate, it does have high levels of polyphenols, which give Amla its activity. This fruit has been used for millennia in India as part of 2 famous rasayana (restorative) formulas, Chyawanaprash and Triphala. Used alone it is strongly antioxidant and anti-inflammatory and useful for inhibiting oxidative disease and inflammation. Amla strengthens the skin, hair, muscles, and connective tissue and helps prevent cancer, gastric ulcers, liver damage, arteriosclerosis, osteoarthritis and degenerative eye diseases such as age-related macular degeneration (AMD).
Tea - 1/2-1 tsp. of the dried powdered fruit to 8 oz. water, decoct 10 minutes, steep 1 hour. Take 2-3 cups per day.
Tincture - 60-100 drops (3-5 ml) TID.

Andrographis *herb (Andrographis paniculata) has* long been used in both Chinese and Ayurvedic medicine, for its antimicrobial activity. The herb is a bitter tonic, alterative, immune stimulant, anthelmintic, hepatoprotective agent, cholagogue, anti-inflammatory and it has pronounced antiviral and antibacterial activity. It can be used to treat colds, influenza, sore throats, hepatitis and topical MRSA infections. In India it is also used to treat malaria. This intensely bitter herb is effective for treating intestinal parasites such as Giardia, Blastocystis hominis and Dientamoeba fragilis when combined with Black Walnut hulls, Elecampane and Quassia. In a human clinical trial it was as effective as mesalazine for treating ulcerative colitis (Tang, et al., 2011).
Tincture - 20-40 drops (1-2 ml) QID.
CONTRAINDICATIONS: Not for use in pregnancy unless otherwise directed by qualified expert.

Angelica *root (Angelica archangelica)* is a time-tested warming bitter useful for deficient gastric hydrochloric acid, gas, nausea and intestinal colic. It also acts as a stimulating diaphoretic, antispasmodic and expectorant effective for colds, influenza, bronchial congestion, intestinal viruses, menstrual cramps, rheumatic pain and cold extremities. Animal studies suggest this herb also has anxiolytic and hepatoprotective activity.
Tea - 1 tsp. of the dried root to 8 oz. water, decoct 5-10 minutes, steep covered 15-20 minutes. Take 4 oz. 3 times per day.
Tincture - 20-40 drops (1-2 ml) TID.
CONTRAINDICATIONS: Not for use in pregnancy unless otherwise directed by qualified expert. Avoid prolonged exposure to sunlight when taking this herb.

Arnica* *fresh herb in flower (Arnica spp.)* is well known as an herbal and homeopathic remedy for trauma injuries such as bruises, sprains, strains, or muscle or nerve pain including fibromyalgia, back pain, whiplash, sciatica, Reflex Sympathetic Dystrophy Syndrome (RSD), and torticollis. It is frequently used topically for these and other painful musculoskeletal conditions. (See Compound Arnica Oil™)
Topical Oil - Apply 2-3 times per day or as needed. Discontinue use if skin irritation or a rash develops.
CONTRAINDICATIONS: Avoid use on abraded or damaged skin and in people with Asteraceae allergies.

Artichoke *fresh and dry leaf (Cynara scolymus)* is a strong bitter that stimulates digestion, absorption and intestinal elimination. It stimulates gastric hydrochloric acid, bile, liver, pancreatic and small intestine juices and has mild hepatoprotective activity. Artichoke is indicated for sluggish liver, impaired digestion, elevated LDL/VLDL cholesterol levels, dyspepsia (Holtmann, et al., 2003) and Metabolic Syndrome (Rondanelli, et al., 2013). It has also been shown to have anti-emetic activity and can help relieve nausea, especially when caused by eating fatty foods.
Tea - 1 tsp. of the dried herb to 8 oz. hot water, steep 40 minutes. Take 4 oz. 3 times per day.
Tincture - 20-30 drops (1-1.5 ml) TID.

Ashwagandha *root (Withania somnifera)* is a traditional Ayurvedic rasayana or rejuvenative remedy. It is a calming adaptogen and nervine used to reduce stress and anxiety while also stimulating libido, sperm count, and thyroid function. It also acts as an anti-inflammatory and antispasmodic. Combined with Black Cohosh, White Peony, and Wood Betony it is effective for fibromyalgia pain. Due to its rich iron content, Withania is used to treat iron-deficient anemia and the resultant fatigue associated with it. In a recent clinical trial Ashwagandha enhanced athletic performance, muscular strength and neuro-muscular co-ordination (Sandhu, et al., 2010).
Tea - 1-2 tsp. of the dried root to 12 oz. water, decoct 15-20 minutes, steep 1/2 hour. Take 4 oz. 2 or 3 times a day.
Tincture - 30-50 drops (1.5 -2.5 ml) TID.
CONTRAINDICATIONS: Not for use in pregnancy unless otherwise directed by qualified expert. Some sources state that it may potentiate the effects of barbiturates, this is theoretical. Avoid use in hyperthyroidism or Graves disease.

Astragalus *root (Astragalus membranaceus)* or Huang Qi strengthens the "immune reservoir" and *Wei Qi* (protective energy). It is a superior tonic used for rebuilding depleted immune activity. Huang Qi is used in Fu Zheng therapy in China for treating cancer and it is an immune amphoteric. It can help relieve allergic rhinitis and allergic asthma. It can be used to treat chronic lung deficiency and for Chronic Fatigue Immune Deficiency Syndrome (CFIDS). Astragalus also lowers blood sugar levels, inhibits gastric ulcers, protects the heart against

Coxsackie B virus and strengthens the upright *Qi*, making it useful for organ pro-lapse. In Traditional Chinese Medicine (TCM), Astragalus is also used for con-gestive heart failure along with Dong Quai, Chinese Salvia, and Tienqi Ginseng.
Tea - 8-12g (about 10-16 pieces) of the dried root to 16 oz. water, decoct 30-40 minutes, steep 1 hour. Take 2 cups per day.
Tincture - 40-80 drops (2-4 ml) TID.

Bacopa *herb (Bacopa monnieri)* is a very effective anxiolytic, nervine, nootropic (cerebral tonic), and thyroid stimulant. It is known as Brahmi in Ayurvedic medicine and is used to treat anxiety, irritability, poor memory (Calabrese, et al., 2008), Alzheimer's disease, ADD/ADHD, and in recovery from head trauma injuries. Research indicates it stimulates thyroid function, making it potentially useful for hypothyroidism.
Tincture - 40-60 drops (2-3 ml) TID.

Bai-Zhu Atractylodes *root (Atractylodes macrocephala)* is a useful tonic for the Chinese stomach and spleen. It dries dampness and stagnation, so it is an effective remedy for gas, diarrhea, dysbiosis and bloating. It is included in many Fu Zheng formulas to improve nutrition in cancer patients and can help prevent cancer induced cachexia as well as diarrhea in AIDS patients. It is also used in Chinese medicine for excessive sweating, cold/damp arthritis and to enhance small intestine motility.
Tea - 1-2 tsp. of the dried root to 12 oz. water, decoct 20 minutes. Take 4 oz. 3 times per day.
Tincture - 30-40 drops (1.5-2 ml) TID.

Barberry *root (Berberis spp.)* is a common weedy shrub that has bright yellow, bitter tasting roots. The primary constituent is the alkaloid berberine, which is antibacterial, a hypoglycemic agent, a bitter tonic, cholagogue and antifungal. The root is used to stimulate bile secretion, increase liver function and improve fat digestion. It is also effective as an antibacterial/antifungal agent (orally and topically) for thrush, bacterial vaginosis, vaginal candidiasis, urinary tract infec-tions, sore throats and sinus infections.
Tincture - 20-40 drops (1-2 ml) QID.
CONTRAINDICATIONS: Not for use in pregnancy unless otherwise directed by qualified expert (theoretical concern).

Bayberry *root bark (Morella cerifera)* has long been used by Native Americans and later by Thomsonian and Eclectic practitioners for excessive mucous dis-charges. It helps dry up boggy mucous membranes, strengthens the tissue and helps re-establish normal gastrointestinal function. It can be used for post nasal drip, head colds, excess bronchial phlegm, diarrhea, gastric bleeding, periodontal disease and leaky gut syndrome.
Tincture - 15-30 drops (.75-1.5 ml) TID.
CONTRAINDICATIONS: Overuse can cause constipation, gastric upset and deplete the yin. (It is drying.)

Bitter Melon *fruit (Mormordica charantia)* is eaten as a food and used as a medicine throughout India, China, Southeast Asia and the Caribbean. It has a long history of use for treating obesity and type II diabetes. Animal and human research have verified its traditional uses, showing that it stimulates insulin release, reduces insulin resistance and improves cellular uptake of glucose by stimulating GLUT-4 (Lo, et al., 2013). In a human study it has also been shown to be beneficial for treating Metabolic Syndrome (Tsai, et al., 2012) and improving unhealthy blood lipids. Other research has shown the unripe melon has anti-inflammatory, antifungal, neuro-protective, gastroprotective and antipyretic activity (Patel, et al., 2010).
Tincture - 30-40 drops (1.5-2 ml) TID.
CONTRAINDICATIONS: Monitor blood sugar levels carefully when using in combination with blood sugar lowering medications.

Black Cohosh *fresh root (Actaea racemosa, syn: Cimicifuga racemosa)* is an analgesic, emmenagogue and antispasmodic indicated for cases of dysmenorrhea with a scanty flow, amenorrhea, postpartum pain and uterine or testicular pain. While this herb has a reputation for relieving menopausal symptoms, its activity is overstated. By itself it is most useful for relieving menopausal, menstrual or andropausal depression. It is much more effective for relieving hot flashes and nightsweats when combined with Chaste Tree, Sage, Licorice and Motherwort. The Eclectics used this herb with Night Blooming Cereus for "doom and gloom depression" caused by hormonal changes or old age. This herb is also indicated for rheumatic neuralgia, fibromyalgia, muscular pain in the back, pelvis or thighs and any condition where "the muscles feel bruised" and sore.
Tea - 1 tsp. of the dried root to 8 oz. water, decoct 15-20 minutes, steep 40 minutes. Take 2-4 oz. 3 times per day.
Tincture - 10-20 drops (.5-1 ml) TID.
CONTRAINDICATIONS: Pregnancy and lactation. It may potentiate antispasmodic or sedative medication. Consult a healthcare professional before use if you have or have had liver problems, frequently use alcoholic beverages, or take any medications.

Black Haw *fresh bark (Viburnum prunifolium)* is antispasmodic especially to the uterus. It is indicated for dysmenorrhea with lumbar pain, for threatened miscarriage, menorrhagia, vaginismus, mittleschmertz (ovulatory pain), uterine and abdominal colic, as well as testicular pain (epididymitis), hiccoughs and intercostal pain (use it with Wild Cherry bark and Pleurisy root).
Tincture - 30-40 drops (1.5-2 ml) QID.
CONTRAINDICATIONS: Individuals with a history of kidney stones should use this herb cautiously, as it is reported to contain calcium oxalate.

Black Walnut *fresh hull (Juglans nigra)* is a strong antifungal and antibacterial agent as well as a vermifuge. It is used externally (diluted) for athlete's foot, ringworm and cradle cap. Internally it can be used to treat amoebic infections (Giardia, Blastocystis hominis, Dientamoeba fragilis, etc.), nematodes (pinworms) and candidiasis when combined with Elecampane, Sweet Annie or Quassia.

Tincture or Glycerite - 20-30 drops (1-1.5 ml) TID.

CONTRAINDICATIONS: Prolonged use is not advised due to the presence of significant quantities of juglone, a known mutagen in animals. Not for use in pregnancy or while nursing. If used topically Black Walnut can stain the skin.

Bladderwrack *seaweed (Fucus vesiculosis)* is a common seaweed, rich in minerals and trace elements. It has a long history of use as an alterative and nutritive herb. In small amounts it can mildly stimulate underactive thyroid function, especially in people with iodine or trace mineral deficiencies. This "brown" seaweed contains immune enhancing polysaccharides as well as potassium iodide, both of which have been shown to inhibit some types of cancer.

Tea - 1-2 tsp. of the dried seaweed to 10 oz. water, decoct 15 minutes, steep 1/2 hour. Take 4 oz. 2 or 3 times per day.

Tincture - 20-30 drops (1-1.5 ml) TID.

CONTRAINDICATIONS: Overuse of Iodine (from seaweeds or other sources) can cause hypo- or hyperthyroidism.

Blessed Thistle *fresh herb (Cnicus benedictus)* is an intense bitter that acts as a digestive stimulant, cholagogue and febrifuge. It increases stomach, small intestine and liver activity, and in this capacity is especially useful for the convalescent elderly. Blessed Thistle is effective in treating liver stagnation, poor fat digestion and rebellious *qi* (hiatal hernia, GERD, hiccoughs).

Tea - 1 tsp. of the dried herb to 8 oz. of hot water, steep 30 minutes. Take 2-4 oz. 3 times a day.

Tincture - 20-40 drops (1-2 ml) TID.

CONTRAINDICATIONS: Not for use in pregnancy unless otherwise directed by qualified expert. It can worsen PMS breast swelling (mastalgia) in women who have this condition.

Bloodroot* *root/rhizome (Sanguinaria canadensis)* is a traditional Native American remedy once popular for treating skin cancers. The Eclectic physicians used it in small doses for harsh, dry coughs, for liver stagnation (hepatic torpor), bilious headaches, and chronic skin conditions. Topically it is still used for athlete's foot and ringworm.

Tincture - 2-5 drops (.10-.25 ml) TID.

CONTRAINDICATIONS: Pregnancy or if breast feeding. It can cause nausea and vomiting. Use only under the supervision of a qualified practitioner.

Blue Vervain *fresh herb (Verbena hastata)* is an underutilized medicine especially useful for spasmodic nervous disorders. It is indicated for some types of petit mal epilepsy (especially if associated with menses), nervous tics (use it with Skullcap), PMS or menopausal anxiety, irritability associated with fevers or influenza, liver migraines, trigeminal neuralgia, restless leg syndrome, tardive dyskinesia and Bell's Palsy (use it with Mullein root and St. John's wort). It is best used with a carminative to prevent nausea.

Tincture - 30-40 drops (1.5-2 ml) QID.
CONTRAINDICATIONS: Not for use in pregnancy unless otherwise directed by qualified expert.

Buchu *leaf (Agathosma betulina)* is an aromatic herb native to South Africa. It is used as an antiseptic diuretic for chronic low grade cystitis, urethritis, bacterial prostatitis and dysuria. It increases uric acid excretion and can be of benefit for gout and gouty arthritis, used with Parsley, Celery seed and Goldenrod.

Tea - 1 tsp. of the dried leaf to 8 oz. hot water, steep 15 minutes. Take 4 oz. 2-3 times per day.
Tincture - 30-40 drops (1.5-2 ml) TID.
CONTRAINDICATIONS: Pregnancy.

Buckthorn *bark (Frangula alnus)* is primarily used as a stimulant laxative. It contains the anthraquinones rhein and emodin, both of which are laxative and also have antibacterial and antitumor activity. Like any stimulant laxative, regular use should be avoided, but occasional use for situational constipation (travel-induced constipation, menstrual constipation) or liver headaches with constipation is appropriate.

Tea - 1/2 tsp. of the *aged* dried bark to 8 oz. water, decoct for 5 minutes, steep for 30 minutes. Take 4 oz. 2 times per day.
Tincture - 20-50 drops (1-2.5 ml) once per day in the evening.
CONTRAINDICATIONS: Do not use if you have or develop diarrhea, loose stools, or abdominal pain because Buckthorn may worsen these conditions. Consult your physician if you have frequent diarrhea or if you are pregnant, nursing, taking medication, or have a medical condition. Not for long-term use.

Bugleweed *flowering tops (Lycopus virginicus)* is a valuable and underutilized herb used for treating hyperthyroidism. It is especially effective for relieving the nervousness, elevated blood pressure and palpitations often associated with hyperthyroidism. Lycopus also inhibits binding of Graves' IgG to the TSH receptor (Winterhoff, et al., 1994) and can be used with Reishi, Lemon Balm, Self Heal and Motherwort for Graves' Disease. Bugleweed is also an astringent, styptic and sedative and can be used for treating chronic coughs, hemoptysis, hematuria and heart palpitations with a rapid "thready" pulse.

Tincture - 20-30 drops (1-1.5 ml) TID.
CONTRAINDICATIONS: Not for use in pregnancy unless otherwise directed by qualified expert. Do not use with people who have hypothyroid conditions.

Bupleurum *root (Bupleurum spp.)* is known in Chinese medicine as Chai Hu and is used for constrained liver *qi* patterns. The symptoms of this include many female reproductive problems such as dysmenorrhea, PMS anxiety or mood swings irregular menstrual cycles and menstrual constipation. It can be used with Cyperus, Chinese Peony, Dong Quai and Chaste Tree. A prominent liver herb, Bupleurum can also be used to treat hepatitis, liver fire rising (liver headaches) and hepatomegaly. This root is indicated for organ prolapse (used with *qi* tonics), is a systemic anti-inflammatory and can be very effective as an immuno-regulator for autoimmune diseases.

Tea - 1/2 tsp. of the dried root to 8 oz. water, decoct 15 minutes, steep 30 minutes. Take 4 oz. 2-3 times per day, mix with Ginger.

Tincture - 20-30 drops (1-1.5 ml) TID.

CONTRAINDICATIONS: Avoid concurrent use with interferon (theoretical concern).

Burdock *root (Arctium lappa)* is a mild alterative gently increasing lymphatic, kidney and liver function. Burdock is indicated for chronic lymphatic swellings, cystic breast disease, chronic skin diseases with inflammation (atopic eczema, psoriasis) and it is an antimutagen with a long history of use in "cancer formulas". Burdock root is a rich source of inulin which contains FOS (fructo-oligerosaccharides) that act as prebiotics and enhance the growth of healthy bowel flora. It also has mild hepatoprotective activity and can be used as a gentle liver tonic.

Tea - 1-2 tsp. of the dried root to 10 oz. water, decoct 15 minutes, steep 45 minutes. Take 4-8 oz., 3 times a day.

Tincture - 60-100 drops (3-5 ml) TID.

Burdock *seed (Arctium lappa)* The specific indications for Arctium seed are skin conditions that are dry, crusty, itchy or flaky. Use it with fish oil (omega 3 fatty acids) and Milk Thistle seed. It is also a non-irritating diuretic useful for cystitis with scalding urine. The seeds are antibacterial and used in TCM to expel wind heat and can be used for sore throats, ticklish or irritating coughs, tonsillitis, colds and influenza. It is one of the ingredients in the classic TCM formula Yin Qiao San, used to treat the flu and upper respiratory tract infections.

Tea - 1-2 tsp. of the dried seed to 10 oz. water, decoct 15 minutes, steep 1/2 hour. Take 1-3 cups per day.

Tincture - 20-30 drops (1-1.5 ml) TID.

Butternut *root bark (Juglans cinerea)* is a relative of the common Black Walnut. The root bark of this tree is the mildest and safest of the stimulant laxatives. It does not cause laxative dependency and mixed with Dandelion root and bitters is a useful therapy for constipation with dry, hard stools or a lack of bile secretion with clay-colored stools. The Eclectic physicians also used Butternut for treating skin conditions with a scaly appearance or for pus filled pimples caused by a slow transit time.

Tea - 1 tsp. of the dried herb to 8 oz. water, decoct 5-10 minutes, steep 45 minutes. Take 4 oz. 2 times per day.

Tincture - 20-40 drops (1-2 ml) TID.

Calendula *flower (Calendula officinalis)* is also known as Pot Marigold, but should not be confused with the unrelated garden flower Marigold (Tagetes). The bright yellow or orange flowers contain abundant carotenoids especially lutein which is an antioxidant to the eyes. Traditionally Calendula is used as a lymph and liver tonic and as an anti-inflammatory. It is a mild alterative and can be used for Lymphatic stagnation, lymphedema (use it with Cleavers and Horse Chestnut) and arthritis. It can also be an effective part of a protocol for gastritis, gastric ulcers or leaky gut syndrome (Use it with Cat's Claw, Plantain leaf, Turmeric and Licorice.) Topically it is antifungal, antibacterial and a styptic.

Topical use - The oil, ointment and powdered herb can be used for cuts, wounds, abrasions, diaper rash (powdered flowers), athlete's foot, bed sores, insect stings, bacterial vaginosis, cervical dysplasia, and vulvodynia.

Tea - 1-2 tsp. of the dried flowers to 8 oz. water, decoct 5 minutes, steep 1/2 hour. Take 1-2 cups per day.

Tincture - 40-60 drops (2-3 ml) QID.

California Poppy *fresh whole plant in flower (Eschscholtzia californica)* is a common West coast wildflower. It is a useful sedative, anxiolytic, and antispasmodic indicated for insomnia, nervous headache, adult ADHD, muscle pain and sleeplessness due to pain and anxiety. It can also be helpful in formulas for gallbladder or intestinal pain, and spasmodic coughs.

Tincture - 30-40 drops (1.5-2 ml) TID.

CONTRAINDICATIONS: Not for use in pregnancy unless otherwise directed by qualified expert.

Cardamom *seed (Elettaria cardamomum)* is a common spice that is rich in essential oils. Cardamom inhibits the growth of yeast, fungi and bacteria and can be useful in formulas for thrush, vaginal candidiasis, and candida overgrowth in the bowel or upper respiratory tract. Traditionally used in Chinese and Ayurvedic medicine, Cardamom is a carminative indicated for "damp spleen" conditions (diarrhea, nausea, poor appetite) as well as flatulence, borborygmus, and impaired fat digestion.

Tea - 1/2 tsp. of the dried seed and pod to 8 oz. hot water, steep covered 30 minutes. Take 4 oz. 3 times per day.

Tincture - 15-20 drops (.75-1 ml) TID.

Catnip *flowering tops (Nepeta cataria)* is specifically indicated for stress-induced gastro-intestinal problems. It is used for nervous dyspepsia, flatulence, nausea, gastritis, gastric ulcers and irritable bowel syndrome (IBS). Research suggest that catnip can inhibit biofilm production by Helicobactor pylori, the main cause of gastric ulcers and gastritis. Catnip is also useful for children's fevers, colic, nausea, insomnia, and hiccoughs.

Tea - 1-2 tsp. of the dried herb to 8 oz. hot water, steep covered 10-15 minutes. Take 1-2 cups per day

Tincture - 40-80 drops (2-4 ml) QID.

Glycerite - 60-100 drops (3-5 ml) QID.

Cat's Claw *bark (Uncaria tomentosa)* or Una de Gato grows in the rain forests of Peru. It shows promise as an immune amphoteric, anti-inflammatory and bowel tonic. It has been traditionally used for treating cancers, arthritis and gastritis. In laboratory and animal research it has shown antiproliferative, chemoprotective, and proapoptotic activity. In a human trial it reduced neutropenia caused by chemotherapy and prevented oxidative damage to the DNA (Santos, et al., 2012) Clinically it is of benefit for leaky gut syndrome, hot-damp arthralgias (Piscoya, et al., 2001) and allergic rhinitis. The belief that there are two different chemotypes of this herb, one that is effective and one that is not, is a widely promulgated myth created by a company selling "the right product".
Tea - 1 tsp. of the dried bark to 10 oz. water, decoct 15 minutes, steep 1/2 hour. Take 4 oz. 3 times per day.
Tincture - 30-50 drops (1.5-2.5 ml) TID.
CONTRAINDICATIONS: Not for use in pregnancy unless otherwise directed by qualified expert.

Cayenne *fruit (Capsicum annuum, syn: Capsicum frutescens)* is both an intense spicy food and as well as a medicine. Cayenne increases digestive fire, promotes circulation and enhances absorption of the other herbs used with it in a formula. Rich in flavonoids and carotenoids, these hot fruits have anti-inflammatory and antioxidant activity. They help prevent atherosclerosis, stimulate metabolism, and reduce histamine response. In a human clinical trial cayenne pepper was found to be effective for relieving gastric pain, nausea and bloating. (Bortolotti, et al., 2002)
Tincture - 5-10 drops (.25-.50 ml) BID/TID diluted in juice or water. Avoid contact with the eyes.

Celandine *fresh herb and root (Chelidonium majus)* is a powerful cholagogue useful for insufficient bile production with clay colored or gray stools and stagnant liver *qi* with flank pain. It inhibits gallstone formation and is used with Fringe Tree, Wild Yam, and California Poppy to help expel biliary calculi. The Eclectic physicians called this herb "the opium of the gallbladder" and it is effective for relieving gallbladder spasms and pain. Celandine also has marked anti-viral activity and the fresh latex is used externally to remove common warts.
Tincture - 5-10 drops (.25-.5 ml) TID. (Larger doses or extended use is not recommended.)
CONTRAINDICATIONS: Not for use in pregnancy unless otherwise directed by qualified expert. Not to be used by children. Excessive use has caused hepatitis.

Celery *seed (Apium graveolens)* The seed of the common celery is a powerful diuretic, urinary antiseptic, carminative and antirheumatic agent. It increases uric acid excretion (use it with Parsley Leaf) and is used for gout and gouty arthritis as well as osteoarthritis. The seed has been shown to have hepatoprotective activity, and it was used traditionally with Damiana and Chaste Tree as a sexual stimulant for women.

Tincture - 30-40 drops (1.5-2 ml) QID.
CONTRAINDICATIONS: Not for use in pregnancy unless otherwise directed by qualified expert. Individuals with renal disorders should use with caution.

Chaga *mushroom (Inonotus obliquus)* is an ancient folk remedy used throughout Siberia, Scandinavia, the northern US and Canada for cancer and immune deficiency. Although few human trials have been done using Chaga, it may turn out to be the most powerful medicinal mushroom of all. It is a rich source of betulin, which has shown broad spectrum antitumor activity with virtually no toxicity as well as immune potentiating mushroom polysaccharides. In laboratory and animal studies this mushroom has been shown to exhibit antitumor, immune amphoteric, anti-inflammatory, antioxidant, hypoglycemic, antimutagenic, antinociceptive and neuroprotective effects.
Tea - 2-3 tsp. of the dried mushroom to 24 oz. water, decoct 1-4 hours. Take 3-4 cups per day.
Tincture - 60-100 drops (3-5 ml) TID.
CONTRAINDICATIONS: Mushroom allergies.

Chamomile *flowers (Matricaria recutita)* is a mild but effective remedy for both children and adults. The flowers have anti-inflammatory, antispasmodic, carminative and mild sedative activity. Children find the taste palatable and readily take it for teething pain, diarrhea, colic, ADHD, cramps, colds, stomach aches, fevers, irritability and night terrors. For adults it is a soothing remedy for frazzled nerves, insomnia, tension headaches, stress-induced digestive upset (use it with Catnip or Hops), irritable bowel syndrome, morning sickness and gastric ulcers.
Tea - 1-2 tsp. of the dried flowers to 8 oz. hot water, steep covered 15-20 minutes. Take 1-3 cups per day.
Tincture - 60-100 drops (3-5 ml) TID.
Glycerite - 80-120 drops (4-6 ml) TID.
CONTRAINDICATIONS: Avoid use in people with severe ragweed allergies.

Chaste Tree *berry (Vitex agnus-castus)* is indicated for menopausal symptoms such as hot flashes, "skin-crawling" or anxiety as well as PMS symptoms such as mood swings, breast tenderness, acne and edema. It is useful to mediate the after effects from long-term use of birth control pills as it helps re-regulate the reproductive hormones. It is believed to work via the pituitary decreasing prolactin levels by binding with the neurotransmitter dopamine and the opioid receptors (enkephalins, endorphins, endomorphins). It regulates the menstrual cycle (polymenorrhea, oligomenorrhea), and is beneficial for hyperprolactinemia, endometriosis, fibroids, functional ovarian cysts and some types of infertility.
Tincture - 40-60 drops (2-3 ml) BID.
CONTRAINDICATIONS: Not for use in pregnancy unless otherwise directed by qualified expert.

Chinese Asparagus *root (Asparagus cochinchinensis)* is a yin tonic that is moistening and tonifying to mucus membrane tissue, the lungs and stomach. It is indicated for dry mouth, dry coughs, dry, sticky, hard-to-expectorate mucus, vaginal dryness, dry constipation, gastric irritation and other common signs of yin deficiency. It can also be used to alleviate urinary irritation and deficient yin fevers.

Tea - 1-2 tsp. of the dried root to 10 oz. water, decoct 15 minutes, steep 1/2 hour. Take 4 oz. 3 time per day.
Tincture - 30-50 drops (1.5-2.5 ml) QID.

Chinese Peony *root (Paeonia lactiflora)* or Bai Shao acts as a sedative, analgesic, anti-inflammatory, antispasmodic and nervine. It reduces spasms, inflammation and pain and is useful for fibromyalgia, restless leg syndrome, menstrual cramps, angina and petit mal seizures. It is helpful for vasodilative migraine headaches combined with Feverfew, Gambir Spines and Fang Feng/Siler. Chinese Peony is effective as a treatment for polycystic ovarian syndrome (PCOS) along with Saw Palmetto, Chaste Tree and Licorice. It is also used to treat night sweats caused by deficient *yin* patterns. Bai Shao builds the blood and is one of the four ingredients in the classic Chinese formula Si Wu Tang (Women's Four Herb Tea), which is frequently utilized for treating uterine fibroids, dysmenorrhea, amenorrhea and menopausal symptoms.

Tea - 1 tsp. of the dried root to 8 oz. water, decoct with Licorice for 15 minutes, then steep 1/2 hour. Take 4 oz. 3 times per day.
Tincture - 30-40 drops (1.5-2 ml) TID.

Chinese Salvia *root (Salvia miltiorrhiza)* or Dan Shen is a prominent Chinese herb used to move blood, regulate the menses, calm the *shen* (mind) and normalize liver function. Chinese Salvia is used for cardiac pain (angina pectoris), to reduce elevated blood pressure, to promote heart function and to reduce damage from myocardial infarctions (heart attack). The reddish root is also prescribed for chronic hepatitis, for delayed, painful or irregular menstruation and to reduce histamine response in allergies. I also use it clinically as an immuno-regulator along with herbs like Huang Qin, Sarsaparilla, Gotu Kola or Bupleurum for treating auto-immune diseases and allergies.

Tea - 1 tsp. of the dried root to 8 oz. water, decoct 1/2 hour, steep 1/2 hour. Take 2 cups per day.
Tincture - 30-50 drops (1.5-2.5 ml) TID.

Chrysanthemum *flower (Dendrathema x grandiflorum)* or Ju Hua has long been used in TCM for eye problems, headaches and dizziness. It cools painful, dry and swollen eyes and can be used for excessive tearing, visual floaters or blurry vision. It is a good source of lutein, the anti-inflammatory and eye strengthening carotenoid. Chrysanthemum can also be used for mild hypertension with dizziness, headaches and it is one of the most effective herbs for treating influenza. Combine it with Andrographis, Elderberry or Elderflower, Yarrow, Isatis or

Honeysuckle flower.
Tea - 1-2 tsp. of the dried flowers to 8 oz. hot water, steep covered 20 minutes. Take 3 cups per day.
Tincture - 30-50 drops (1.5-2.5 ml) TID.
CONTRAINDICATIONS: Avoid use with ragweed allergies.

Cilantro *fresh herb (Coriandrum sativum)* The seed of this herb is the popular spice coriander. The leaves are used in Mexican, Indian and Thai cuisine for their unique spicy flavor and to prevent and relieve gas, abdominal bloating and nausea. Recent use has focused on this plant's alleged ability to increase heavy metal excretion, especially mercury. While some clinicians claim to have seen benefits in practice, there is no scientific data to support this belief. Cilantro is useful for treating borborygmus, intestinal viruses, and bacterial diarrhea. In animal studies the leaves had memory enhancing, antioxidant and antimutagenic activity.
Tea - 1 tsp. of the dried herb to 8 oz. hot water, steep covered 15 minutes. Take 4 oz. 3 times per day.
Tincture - 40-60 drops (2-3 ml) TID.

Cinnamon *bark (Cinnamomum verum)* is an effective and pleasant tasting circulatory stimulant. It improves peripheral circulation especially to the small capillaries and is useful for spider veins, early stage varicose veins, and Raynaud's disease. Cinnamon decreases insulin resistance and blood sugar levels, thus benefiting insulin-resistant diabetes and Metabolic Syndrome (hyperinsulinemia). Cinnamon also has antibacterial, antiviral, and astringent activity, making it useful for diarrhea, digestive upsets, intestinal viruses, sore throats and gum disease.
Tea - 1/2 to 1 tsp. of the freshly ground dried bark to 8 oz. hot water, steep covered 15-20 minutes. Take 4 oz. 3-4 times per day.
Tincture - 20-40 drops (1-2 ml) QID.
CONTRAINDICATIONS: Avoid using large quantities during pregnancy.

Cleavers *fresh herb (Galium aparine)* is a mild but effective medicine that primarily affects the genito-urinary tract and lymphatic system. Cleavers is a non-irritating diuretic used for irritation and inflammation of the bladder, urethra, vas deferens and spermatic cord. It is useful for cystitis, benign prostatic hyperplasia, prostatitis, epididymitis, urethritis and interstitial cystitis. Cleavers is also effective for enlarged lymph nodes in children and lymphedema (use it with Horse Chestnut) in post-mastectomy patients.
Tincture - 40-60 drops (2-3 ml) TID.

Codonopsis *root (Codonopsis pilosula, C. tangshen)* or Dang Shen is a mild adaptogen commonly used in China as an inexpensive substitute for Ginseng. Codonopsis tonifies the Chinese stomach/spleen, strengthens endocrine function (adrenals, hypothalamus, Pancreatic beta cells) and nourishes the immune system. It is used for fatigue, immune deficiency, and type II diabetes. Dang Shen is commonly used in Fu Zheng formulas to enhance immune function and treat

121

cancer. It also protects against chemotherapy or radiation-induced leukopenia and anemia. Dang Shen can be utilized in formulas for treating CFIDS (Chronic Fatigue Immune Dysfunction Syndrome), mononucleosis (with Astragalus) and adrenal/HPA axis depletion.
Tea - 2 tsp. of the dried root to 16 oz. water, decoct 1 hour. Take 2-3 cups per day.
Tincture - 60-100 drops (3-5 ml) TID.

Collinsonia *fresh root, leaf and flower (Collinsonia canadensis)* is also commonly known as Stone Root. It is indicated primarily for conditions with pelvic or venous stagnation with congestion including hemorrhoids, varicose veins, benign prostatic hyperplasia, tracheitis, and chronic laryngitis (minister's throat). It is also used for treating gastritis, allergic rhinitis, diarrhea, urinary irritation, mitral valve prolapse and chronic heart weakness (use it with Hawthorn and Night Blooming Cereus.)
Tincture - 30-40 drops (1.5-2 ml) QID.

Cordyceps *mycelium and/or mushroom (Cordyceps Ophiocordyceps sinensis (a.k.a. Cordyceps sinensis) or Cordyceps militaris)* was once reserved for the royal family of China as a powerful tonic to the blood (*xue*), kidneys (*yin and yang*) and lungs. Cordyceps is an adaptogen, immune amphoteric and kidney trophorestorative used by Chinese Olympic teams to enhance performance, stimulate endocrine function, reduce fatigue and calm nervousness. It can also be useful for treating glomerulonephritis (with Nettle seed), loss of libido, infertility, asthma, chronic coughs, allergies and auto-immune diseases. In human clinical trials, Cordyceps was given to renal transplant patients along with cyclosporine. Not only did it not interfere with the antirejection medication, the patients who took both had fewer complications and needed a lower dose of the drug (Ding, et al., 2011 & 2009).
Tea - 1 tsp. dried mycelium to 12 oz. hot water, simmer slowly until reduced to 6 oz. Take 2-4 oz. 2 times per day.
Tincture - 20-40 drops (1-2 ml) TID.
CONTRAINDICATIONS: Mushroom allergies.

Corn Silk *fresh silk (Zea mays)* is a soothing, mildly antiseptic diuretic used for inflammation of the urinary tract. It combines well with more active antiseptic diuretics such as Pipsissewa or Goldenseal for treating nephritis, urethritis, prostatitis, and cystitis. Use it with Reishi, Marshmallow, Hydrangea, and Kava for interstitial cystitis. Corn Silk also enhances uric acid excretion and can be used with Parsley and Celery seed to treat gout and gouty arthritis.
Tincture - 60-100 drops (3-5 ml) QID.

Corydalis yanhusuo *rhizome (Corydalis yanhusuo, syn: Corydalis ambigua)* is known in TCM as Yan Hu Suo and is an analgesic used for blood stasis with pain. It is effective for dysmenorrhea, gallbladder spasms, cancer pain (with Indian Pipe), angina, hernia pain, insomnia due to pain (with California Poppy) and for hepatic, abdominal, or intestinal pain. It is often combined with Bai Zhi (Angelica dahurica) which enhances its pain relieving effects.

Tea - 1 tsp. of the dried tuber to 10 oz. water, decoct 15 minutes, steep 1/2 hour. Take 4 oz. 3 times a day.
Tincture - 30-50 drops (1.5-2.5 ml) TID/QID.

Cramp Bark *fresh bark (Viburnum opulus)* is an antispasmodic and nervine primarily affecting the uterus. Cramp bark is used for dysmenorrhea (painful menstrual cramps), PMS irritability, low back pain and muscle pain associated with menopause. It can also be used for restless leg syndrome (with Skullcap, Blue Vervain, and White Peony), back pain, bladder spasms and "liver wind" patterns (spasms, nervous tics).
Tea - 1-2 tsp. of the dried bark to 10 oz. water, decoct 5-10 minutes, steep 1/2 hour. Take 4-8 oz. 2 or 3 times per day.
Tincture - 40-60 drops (2-3 ml) QID.

Culver's Root *root (Veronicastrum virginicum)* was formerly known as Leptandra, and was a popular Eclectic medicine. The root is a bitter tonic, aperient and cholagogue. It is a slow acting laxative used for liver congestion with non-obstructive jaundice, poor fat metabolism, liver headaches with constipation and clay colored stools. This herb works well with other mild liver herbs such as Dandelion root, Artichoke leaf or Turmeric. It is also used along with Evening Primrose herb, St. Johns wort or Wormwood for GI-Based depression.
Tincture - 20-30 drops (1-1.5 ml) TID.
CONTRAINDICATIONS: Pregnancy or if breast feeding. Blockage of the bile ducts, acute gallbladder inflammation or intestinal blockage.

Cynomorium/Suo Yang *stem (Cynomorium songaricum)* is used in Chinese medicine to tonify the kidney and nourish the blood. It is often used along with a second herb called Rou Cong Rong (Cistanche salsa) to treat impotence, low sperm count, impaired sperm motility, and lack of libido. It is also used for infertility in women and to enhance female libido as well.
Tea - 1 tsp. of the dried herb to 10 oz. water, decoct 10-15 minutes, steep 40 minutes. Take 4 oz. 3 times per day.
Tincture - 30-50 drops (1.5-2.5 ml) TID

Cyperus *root (Cyperus rotundus)* or Xiang Fu has a long history of use in both Chinese and Ayurvedic medicine. This herb is considered especially effective for gynecological or abdominal pain. It regulates the *qi* of the "Chinese liver", making it useful for symptoms of GI stagnation such as cramping, gas, nausea and vomiting. It has been shown to increase the pain threshold and can be used in many protocols for uterine, gastro-intestinal or cardiac pain. I regularly use it for treating irritable bowel syndrome, ovulatory pain, gallbladder spasms, dysmenorrhea and pain due to endometriosis, uterine fibroids, ovarian cysts or IBD.
Tea - 1 tsp. of the dried root to 8 oz. water, simmer 5 minutes, then steep covered for 30 minutes. Take 4 oz. 3 times per day.
Tincture - 30-60 drops (1.5-3 ml) QID.

Damiana *herb (Turnera diffusa)* has an interesting history and has long been used as an aphrodisiac. While no human studies confirm this, an animal study found that it stimulated sexual activity. It is also an antidepressant and used for mild depression with loss of libido, old-age depression and for "stagnant" depression along with Lavender, Holy Basil, and Rosemary. It is a carminative used for flatulence, dyspepsia, and biliousness.

Tea - 1 tsp. of the dried herb to 8 oz. hot water, steep covered 15 minutes. Take 4 oz. 2-3 times per day.

Tincture - 20-40 drops (1-2 ml) TID.

Dandelion *fresh leaf (Taraxacum officinale)* is an outstanding nutritive diuretic (aquaretic) that increases elimination of urine without depleting potassium. It is appropriate for long term use for edema (cardiac, circulatory, PMS, pulmonary), hypertension, and was found to reduce weight in an animal study, more than its diuretic activity could account for. It is also a bitter tonic and can enhance digestion and absorption of foods.

Tea - 1-2 tsp. of the dried leaf to 8 oz. hot water, steep 20-30 minutes. Take 2-3 cups per day.

Tincture - 60-100 drops (3-5 ml) QID.

Dandelion *fresh root (Taraxacum officinale)* is an excellent bitter tonic that stimulates secretion of gastric hydrochloric acid, bile, and liver, pancreatic and small intestine juices. It is indicated for chronic constipation with clay colored stools, impaired absorption of fats and sluggish liver function. The root is a rich source of inulin which contains fructo-oligosaccharides (FOS), which stimulate the growth of healthy bowel flora. Dandelion is also an effective liver tonic, a mild hepatoprotective agent and cholagogue.

Tea - 1-2 tsp. of the dried root to 8 oz. hot water, steep 40 minutes. Take 4 oz. 3 times per day.

Tincture - 40-60 drops (2-3 ml) QID.

Glycerite - 60-80 drops (3-4 ml) QID.

CONTRAINDICATIONS: Blockage of the bile ducts, acute gallbladder inflammation, or intestinal blockage.

Devil's Claw *tuber (Harpagophytum procumbens)* is a South African herb that is primarily used for osteoarthritis. The tuber is an anti-inflammatory, a cholagogue, and an analgesic. The specific indications are arthralgias with stiff, painful joints (Warnock, et al., 2007), as well as neuralgia, tendonitis and lumbago. It is also a bitter tonic used for dyspepsia, lack of appetite and flatulence.

Tincture - 20-30 drops (1-1.5 ml) TID.

CONTRAINDICATIONS: Pregnancy. Gastric and duodenal ulcers.

Devil's Club *root bark (Oplopanax horridus)* is indicated in cases of impaired sugar metabolism especially in people of color or those who are short and obese, with elevated triglyceride levels. It is used to treat type II diabetes (under medical supervision). It is also a laxative and an anti-inflammatory agent used by native peoples in the Pacific Northwest as a spring tonic and for treating arthritis, bursitis, and obesity.

Tea - 1 tsp of the dried root bark to 10 oz. water, decoct 10-15 minutes, steep 1/2 hour. Take 4 oz. 3 times per day.

Tincture - 20-30 drops (1-1.5 ml) TID.

Dong Quai *root (Angelica sinensis)* or Dang Gui (Pinyin spelling) is a popular Chinese herb that revitalizes and moves blood (*xue*). Because of this activity it is often used for female reproductive problems such as uterine fibroids, ovarian cysts, menopausal discomfort, PMS, amenorrhea and dysmenorrhea. It is frequently used with three other herbs in classic formula known as Si Wu Tang or Women's Four Precious Tea. Because of its moistening qualities it can also be effective for menstrual or menopausal constipation and vaginal dryness. Dong Quai is a common ingredient in Chinese formulas for cardiac problems such as angina and mild congestive heart failure (used with Chinese Salvia, Astragalus, and Tienqi Ginseng). It enhances cardiac function and promotes circulation.

Tea - 1-2 tsp. of the dried root to 10 oz. water, decoct 20 minutes, steep covered 1/2 hour. Take 2-3 cups per day.

Tincture - 40-60 drops (2-3 ml) TID.

CONTRAINDICATIONS: Not for use in pregnancy unless otherwise directed by qualified expert.

Echinacea *fresh root (E. angustifolia, E. purpurea, E. pallida)* is indicated for acute viral or bacterial infection such as influenza, colds, bronchitis, sinusitis, tonsillitis, and laryngitis. Several studies indicate that it can help prevent, treat or shorten the duration of viral illnesses (Jawad, et al., 2012, Schoop, et al., 2006). It can also be used for acute prostatitis, allergic rhinitis, otitis media, aphthous stomatitis, and gingivitis. The Eclectic physicians used this root as an alterative for blood dyscrasias with dirty, sallow skin and a tendency to form boils, styes, and develop enlarged lymph nodes. Topically it is used for infections, insect bites, abscesses, and psoriasis.

Tincture - (acute) 40-60 drops (2-3 ml) every 2-3 hours.

Glycerite - (acute) 60-80 drops (3-4 ml) every 2-3 hours.

Elderberry *fruit (Sambucus nigra, S. canadensis)* These small black berries are a rich source of vitamin C, proanthocyanadin flavonoids and antiviral proteins. Elderberry syrup, extract or glycerite is very useful for treating colds, influenza and other viral respiratory disorders. The flavonoids help to strengthen capillary integrity especially in the eyes and help stabilize mast cells and reduce histamine production. This reduces allergic symptoms and mucosal inflammation.

Tincture - 60-90 drops (3-4.5 ml) QID.

Glycerite - 1-2 tsp. (5-10 ml) QID.

Elderflower *blossoms (Sambucus nigra, S.canadensis)* are a mild remedy often used with Peppermint for children's colds and influenza. The flowers have antiviral, diaphoretic, emollient and mild diuretic effects. The Eclectic specific indications for Sambucus are indolent ulcers (bedsores or impetigo) with boggy borders and a serous discharge that forms crusts.
Tea - 1-2 tsp. of the dried flowers to 8 oz. hot water, steep 10-15 minutes. Take 1-2 cups per day.
Tincture - 40-60 drops (2-3 ml) TID.

Elecampane *fresh root (Inula helenium)* is an antiseptic expectorant for bronchitis, pneumonia and pertussis, especially if the person has a persistent ticklish cough with pain in the chest or ribs. It also stimulates digestion, liver function and is active against Giardia and other amoebas.
Tea - 1-2 tsp. dried root to 8 oz. hot water, steep 1 hour covered. Take 4 oz. 3 times per day.
Tincture - 20-30 drops (1-1.5 ml) QID.

Eleuthero *root (Eleutherococcus senticosus)* is a mild, yet effective adaptogen, and immune amphoteric. It reduces fatigue, the effects of chronic stress (elevated cortisol levels), and depression. Eleuthero is a well-researched herb and has been found to enhance endocrine activity, promote strength and energy, and improve work or athletic performance. It acts on the HPA Axis and SAS and recent studies suggest that adaptogens also work on a cellular level preventing stress-induced mitochondrial dysfunction (Panossian, et al., 2012, Panossian, et al., 2009).
Tea - 2 tsp. of the dried root to 8 oz. water, decoct 15-20 minutes, steep 1 hour. Take 2-3 cups per day.
Tincture - 50-60 drops (2.5-3 ml) TID.

Epimedium *herb (Epimedium grandiflorum)* is also known in China Yin Yang Huo, which translates to lustful sheep plant or horny goat weed. Both names are obvious references to its ability to enhance libido. In clinical studies this herb has been shown to be effective for improving lack of libido and quality of life in people undergoing dialysis (Liao, et al., 1995). It is also used for treating low testosterone levels, neurasthenia, chronic bronchitis, arthritis, and neutropenia. In animal studies, Epimedium has been shown to have neuroprotective, osteoprotective and immune enhancing activity. Some preliminary research suggests it may have adaptogenic effects as well.
Tea - 1/2-1 tsp. of the dried leaf to 8 oz. hot water, steep 30 minutes. Take 4 oz. 2 times per day.
Tincture - 10-30 drops (.5-1.5 ml) BID/TID.

European Mistletoe *herb (Viscum album)* is an ancient remedy long used in Great Britain, Germany and France. It is a powerful sedative and hypotensive agent, used for hypertension, temporal arteritis, tinnitus and vascular headaches. It is also indicated for an atonic bladder, uterus or intestine with prolapse or constipation.

Tincture - 20-40 drops (1-2 ml) TID.

CONTRAINDICATIONS: Not for use in pregnancy or while lactating. Do not mix with pharmaceutical hypotensive agents.

Eyebright *herb (Euphrasia officinalis)* contrary to popular belief Eyebright is not really an "eye herb". It is primarily used for inflammation and irritation of the sinuses, with an excessive mucus discharge. As a simple or in formulas with Collinsonia, Kudzu, Bayberry bark or Osha, I use it to treat allergic rhinitis (hay fever), post-nasal drip, head colds with excessive clear or white mucous or Otitis media. Taken orally there is one situation where Eyebright has benefits for the eyes and that is the itchy, scratchy, red eyes caused by pollen allergies. It often can help reduce the inflammation, itching and redness in a day or two.

Tincture - 20-30 drops (1-1.5 ml) TID.

Fennel *seed (Foeniculum vulgare)* is a pleasant tasting and effective carminative. It is very useful for treating flatulence, nausea, vomiting, colic (via breastfeeding) and motion sickness (use it with Ginger). Fennel is also a galactagogue (it stimulates milk production) and a useful flavoring for children's formulas. The seed combined with Spicebush and Fenugreek seed is used in Chinese medicine for testicular and lower abdominal pain (hernia pain).

Tea - Take 1/2-1 tsp. of the dried seed to 8 oz. hot water, steep covered 10 minutes. Take 4 oz. up to 4 times per day.

Tincture - 30-40 drops (1.5-2 ml) QID.

Fenugreek *seed (Trigonella foenum-graecum)* is a warming bitter, with a long history of use as a food and medicine throughout northern Africa, India, China and the Middle East. It is used as a spice in Indian cuisine, both for its flavor and its ability to reduce nausea, gas and gastric irritation. It is also used to lower blood sugar levels in adult onset diabetes and it decreases insulin resistance in people with metabolic syndrome (Gupta, et al., 2001). Fenugreek is an important GI herb, it helps heal excessive gut permeability (leaky gut syndrome), it binds endotoxins in the intestine enhancing their excretion and it can help to lower LDL/VLDL cholesterol levels.

Tea - Take 1-2 tsp. of the dried seeds to 8 oz. hot water, steep 1/2 hour. Take 4 oz. 3 times per day.

Tincture - 30-40 drops (1.5-2 ml) TID.

CONTRAINDICATIONS: Not for use in pregnancy unless otherwise directed by qualified expert. Taking this herb can cause the urine to smell like maple syrup which could be misdiagnosed as maple syrup urine disease, a rare genetic disorder.

Feverfew *fresh herb in flower (Tanacetum parthenium)* has been shown in clinical studies to reduce the number and severity of migraine headaches (Diener, et al., 2005). It is most effective for vaso-dilative headaches and can be used with

Fang Feng/Siler, White Peony and Gambir Spines. The parthenolides found in this plant inhibit inflammatory prostaglandins and it has been shown to have some activity in treating rheumatoid arthritis.

Tincture - 30-40 drops (1.5-2 ml) TID.

CONTRAINDICATIONS: Not for use in pregnancy unless otherwise directed by qualified expert. Avoid use in severe ragweed allergies.

Figwort *herb (Scrophularia nodosa)* is an alterative affecting the lymph, blood and skin. It is indicated for chronic skin conditions such as eczema, psoriasis and acne. It is also effective for lymphatic stagnation with heat i.e., hemorrhoids, cystic breast disease, lymphadenitis, and lipomas (with Self Heal, Chickweed and Red Root). It is used in TCM for blood heat conditions such as thrombophlebitis, cellulitis, mastitis or splenomegaly.

Tea - 1-2 tsp. of the dried root to 10 oz. water, decoct 15 minutes. Take 4 oz. 2-3 times per day.

Tincture - 20-40 drops (1-2 ml) TID.

CONTRAINDICATIONS: Ventricular tachycardia.

Gentian *root (Gentiana lutea)* is a powerful digestive bitter that is very effective for stimulating digestion, absorption and elimination. It is indicated for atony of the GI tract, including the stomach, small intestines and colon. It can also be used for GI dysbiosis, anorexia, and elevated LDL/VLDL cholesterol levels. Bitters mildly reduce blood sugar levels, so can be used as part of a protocol of treating metabolic syndrome.

Tincture - 20-30 drops (1-1.5 ml) TID.

CONTRAINDICATIONS: Gastric or duodenal ulcers and gastritis.

Ginger *rhizome (Zingiber officinale)* increases circulation of blood and *qi*, improves digestion (it stimulates gastric HCL) and is useful for nausea, gas, and motion sickness. This spicy herb is also an anti-inflammatory, expectorant, and a diaphoretic. Because of its anti-inflammatory and warming nature, it is useful for cold/damp osteoarthritis and for treating impaired peripheral circulation or Raynaud's Syndrome. I frequently use Ginger with Orange Peel for cold/damp lung conditions.

Tea - 1/2 tsp. of the dried rhizome to 8 oz. hot water, steep covered 20 minutes. Take 2-3 cups per day.

Tincture - 20-30 drops (1-1.5 ml) TID/QID.

Glycerite - 40-60 drops (2-3 ml) TID/QID.

Ginkgo *leaf (Ginkgo biloba)* enhances cerebral and peripheral blood flow and can be used for vascular insufficiency headaches, tinnitus, poor memory, early-stage memory loss, peripheral arterial insufficiency, varicose veins, impotence caused by impaired circulation, and to prevent diabetic retinopathy. It has both bronchiodilator and anti-inflammatory (PAF antagonist) properties making it useful as part of a protocol for treating asthma. Most research on this herb

has been done using highly concentrated standardized extracts. A recent study using a whole plant extract found that it enhanced vascular microcirculation and improved antioxidant status in elderly patients (Suter, et al., 2011).
Tincture - 30-60 drops (1.5-3 ml) QID.
Capsules (standardized extract) - 80-240 mg per day

Goldenseal *root (Hydrastis canadensis)* is a powerful antibacterial and anti-fungal agent. The specific indications for Hydrastis are boggy, atonic mucous membranes with a tendency to oversecrete, bleed, or become infected. It is useful for upper respiratory tract and mucous membrane infections including tonsil-litis, strep throat, sore throat, sinus infections (bacterial or fungal), gum disease, uvulitis and post nasal drip. Goldenseal has a long tradition of use as a local antibacterial, especially to the skin, throat, sinuses, GI tract, and urinary tract. It is rich in isoquinoline alkaloids, especially the bright yellow colored alkaloid berberine, which has shown activity against a wide range of pathogens including Helicobacter pylori, Staphylococcus aureus, and Streptococcus spp. Because it is bitter, Goldenseal will stimulate digestion and absorption. In clinical practice, Goldenseal is used to treat cystitis, acute gastroenteritis, gastric ulcers, bacillary dysentery, conjunctivitis (as a saline eye-wash). The famed American Herbalist Dr. Christopher used Goldenseal to lower blood sugar levels. Research has found that Berberine does have hypoglycemic activity providing a possible basis for this traditional use.
Tincture - 15-20 drops (0.75-1 ml) BID. (Short-term use is advised)
CONTRAINDICATIONS: Not for use in pregnancy unless otherwise directed by qualified expert (theoretical concern).

Gotu Kola *herb (Centella asiatica)* acts as a systemic anti-inflammatory and is an important medicine for autoimmune conditions. It strengthens connective tis-sue and is indicated for connective tissue disorders and skin conditions where the tissue is red, hot and inflamed. It can be used to treat eczema, psoriasis, psoriatic arthritis, rheumatoid arthritis and cellulitis. It is used in Ayurvedic medicine as a rasayana and a "brain tonic". It increases circulation to the brain and has been shown to have anxiolytic, nootropic and antidepressant activity. Gotu Kola can also be used orally with Hawthorn and Horse Chestnut for varicose veins and peripheral insufficiency. Topically it is used to enhance healing and prevent scar-ring from burns or surgery.
Tincture - 40-60 drops (2-3 ml) TID.

Ground Ivy *fresh herb (Glechoma hederacea)* is a common weed of lawns and gardens and fortunately is also a useful medicinal herb. It has antiviral, expectorant, bitter tonic, cholagogue, diuretic, diaphoretic and anti-inflammatory activities. Ground Ivy is useful for treating bronchitis, viral pneumonia, sinusitis, ear infections and tinnitus. It also stimulates digestion and is used in Chinese medicine to help expel renal or biliary calculi. Based on information found in Maud Grieve's *A Modern Herbal* (1931), this herb has been used clinically for

increasing lead excretion from the body with positive laboratory results.
Tincture - 30-40 drops (1.5-2 ml) TID.
CONTRAINDICATIONS: Pregnancy.

Guaiacum *resin or wood (Guaiacum officinale)* is also known as Lignum vitae and is anti-inflammatory, a diuretic and an alterative. The wood and resin were once used with Sarsaparilla to treat syphilis and it is now used to treat osteoarthritis, rheumatoid arthritis and Lyme disease.
Tincture - 20-30 drops (1-1.5 ml) TID.
CONTRAINDICATIONS: Pregnancy. Gastric irritation or ulcers.

Guggul *gum resin (Commiphora mukul)* is a relative of Myrrh, that is used to modestly lower LDL/VLDL cholesterol levels. It acts as a systemic anti-inflammatory, enhances circulation, and stimulates thyroid function by enhancing peripheral conversion of T-4 to T-3. It is used to treat hyperlipidemia, hypothyroidism, obesity, arthritis, acne and impaired circulation.
Tincture - 30-40 drops (1.5-2 ml) TID.
CONTRAINDICATIONS: Not for use in pregnancy unless otherwise directed by qualified expert.

Gymnema *herb (Gymnema sylvestre)* or Gurmar (sugar destroyer) is used in Ayurvedic medicine to treat glycosuria (sugar in the urine) and diabetes mellitus. Research shows that it increases insulin sensitivity, lowers blood sugar levels, hemoglobin A1c and reduces fatigue and appetite in diabetics and obese people (Kumar, et al., 2010). The herb is also used as a diuretic, astringent, gastroprotective and as a treatment for fevers and colds.
Tincture - 30-50 drops (1.5-2.5 ml) TID.
CONTRAINDICATIONS: Monitor blood sugar levels carefully when using this herb in combination with blood sugar lowering medications.

Hawthorn *fruit, leaf and flower (Crataegus spp.)* Indications for this herb include functional and organic heart weakness with pain, or a lack of tonus of the heart muscle. It is used to treat angina, valvular insufficiency, mitral valve prolapse, mild congestive heart failure (Habs, 2004, Tauchert, 2002), venous stasis, poor capillary and venous integrity and varicose veins. Hawthorn lowers cholesterol levels, mildly reduces blood pressure and inhibits deposition of plaque on arterial walls as well as stabilizing plaques. Hawthorn is also of benefit for connective tissue disorders and ADHD (disturbed Shen).
Tea - 1-2 tsp. dried fruit/flowers to 10 oz. water, decoct 10 minutes, steep 1/2 hour. Take 1-3 cups per day.
Tincture - 60-100 drops (3-5 ml) QID.
CONTRAINDICATIONS: Consult with a physician before using in patients with serious heart disease. This herb may potentiate beta-blockers and it interfered with accurate testing for cardiac glycoside medications in an in-vitro study (Dasgupta, et al., 2010).

He Shou Wu *root (Polygonum multiflorum)* is a major Chinese tonic herb, also incorrectly known as Fo Ti. The processed root nourishes the Chinese kidney, liver and the blood *(xue)*. It is used to stimulate male reproductive function, improve sports performance, stimulate liver and bowel function and lower cholesterol levels. In animal studies this herb has been shown to have neuroprotective activity.

Tea - 1 tsp. of the dried root to 10 oz. water, decoct 15 minutes, steep 40 minutes. Take 4 oz. 2-3 time per day.
Tincture - 30-40 drops (1.5-2 ml) TID.
CONTRAINDICATIONS: Pregnancy, liver disease. Short term use of this herb is most appropriate as long-term use may be responsible for liver damage.

Holy Basil (Tulsi) *fresh herb (Ocimum tenuiflorum)* has long been used in Ayurvedic medicine as a tonic to the brain and nervous system. It lifts the spirits while increasing clarity of thought and dispelling depression. This mild adaptogenic spice reduces mental fog associated with drug use, menopause or chronic stress, relieves anxiety and can be useful for ADHD. It also has antiviral, antibacterial, carminative, anti-inflammatory, galactagogue, immune amphoteric, hypoglycemic and mild hepaprotective activity. The tea or tincture of the herb can be useful as part of a protocol for digestive upset, diabetes (Agrawal, et al., 1996) or metabolic syndrome.

Tea - 1-2 tsp. of the herb to 8 oz. hot water, steep covered 15 minutes. Take 2-3 cups per day.
Tincture - 30-60 drops (1.5-3 ml) QID.
CONTRAINDICATIONS: If you are pregnant, consult a practitioner before using this product.

Hops *fresh strobiles (Humulus lupulus)* is a well known ingredient of beer whose bitterness comes from a resin known as lupulin. This herb is a sedative and mild analgesic; Hops is used for nervousness, anxiety, nervous stomach, insomnia and muscle spasms. Its intense bitterness stimulates digestive function, bile secretion and enhances absorption of nutrients. Hops can also be used with Hydrangea, Kava, Khella and Lobelia to help relieve pain and ease the passage of small kidney stones.(<4mm)

Tea - 1-2 tsp. of the dried herb to 8 oz. hot water, steep 20 minutes. Take 4 oz. 3 or 4 times per day.
Tincture - 20-30 drops (1-1.5 ml) TID.

Horehound *flowering tops (Marrubium vulgare)* is best known as a lung herb, used as an expectorant and cough suppressant. It is appropriate for dry sticky mucus, spasmodic coughs and coughing caused by viral diseases (chest colds, bronchitis). Horehound is also an effective digestive bitter, stimulating bile and pancreatic secretions, as well as stimulating hepatic function. In preliminary research, Horehound has also been shown to have gastroprotective and blood sugar lowering effects (Boudjelal, et al., 2012).

Tea - 1-2 tsp. of the dried herb to 8 oz. hot water, steep 20 minutes. Take 4 oz.

3 or 4 times per day.

Tincture - 20-40 drops (1-2 ml) TID.

CONTRAINDICATIONS: Not for use in pregnancy unless otherwise directed by qualified expert.

Horse Chestnut *seed (Aesculus hippocastanum)* has been researched extensively in Europe and has been found to be an effective remedy for varicose veins, spider veins and hemorrhoids. It is a powerful vasoprotective agent used to increase the tonus and integrity of the veins, arteries and capillaries. The specific indications for Aesculus are dull throbbing pain, where the tissue is full and edematous. It can be useful for sciatica, Raynaud's Syndrome, intermittent claudication, poor circulation to the extremities, lymphedema (use it with Cleavers and Gotu Kola) and peripheral nerve pain.

Tincture - 5-15 drops (.25-.75 ml) TID

CONTRAINDICATIONS: Pregnancy.

Horseradish *fresh root (Armoracia rusticana)* is a rich source of antibacterial and antimutagenic sulfur compounds. It is a powerful bronchiodilator, antibacterial, diuretic and respiratory antispasmodic. Horseradish can be used for sinus congestion, asthma, allergic rhinitis, cold/damp coughs and cold/damp lung conditions such as pneumonia, and post nasal drip. Regular intake of glucosinolates found in Horseradish have been linked to reduce risk of developing cancer (Conoway, et al., 2002).

Tincture - 10-15 drops (.5-.75 ml) diluted in water or juice TID/QID

Horsetail *spring gathered herb (Equisetum arvense)* is a rich source of silicic acid which is a co-factor with calcium to increase bone mass and density. The herb also stimulates the maturation of the osteoblasts. It gradually helps to reverse early stage osteoporosis, speeds the healing of fractures and improves the strength and growth of the skin, hair, and nails. Horsetail is also a diuretic useful for urinary tract infections especially with bladder irritation and blood in the urine.

Tea - 1-2 tsp. of the dried spring gathered herb to 8 oz. of hot water, steep 30-40 minutes. Take 4 oz. 3 times per day.

Tincture - 20-30 drops (1-1.5 ml) TID.

Capsules - Two size 00 capsules BID.

Houttuynia *leaf (Houttuynia cordata)* is known as Yu Xing Cao (fishy-smelling herb) in Chinese medicine. It is used to clear heat (antibacterial), to eliminate toxins, and topically to heal infections. In TCM, Houttuynia is often used to treat bronchitis, cervicitis, sinusitis, pneumonia, enteritis, urinary tract infections, cervical dysplasia, and SARS. In a human clinical trial, it was found to be effective for treating ulcerative colitis (Jang & Cui, 2004)

Tea - 1-2 tsp. of the dried herb to 8 oz. water, decoct 5 minutes, steep 30 minutes. Take 2 cups per day.

Tincture - 40-45 drops (2-2.25 ml) TID.

Huang Qin (Baikal Skullcap) *root (Scutellaria baicalensis)* is commonly used in TCM for excess heat symptoms such as fevers, hypertension, red inflamed skin or eyes, nosebleeds, uterine bleeding and fire poison (shingles, boils, Staph infections). This root is antibacterial and antiviral, making it useful for treating colds, influenza, herpes, bronchitis and Staphylococcus aureus infections. Huang Qin is also hepatoprotective and I use it along with Milk Thistle, Turmeric and Schisandra for treating Hepatitis A, B or C. It reduces the inflammatory cascade and can be a useful part of a protocol for allergies and autoimmune disease (rheumatoid arthritis, ankylosing spondylitis, scleroderma, lupus, allergic hives) when used with other immuno-regulatory herbs and immune amphoterics.
Tea - 1 tsp. of the dried root to 8 oz. water, decoct 15 minutes, steep 1 hour. Take 2 cups per day.
Tincture - 30-50 drops (1.5-2.5 ml) QID.

Hydrangea *root (Hydrangea arborescens)* is a wild relative of the showy garden shrub Hydrangea. The root of the wild plant is an effective urinary analgesic and is indicated for urethritis or cystitis with pain, pain associated with low grade nephritis and to ease the pain and expulsion of urinary calculi (gravel). It can also be useful for renal colic, bladder spasms, benign prostatic hyperplasia, and interstitial cystitis.
Tincture - 20-40 drops (1-2 ml) QID.
CONTRAINDICATIONS: Use with caution during pregnancy.

Hyssop *fresh flowering herb (Hyssopus officinalis)* is a valuable, if underutilized, European herb with many uses. It is an antiviral agent especially effective for inhibiting herpes and influenza viruses. This fragrant herb is also a carminative, emmenagogue and diaphoretic. Hyssop is appropriate for intestinal viruses, colds, influenza, nausea, flatulence and delayed menses. It is used in the UK for treating hypotension, anxiety and petit mal seizures. Topically it can be useful for herpetic sores along with Lemon Balm and Licorice.
Tea - 1 tsp. of the dried flowering herb to 8 oz. hot water, steep covered 15-20 minutes. Take 4 oz. 3 times per day.
Tincture - 20-40 drops (1-2 ml) QID.
CONTRAINDICATIONS: Not for use in pregnancy unless otherwise directed by qualified expert.

Indian Pipe *fresh whole plant (Monotropa uniflora)* is an unusual plant, it contains no chlorophyll and is parasitic on the roots of several species of trees. It was used by Native Americans and the Eclectic physicians for pain. Its action is similar in effect to nitrous oxide at the dentist, you are conscious and aware of pain, but distant from it. It is antinoceptive which means it increases the pain threshold and, used along with analgesics and anti-inflammatory herbs, can be an effective part of a pain management protocol. Indian Pipe and Corydalis can be very useful in helping to control cancer pain especially in terminal patients who have reached their maximum dosage of morphine and are still in pain.

Tincture - 20-30 drops (1-1.5 ml) QID.
CONTRAINDICATIONS: Pregnancy or breast feeding (theoretical concern).

Isatis *root (Isatis tinctoria, I. indigotica)* or Ban Lan Gen is used in TCM to clear "pathogenic heat" (infections) from the blood. In Western terms Isatis is antibacterial and antiviral and is used to treat acute conjunctivitis, pharyngitis, influenza, acute hepatitis, painful UTIs, damp heat pneumonia, sinusitis, tonsillitis, IBD and damp heat diarrhea. It can be used orally and topically for herpes, shingles, acne rosacea, erysipelas and impetigo.
Tea - 1 tsp. of the dried root to 10 oz. water, decoct 10 minutes, steep 1/2 hour. Take 4 oz. 2-3 times per day.
Tincture - 30-60 drops (1.5-3 ml) TID.

Jamaica Dogwood *bark (Piscidia piscipula)* is one of the strongest non-narcotic herbal analgesics; it also has pronounced antispasmodic activity. Piscidia is especially useful for severe menstrual pain (dysmenorrhea) and facial nerve pain or paralysis (Bell's palsy, trigeminal neuralgia, temporomandibular joint pain). The bark of this tropical tree can also be used for back pain, acute pain and spasms of the bladder, vagina or neck (torticollis).
Tincture - 10-20 drops (.5-1 ml) TID.
CONTRAINDICATIONS: Pregnancy or breast feeding. It may potentiate sedative medications.

Japanese Honeysuckle *flower (Lonicera japonica)* is a common weedy plant with fragrant flowers. As a child you may have sucked the sweet nectar from these blossoms. In Chinese medicine the unopened flower buds are known as Jin Yin Hua. They are used as a powerful antibacterial and antiviral agent. They are effective in treating influenza, sinusitis, otitis media, sore throat, colds, urinary and intestinal infections, painful mastitis, damp heat dysentery, and conjunctivitis. Barefoot Doctors in China combined Lonicera with Coptis to make a "poor man's penicillin".
Tea - 1-2 tsp. of the dried flowers to 8 oz. hot water, steep 30-40 minutes. Take 4 oz. 4 times per day.
Tincture - 30-40 drops (1.5-2 ml) QID.

Juniper *berry (Juniperus communis)* is a urinary antiseptic, diuretic, alterative, carminative, expectorant and emmenagogue. The essential oils are responsible for much of its activity. Juniper can be used for cystitis with a mucus discharge, deficient gastic HCL production and cold/damp lung conditions. Sebastian Kneipp, a Bavarian priest and a founder of Nature Cure, (naturopathy) used Juniper berries for a two week "cleansing" program for his most difficult cases. He felt this helped to increase the elimination of metabolic wastes and promote the vital force within.
Tincture - 20-40 drops (1-2 ml) TID. (Long term use is not recommended)
CONTRAINDICATIONS: Not for use in pregnancy unless otherwise directed

by qualified expert. Do not for use for more than 4-6 weeks. Avoid use with inflammatory kidney disease.

Kava *root (Piper methysticum)* is a mucous membrane analgesic. It reduces pain in the throat, stomach and urinary tract. Kava is very effective for relieving genito-urinary pain caused by cystitis, urethritis, interstitial cystitis, prostatitis and inflammation of the vas deferens or spasmatic cord. It is also a muscle relaxant useful for fibromyalgia, restless leg syndrome, muscle spasms and insomnia with muscular tension. Kava has also been shown to have anxiolytic activity in many clinical trials (Sarris, et al., 2009, Geier & Konstantinowicz, 2004, Gastpar & Klimm, 2003) and it was found to improve mood and cognitive function (Thompson, et al., 2004).

Tincture - 30-40 drops (1.5-2 ml) QID.

CONTRAINDICATIONS: The FDA advises that a potential risk of rare, but severe, liver injury may be associated with kava-containing dietary supplements. Ask a healthcare professional before use if you have or have had liver problems, frequently use alcoholic beverages, or are taking any medications. Stop use and see a doctor if you develop symptoms that may signal liver problems (e.g., unexplained fatigue, abdominal pain, loss of appetite, fever, vomiting, dark urine, pale stools, yellow eyes or skin). Not for use by persons under 18 years of age, or by pregnant or breastfeeding women. Not for use with alcoholic beverages. Excessive use, or use with products that cause drowsiness, may impair your ability to operate a vehicle or dangerous equipment. Not for use in pregnancy unless otherwise directed by qualified expert. Do not exceed recommended dose.

Khella *seed (Ammi visnaga)* has long been used as a medicine in Northern Africa and the Middle East. It contains a chemical called Khellin which acts as a powerful antispasmodic to the small bronchi in the lungs. Its effects are long lasting and are useful in preventing asthma attacks, especially at night. It also acts as a spasmolytic agent to the intestines, gallbladder, genito-urinary tract, and cardiovascular systems. Khella is a useful part of a protocol for intestinal or bladder spasms, renal colic, angina pectoris, and gallbladder spasms. I also use Khella with Hydrangea, Kava, Lobelia and Hops to help ease the passage of small kidney stones.

Tea - 1 tsp. of the dried seed to 8 oz. hot water, steep 45 minutes. Take 2 oz. 3-4 times per day.

Tincture - 10-20 drops (.5-1 ml) TID.

CONTRAINDICATIONS: It may cause photosensitivity in fair skinned people.

Kudzu *root (P. montana)* is an aggressive weed that has taken over much of the southeastern United States. It is unfortunate that people are unfamiliar with this plant's many uses. Instead of cursing the plant, we need to learn how to utilize this invasive "gift", as frequently as possible. Kudzu is a demulcent, antispasmodic, cardiotonic and decongestant. The root is used to treat torticollis, back spasms, angina pain, mild congestive heart failure, for sinus congestion, sinus and cluster headaches, irritable bowel syndrome and diarrhea. The flowers are traditionally used for alcohol poisoning (hangovers) and the root has shown some ability to modestly reduce alcohol cravings (Lukas, et al., 2012).

Tea - 1-2 tsp. of the dried root to 10 oz. water, decoct 15-20 minutes, steep 30 minutes. Take 4 oz. 2 times per day.

Tincture - 40-60 drops (2-3 ml) TID.

Lavender *flowers (Lavendula angustifolia)* is a fragrant, aromatic herb that has antiviral, antibacterial, antidepressant, carminative and nervine properties. Lavender is useful for gas, nausea, dysbiosis, damp spleen (chronic low grade diarrhea), and intestinal viruses. The flowers are also of benefit for "stagnant" depression (with Rosemary, Holy Basil and Damiana), mild anxiety, and to decrease sleep latency while improving sleep quality. In a RCT, Lavender tincture enhanced the efficacy of imipramine for treating mild to moderate depression (Akhondzadeh, et al., 2003).

Tea - 1/4-1/2 tsp. of the dried flowers to 8 oz. hot water, steep covered 15 minutes. Take 4 oz. 2-3 times per day.

Tincture - 30-40 drops (1.5-2 ml) QID.

Lemon Balm *fresh herb (Melissa officinalis)* is a mild, flavorful remedy appropriate for children's colds, stomachaches, hyperchlorhydria (heart burn) and tension headaches. It acts as a carminative, antiviral agent, nervine, mood elevator, and a mild thyroxin antagonist. Lemon Balm is useful for depression, especially seasonal affective disorder (SAD) when combined with St. John's wort. It can also be useful for treating mild hypertension, anxiety, herpes (topically), and hyperthyroidism (use it with Bugleweed, Self Heal and Motherwort).

Tea - 1-2 tsp. of the dried herb to 8 oz. hot water, steep 15 minutes. Take 1-3 cups per day.

Tincture - 60-100 drops (3-5 ml) QID.

Glycerite - children 30-40 drops (1.5-2 ml) QID, adult 80-120 drops (4-6 ml) QID.

Licorice *root (Glycyrrhiza glabra or G. uralensis)* has an ancient history of use in China and the Middle East. This intensely sweet root is an adaptogen, demulcent, hepatoprotective agent, immune amphoteric, expectorant, pectoral, antiviral and antidepressant. Licorice strengthens endocrine function, especially the adrenals, ovaries, pancreatic beta cells and the hypothalamus. It can be combined with Cordyceps and Red Ginseng for adrenal exhaustion (Addison's Disease). It is often used in TCM in small amounts to harmonize a formula, improve the flavor and reduce the toxicity of harsh herbs. It can be an effective part of a protocol for treating CFIDS, menopausal symptoms, hypoglycemia, animal dander allergies and many autoimmune diseases. The demulcent action heals mucous membrane tissue especially the stomach (gastric ulcers, gastritis), large and small intestine (duodenal ulcers, IBS, or IBD) and the lungs (dry, irritative coughs).

Tea - 1/2 tsp. of the dried root to 8 oz. hot water, steep 40 minutes. Take 2 oz. 3 times per day.

Tincture - 10-20 drops (.5-1 ml) BID/TID.

CONTRAINDICATIONS: Excessive use of Licorice can elevate blood pressure. Not for use in pregnancy unless otherwise directed by qualified expert. Not for prolonged use or in high doses except under supervision of a qualified health practitioner. It is contraindicated in hypertension, severe kidney insufficiency and hypokalemia. Licorice can potentiate potassium depletion caused by thiazide diuretics and stimulant laxatives. It may also potentiate the effects of cardiac glycosides and cortisol. When taking licorice, use small amounts and increase potassium intake while decreasing sodium consumption.

Ligustrum *fruit (Ligustrum lucidum)* or Nu Zhen Zi is used as a tonic for deficient Yin of the Chinese kidney and liver. Symptoms of this include dizziness, lower back pain and tinnitus. It also stimulates immune activity especially increasing white blood cell counts depleted by chemotherapy or radiation (leukopenia). Ligustrum may also offer relief of female reproductive problems such as vaginal dryness and infertility, especially when combined with Shatavari, Dong Quai and fresh Oat.

Tea - 1-2 tsp. of the dried herb to 8 oz. water, decoct 15 minutes, steep 45 minutes. Take 4 oz. 3 times per day.

Tincture - 40-60 drops (2-3 ml) TID.

Linden *flower and leaf (Tilia sp.)* is a very pleasant tasting herb with nervine qualities. It is used for mild hypertension (use it with Chrysanthemum flower, Olive leaf, Motherwort, and Hawthorn), irritability, stress headaches, stress-induced palpitations, insomnia, anxiety and nervous stomach.

Tea - 1-2 tsp. of the dried flowers to 8 oz. hot water, steep covered 15 minutes. Take 2-3 cups per day.

Tincture - 30-40 drops (1.5-2 ml) TID.

Lobelia *fresh herb in flower and seed (Lobelia inflata)* has been used for thousands of years by Native Americans and later by Thomsonian and Eclectic physicians as a strong antispasmodic to the lungs, heart and musculo-skeletal system. It can be used effectively in combination with other herbs for spasmodic coughing (bronchitis, asthma, pertussis), muscle spasms, petit mal epilepsy, hiccoughs, and angina pain.

Topical use - Lobelia seed oil is a useful antispasmodic and antibacterial agent. It is used for "body armor", muscle tension, muscle spasms, back pain and neck pain. The oil can also be applied to boils and local infections.

Tincture - 5-15 drops (.25-.75 ml) QID.

CONTRAINDICATIONS: Not for use in pregnancy unless otherwise directed by qualified expert. May cause nausea and vomiting. Not to be taken in large doses.

Lomatium *root (Lomatium dissectum)* has been used extensively by native peoples of the Western US but remains little-known to the general public. It is a powerful antiviral agent, that is used to inhibit viruses in chronic conditions such as Epstein Barr Virus (EBV), Cytomegalovirus (CMV), Human Papilloma Virus (HPV), and herpes. It is also an active respiratory antibacterial/antiviral agent and is effective for treating colds, damp coughs and influenza. Lomatium may also have some benefit for treating Lyme disease, when used with other herbs for clearing "blood heat".

Tincture - 15-20 drops (.75-1 ml) TID.

CONTRAINDICATIONS: Not for use in pregnancy unless otherwise directed by qualified expert. Long term use may induce a wide spread rash and a low-grade fever in sensitive individuals. Discontinue if you develop a rash. Some herbalists state that taking Dandelion root tea or capsules helps to more quickly resolve a Lomatium-induced rash.

Long Pepper *fruit (Piper longum)* also known as Pippali, is related to black pepper (Piper spp.) and is used as a spice and for its medicinal activity. It is a major tonic herb or rasayana in Ayurvedic medicine. The fruits act as an anti-inflammatory, carminative and expectorant and can be used for cold/damp coughs, dyspepsia, flatulence, head colds, and abdominal bloating. It also enhances circulation and promotes absorption of other herbs when used in a formula. In animal studies Pippali has been shown to have significant anti-amoebic (Sawangjaroen, et al., 2004, Ghoshal, et al., 1986), hepatoprotective (Rojeswary, et al., 2011), radioprotective (Sunila & Kuttan, 2005) and gastroprotective (Agrawal, et al., 2000) effects

Tea - 1/2 tsp. of the dry powdered fruit to 8 oz. hot water, steep covered 30 minutes. Take 2-4 oz. 2-3 times per day.

Tincture - 30-50 drops (1.5-2.5 ml) TID.

CONTRAINDICATIONS: Pippalli, Black Pepper and Cubeb berry all contain piperine which can increase absorption of herbs, as well as pharmaceutical medications. It may increase blood levels of some medications.

Lycium *fruit (Lycium barbarum)* also known as Goji berry, is a rich source of anti-inflammatory flavonoids which give this herb antioxidant, anti-inflammatory and vasoprotective effects. In TCM it is used to increase circulation to the lower extremities, i.e. cold feet, varicose veins and peripheral neuropathy. Lycium is also used to strengthen the eyes and enhance visual acuity as well as protect the liver against oxidative damage. Lycium also acts as a prebiotic enhancing the growth of healthy bowel flora.

Tea - 2 tsp. of the dried berries to 10 oz. water, decoct 10 minutes, steep 40 minutes. Take 2-3 cups per day.

Tincture - 60-100 drops (3-5 ml) TID.

CONTRAINDICATIONS: Do not use if you have a nightshade sensitivity or are allergic to peaches (Larramendi, et al., 2012).

Maca *root (Lepidium meyenii)* has gained quite a reputation as a sexual tonic for men and women. According to popular accounts it has a long history of use in the Andes for infertility, impotence, and sexual lassitude. The reality is that it has a long history of use as a nourishing food, but its use as a medicine is a much more recent occurrence. While animal studies suggest the herb has activity, human studies until recently were lacking. In two clinical trials large doses of Maca enhanced feelings of well being and sexual performance in men with mild erectile dysfunction (Zencio, et al., 2009) and SSRI-induced sexual dysfunction (Dording, et al., 2008). Be sure your Maca is grown in Peru at high altitude. A recent study found Maca grown in a low altitude had no or very low levels of active constituents (Melnikovova, et al., 2012).
Tincture - 60-100 drops (3-5 ml) TID/QID.

Maitake *mushroom (Grifola frondosa)* is a fungus that like Reishi, is an immune amphoteric (immunomodulator). It is indicated for hyper-immune response (allergies), hypo-/hyperimmune conditions such as auto-immune disease or decreased immune activity (cancer, HIV/AIDS, CFIDS). Maitake is an important immune modulator that enhances macrophage, NK cell, and T-cell activity. It is used in protocols for treating allergic rhinitis, to promote immune competence in cancer patients and for autoimmune hepatitis and lupus. Maitake's hepatoprotective activity and its ability to lower VLDL cholesterol levels and triglycerides makes it a useful part of protocols for treating type IV hyperlipidemia and non-alchoholic fatty liver disease. It has also been used to induce ovulation in women with PCOS (Chen, et al., 2010). This may be due to it's ability to reduce blood sugar levels and alleviate insulin resistance.
Tincture - 60-100 drops (3-5 ml) QID.
CONTRAINDICATIONS: Mushroom allergies.

Marshmallow *root (Althea officinalis)* is the original source of the confection marshmallows. The root is demulcent and a soothing diuretic and it is wonderful for irritated, inflamed mucous membranes in the bladder, stomach, small and large intestines and throat. It is the most soothing of all urinary herbs and the root is effective for treating interstitial cystitis, urethritis and common cystitis. It can also be utilized for healing gastric ulcers, esophagitis, hiatal hernia, GERD, gastritis, and dry irritating coughs.
Tea - 1-2 tsp. of the dried root to 12 oz. water, decoct 20 minutes, steep 1 hour. Take 1-3 cups per day.
Tincture - 60-100 drops (3-5 ml) QID.

Meadowsweet *flowering tops (Filipendula ulmaria)* is a gentle pain reliever that contains methyl salicylate, an aspirin-like chemical. Unlike aspirin, it does not irritate the gastrointestinal tract, nor does it significantly thin the blood. Meadowsweet is anti-inflammatory and is used for excessive gastric acid secretion (with Marshmallow, Licorice and Lemon Balm), gastric ulcers, hiatal hernia and nausea. In laboratory studies Filipendula strongly inhibited Helicobacter pylori, the cause of most gastric ulcers and gastritis. Filipendula can also be used for arthritis pain, headaches and muscle or back pain.

Tea - 1-2 tsp. of the dried herb to 8 oz. hot water, steep 20 minutes. Take 1-2 cups per day.

Tincture - 40-60 drops (2-3 ml) QID.

Milk Thistle *seed (Silybum marianum)* contains the silymarin complex which are hepatoprotective flavonolignans used to prevent and treat liver damage caused by chemicals, viruses or mushroom poisoning. It is indicated for cirrhosis of the liver as well as preventing drug-induced nephrotoxicity, psoriasis and as a supportive remedy for Hepatitis A, B or C. Milk Thistle also acts as a cholagogue and a galactogogue. It combines well with Burdock seed for dry, scaly skin conditions. The primary flavo-lignan in Milk Thistle, Silybinin, is being studied for its ability in laboratory and animal studies to inhibit carcinogenesis, promote apoptosis and prevent metastasis in many types of cancer.

Tincture - 30-40 drops (1.5-2 ml) TID.

Capsule (standardized capsule) - 120 mg 2-3 times per day.

Mimosa *bark (Albizia julibrissin)* is known in TCM as He Huan Pi or collective happiness bark. It calms disturbed shen (anxiety, insomnia, bad dreams) and is an incredibly effective mood elevator. Mimosa is also used for irritability, depression, mood swings, poor memory, and excessive anger. I use it with Hawthorn flower/fruit and Rose Petals for treating stagnant depression, broken heart, chronic grief and PTSD. In TCM Albizia is also used to treat trauma injuries (bruises, sprains) and back pain.

Tea - 1-2 tsp. of the dried bark to 8 oz. water, decoct 10 minutes, steep 30 minutes. Take 4 oz. 3 times per day.

Tincture - 40-80 drops (2-4 ml) TID.

CONTRAINDICATIONS: Do not use if you have bipolar disorder.

Motherwort *fresh herb (Leonurus cardiaca)* is an anxiolytic, analgesic, nervine, antispasmodic and emmenagogue useful for treating PMS symptoms, dysmenorrhea, palpitations caused by hyperthyroidism or nervousness, stress-induced hypertension, and neuralgias. It is often used for post-partum pain, PMS and menopausal anxiety and generalized anxiety disorder (use it with Blue Vervain, Fresh Oat, Bacopa and Chinese Polygala).

Tea - 1 tsp. of the dried herb to 8 oz. hot water, steep 15-20 minutes. Take 4-8 oz. 3 times per day.

Tincture - 30-40 drops (1.5-2 ml) TID.

CONTRAINDICATIONS: Not to be used in pregnancy unless otherwise directed by qualified expert.

Mullein *leaf (Verbascum thapsus)* is used as a mild, non-irritating expectorant. It increases activity of the cilia stimulating expectoration of mucus and it soothes irritated mucous membranes. Verbascum is energetically neutral so it can be

used for hot, cold, dry or damp lung conditions. It is usually combined with stronger expectorants such as Elecampane, Yerba Santa, Horehound or Grindelia.
Tea - 1-2 tsp. of the dried leaf to 8 oz. hot water, steep 15-20 minutes. Strain carefully and take 1-3 cups per day.
Tincture - 40-60 drops (2-3 ml) TID.

Myrrh *gum resin (Commiphora molmol)* is an excellent astringent, anti-inflammatory, and antiseptic used topically for bedsores and herpes, and as a gargle for strep throat, laryngitis and aphthous stomatitis. Used internally Myrrh enhances white blood cell counts and is specifically indicated for acute infections or inflammation of the mucous membranes of the throat, upper respiratory tract, stomach and bowels. It can be used to treat bronchitis, leaky gut syndrome, ulcerative colitis, ileitis, gastric ulcers, diarrhea and gastritis. In TCM, Myrrh is used internally and topically to "move blood" and relieve stagnation and is often used to treat painful bruises, angina pain, dysmenorrhea and arthritic pain.
Tincture - 15-30 drops (.75-1.5 ml) TID.
CONTRAINDICATIONS: Not for use in pregnancy unless otherwise directed by qualified expert.

Night Blooming Cereus *fresh stem (Selenicereus pteranthus, S. grandiflorus)* is a cardiotonic indicated for heart disease of nervous or drug origin (excess caffeine, tobacco, etc.). Combined with Hawthorn, it is beneficial for nervous tachycardia, palpitations, and a feeble and irregular pulse with shortness of breath with mild exertion. Combined with Collinsonia and Hawthorn it can be used to treat mild to moderate mitral valve prolapse. It is also effective for menopausal or old-age induced depression taken with Black Cohosh and for Grave's Disease used with Bugleweed, Motherwort and Lemon Balm.
Tincture - 5-15 drops (.25-.75 ml) TID.

Oat *fresh milky seed (Avena sativa)* is one of our most useful nervous system trophorestoratives, as it strengthens and nourishes the nervous system. It is indicated for nervous exhaustion, sexual neurasthenia and occipital pain extending toward the spine. Avena helps to relieve withdrawal symptoms from either nicotine or caffeine. Fresh Oat soothes overwrought, frazzled emotions caused by "burning the candle at both ends." It can help to restore a person's emotional foundation and reduce labile emotions. It is also effective for treating anxiety, poor quality sleep due to stress, ADHD and OCD behaviors.
Tincture - 60-100 drops (3-5 ml) QID.
Glycerite - 80-120 drops (4-6 ml) QID.

Olive *leaf (Olea europaea)* is used in Europe for hypertension, impaired circulation, diabetes and as a diuretic. Its effects on high blood pressure are slow acting but definite and long lasting especially when used in combination with Mistletoe, Motherwort, Linden, or Chrysanthemum flower. It not only lowered blood pressure, but it reduced triglyceride levels as well (Susalit, et al., 2011).

Olive leaf also has shown antiviral activity in test tube studies, but there is little to no research showing efficacy when taken internally by humans or even animals. *Tea* - 2 tsp. of the dried leaf to 8 oz. hot water, steep 40 minutes. Take 4-8 oz. 2-3 times per day.
Tincture - 40-60 drops (2-3 ml) TID.

Orange Peel *(Citrus spp.)* is a superb digestive stimulant and carminative. It stimulates gastric HCL production, making it an effective remedy for achlorhydria (lack of gastric HCL). Orange Peel also relieves gas, nausea and borborygmus. I usually combine Orange Peel with Angelica root, Artichoke leaf and Dandelion root to make a highly effective digestive bitter, which can be used on a daily basis. Orange Peel with Ginger is a lovely tasting remedy for cold/damp coughs and head colds. Some of the essential oil compounds found in this herb such as limonene have shown the ability to suppress tumor growth in laboratory studies.
Tea - 1/4-1/2 tsp. of the dried peel to 8 oz. hot water, steep covered 15-20 minutes. Take 2 oz. 3-4 times per day.
Tincture - 20-30 drops (1-1.5 ml) TID.

Oregon Grape *root (Mahonia nervosa, M. aquafolium, M. repens)* is a liver tonic and cholagogue used to increase digestion and absorption, especially of fats. It is indicated for dyspepsia, GI dysbiosis, jaundice, elevated bilirubin levels, and a lack of bile secretion. Oregon Grape is also antibacterial, antifungal, and antiviral. It can be used to treat urinary tract infections, Strep and Staph infections, intestinal viruses and skin conditions such as acne rosacea, psoriasis, and large, red pimples on the neck, back, or buttocks (topically and orally). Mahonia, while not as effective as Goldenseal can be used for inhibiting Helicobacter pylori, a major cause of gastritis and gastric ulcers.
Tea - 1 tsp. of the dried root to 10 oz. of water, decoct 15-20 minutes, steep 1/2 hour. Take 4 oz. 3 times per day.
Tincture - 20-40 drops (1-2 ml) TID.
CONTRAINDICATIONS: Not for use in pregnancy (theoretical concern) unless otherwise directed by qualified expert.

Osha *root (Ligusticum porteri)* has finally gained recognition as a major medicinal plant after a long history of use by Native American and Hispanic people. It is an antibacterial expectorant and bronchiodilator useful for cold/damp lung conditions. It has mild antihistamine activity which makes it useful for allergic rhinitis, head colds and allergies. It can be useful to help treat mild causes of altitude sickness. This aromatic root is also a carminative, diaphoretic and emmenagogue.
Tincture - 20-40 drops (1-2 ml) TID.
CONTRAINDICATIONS: Not for use in pregnancy unless otherwise directed by qualified expert.

Parsley *fresh whole plant (Petroselinum crispum)* is a common culinary herb that also has many medicinal qualities. Not only is the plant highly nutritious, it is also a diuretic, urinary antiseptic, emmenagogue and carminative. Parsley can be used for dysuria, amenorrhea, gas, infant colic (via breastmilk) and bilious colic. Combined with Celery seed, it is one of the most effective remedies for gout and gouty arthritis.
Tea - 1/2 tsp. of the dried herb to 8 oz. hot water, steep covered 15-20 minutes. Take 4 oz. 3 times per day.
Tincture - 30-40 drops (1.5-2 ml) QID.

Passionflower *fresh herb (Passiflora incarnata)* is a mild sedative, nervine, antispasmodic and anxiolytic useful for anxiety, insomnia, nervous or occipital headaches, neuralgia, teething children, muscle/nerve pain, facial tics, pelvic and spasmodic pain. It is very effective for people who cannot fall asleep because of mental chatter or repetitive thoughts.
Tea - 1-2 tsp. of the dried herb to 8 oz. hot water, steep 1/2 hour. Take 1-3 cups per day.
Tincture - 30-40 drops (1.5-2 ml) TID.

Pau D'Arco *bark (Tabebuia impetiginosa)* has been used in South America as an immune tonic, antimicrobial, antifungal, anti-inflammatory and astringent. Laboratory and animal research suggests that it does have antitumor activity as well as wound healing, antiulcerogenic, and antibacterial effects. The herb is widely touted for its effects on Candida overgrowth. Clinical results are variable, with some reports of great success and other clinicians seeing little activity or benefit.
Tincture - 30-60 drops (1.5-3 ml) TID.

Peppermint *fresh herb (Mentha x piperita)* is a time-tested carminative used for millennia to relieve nausea, gas, abdominal bloating and intestinal colic. It is a pleasant tasting flavoring agent and can be given with laxatives to prevent gripping. Peppermint combined with Elderflower has a long history of use for treating colds or influenza in children. The essential oil (EO) taken in enteric-coated capsules has been found to be effective for relieving IBS symptoms (McKay and Blumberg, 2006).
Tea - 1 tsp. of the dried herb to 8 oz. hot water, steep 10-15 minutes. Take 1-3 cups per day.
Tincture - 40-60 drops (2-3 ml) QID.
CONTRAINDICATIONS: GERD.

Pipsissewa *fresh herb (Chimaphila umbellata)* is a non-irritating, antiseptic diuretic that is used for genito-urinary infections especially if of a chronic nature. It is appropriate for chronic nephritis or cystitis, bacterial vaginosis, prostatitis, and urethritis. Pipsissewa is also used as an alterative (antidyscratic) used for treating gouty arthritis, gout and rheumatic pain. The dried leaf loses most of its activity and the most effective preparation is a tincture made from the fresh leaf. *Tincture* - 20-40 drops (1-2 ml) TID.

Plantain *fresh leaf (Plantago major)* is a vulnerary, primarily used for its demulcent, healing qualities both internally and externally. It is a rich source of chlorophyll and allantoin which speed healing of skin and mucous membrane tissue especially in the stomach, bladder and vaginal tract. Plantain is useful for treating gastritis, gastric and duodenal ulcers, ulcerative colitis, and interstitial cystitis. It can be applied topically for toothache pain, insect bites, bruises and rashes. Plantago is also noted in the Homeopathic literature for helping to reduce tobacco cravings. *Tea* - 1-2 tsp. of the dried leaf to 8 oz. hot water, steep 20-30 minutes. Take 2-3 cups per day
Tincture - 60-100 drops (3-5 ml) QID.

Platycodon *root (Platycodon grandiflorum)* or Jie Geng is one of the most important lung remedies in TCM. It is an active expectorant, antitussive, anti-inflammatory, and antipyretic. It is used for sore throats, coughs, laryngitis, pneumonia, bronchitis, lung abscesses, allergic asthma, and allergic rhinitis. It can also be used to treat diarrhea, IBS and rectal or intestinal spasms (use it with Wild Yam, Kudzu, and Chamomile).
Tea-1 tsp. of the dried root to 8 oz. water, decoct 5-10 minutes, steep 45 minutes. Take 4 oz. 3 times per day
Tincture - 40-60 drops (2-3 ml.) TID

Pleurisy root *fresh root (Asclepias tuberosa)* or Butterfly weed is indicated for lung conditions where breathing is painful and there is a fever with little or no sweating. It can be used to treat pleurisy, pneumonia, pericarditis, bronchitis and pneumonitis. Pleurisy root increases diaphoresis, expels mucus, slows a rapid pulse and reduces respiratory pain. It is also effective combined with Black Haw and Wild Cherry bark for intercostal pain.
Tincture - 20-40 drops (1-2 ml) in hot water QID.
CONTRAINDICATIONS: Not for use in pregnancy unless otherwise directed by qualified expert. In sensitive people larger doses may cause nausea or vomiting.

Poke* *root (Phytolacca americana)* is used in many traditional alterative formulas including the Hoxsey Formula for treating chronic skin conditions, arthritis and cancer. Internally, very small doses of Poke root tincture can be used as a powerful alterative for lymphatic stagnation especially mastitis and cystic breast disease. Topically, Phytolacca infused oil is used to increase lymphatic drainage. It can be massaged into the breasts for cystic breast disease, mastitis and calcium deposits in the milk ducts. The oil is also used for lymphatic stagnation with benign, hard, swollen lymph nodes.
Tincture - 3-5 drops (.15-.25 ml) BID/QID
CONTRAINDICATIONS: Pregnancy or breast feeding. Use only under a practitioner's supervision.

Polygala root (Polygala tenuifolia) or Yuan Zhi is used in TCM to calm disturbed Shen. Symptoms of disturbed Shen include restlessness, anxiety, irritability, insomnia and bad dreams. The saponins contained in the root exhibit dopamine and serotonin receptor antagonist properties. This give credence to its traditional use for psychiatric disorders such as OCD, Mania, ADHD, and Paranoia. Preclinical tests have shown that Polygala exerts protective effects against neuronal death and it can also reduce insomnia, possibly by acting on the proliferation and outgrowth of neuronal cells. I find Chinese Polygala along with Bacopa, Motherwort, Fresh Oat and Blue Vervain to be very effective for treating generalized anxiety disorder (GAD).

Tea - 1/2 tsp. of the dried root to 8 oz. water, decoct 10 minutes, steep 40 minutes. Take 4 oz. 2 times per day.

Tincture - 20-40 drops (1-2 ml) TID/QID.

CONTRAINDICATIONS: Do not use during pregnancy or lactation. Use cautiously with gastric ulcers or gastritis. It can cause nausea in overdose.

Prickly Ash *bark (Zanthoxylum clava-herculis)* is a pungent carminative and circulatory stimulant. It increases digestion and absorption in people with deficient gastric HCL, gas and malabsorption. Prickly Ash also increases peripheral circulation and relieves nerve pain. It is indicated for people with cold extremities, Raynaud's disease, peripheral neuropathies, and sciatica. (Use it with St. John's wort, Teasel root, Sweet Melilot and Horse Chestnut.)

Tincture - 10-20 drops (.5-1 ml) TID.

CONTRAINDICATIONS: Not for use in pregnancy unless otherwise directed by qualified expert.

Prince Seng *root (Pseudostellaria heterophylla)* or Tai Zi Shen is known as the "Ginseng of the Lungs" in Chinese medicine. It is a *yin* tonic, mild adaptogen, demulcent and nutritive. It is useful for dry, irritated mucous membranes, dry coughs, emphysema, post-pneumonia debility, fatigue (with Schisandra) and deficient spleen patterns with symptoms such as weakness, malaise and lack of appetite.

Tea - 2 tsp. of the dried root to 10 oz. water, decoct 20 minutes, steep 40 minutes. Take 2-3 cups per day.

Tincture - 60-80 drops (3-4 ml) TID.

Propolis *(bee gathered tree resin)* is an antimicrobial and anti-fungal agent with activity against Streptococcus mutans, Candida albicans, Enterococcus faecalis, Staphylococcus aureus and Campylobacter jejuni. It is indicated for Strep throat, gum disease, herpes, Staph infections and upper respiratory infections. It is often used in gargles and throat sprays, for treating laryngitis, pharyngitis, uvulitis and esophagitis.

Tincture - 20-30 drops (1-1.5 ml) TID.

CONTRAINDICATIONS: Do not use if you have allergies to bee stings or bee-based products.

Pulsatilla* *fresh or dried aerial parts or root (Anemone pulsatilla)* is a powerful medicinal plant with a long history of use by the Eclectic physicians. It is used for overly emotional people who constantly cry, are anxious, moody, or depressed. For menopausal depression it can be used with Black Cohosh and Night Blooming Cereus. For grumpy old man syndrome (andropausal depression), use it with Saw Palmetto and Black Cohosh. It also has benefit for stress-induced headaches, night terrors, anxiety attacks and dysmenorrhea.

Tincture - 3-5 drops (.15-.25 ml) BID/TID (Toxic in overdose).
CONTRAINDICATIONS: Pregnancy or breast feeding. Use only under a practitioner's supervision.

Quassia *wood (Picrasma excelsa)* was introduced into European medicine in the 16th Century. It is a powerful bitter that stimulates digestion and absorption by increasing gastric hydrochloric acid production, bile secretion, and small intestine and pancreatic secretions. Quassia has strong antiamoebic activity and is useful for treating Giardia, Blastocystis hominus, Dientamoeba fragilis and Cryptosporidium infections. It has also been used to kill intestinal parasites such as pin worms.

Tincture - 15-20 drops (.75-1 ml) TID.
CONTRAINDICATIONS: Not for use in pregnancy or with young children unless otherwise directed by qualified expert.

Raspberry *leaf (Rubus idaeus)* is rich in minerals as well as being a mild astringent. Raspberry leaf is a tonic to smooth muscle tissue, especially the uterus and large intestine. It is a pregnancy tonic used to reduce morning sickness, prevent miscarriage and post partum bleeding. Raspberry is also indicated for menorrhagia, uterine and bladder prolapse, diarrhea, BPH and urinary frequency.

Tea - 1-2 tsp. of the dried herb to 8 oz. hot water, steep 20 minutes. Take 1-3 cups per day.
Tincture - 40-60 drops (2-3 ml) QID.

Red Alder *bark (Alnus rubra)* is used as an alterative, mild laxative, cholagogue and antibacterial. Red Alder bark is considered specific for skin conditions where the eruptions (pimples) are red, raised and never come to a head. It can be used orally and topically for boils, carbuncles, Staph infections, acne rosacea, and large painful pimples on the back, buttocks, face or neck. It is also of benefit for constipation with clay colored stools, and impaired fat digestion.

Tea - 1 tsp. of the dried bark to 10 oz. water, decoct 10-15 minutes, steep 1/2 hour. Take 4 oz. 3 times per day.
Tincture - 20-40 drops (1-2 ml) TID.
CONTRAINDICATIONS: Not for use in pregnancy unless otherwise directed by qualified expert. Lactation. Diarrhea.

Red Clover *blossom (Trifolium pratense)* has a long history of use in alterative formulas for treating cancer. It contains genistein which inhibits cancer cell growth and metastasis in laboratory studies. Red Clover is a mild lung, lymphatic and liver remedy indicated for cases of irritable coughs, especially if caused by measles or whooping cough. It is also used to treat lymphatic congestion, tonsillitis, cystic breast disease, and lymphedema.

Tea - 1-2 tsp. of the dried blossoms to 8 oz. hot water, steep 30 minutes. Take 1-3 cups per day.

Tincture - 60-100 drops (3-5 ml) QID.

Red Ginseng *root (Panax ginseng)* is the best known and well researched adaptogenic herb in the world. Asian Ginseng is used to enhance immune function, (it is an immune amphoteric) and normalize an overactive stress response (it lowers excessive cortisol levels). It increases physical and mental performance and has been shown in clinical trials to improve erectile dysfunction in men (Kim, et al., 2009, Jang, et al., 2008) and lack of libido in post-menopausal women (Oh, et al., 2010). Red Ginseng is most appropriate for older, deficient people suffering from exhaustion, depression, adrenal insufficiency and chronic fatigue immune deficiency syndrome (CFIDS). I use it with Cordyceps and Licorice for treating Addison's Disease.

Tea - 1 tsp. of the dried root to 12 oz. water, decoct 15-20 minutes, steep 1 hour. Take 4 oz. 3 times per day.

Tincture - 20-40 drops (1-2 ml) TID/QID.

CONTRAINDICATIONS: Excess doses of Red Ginseng, especially in people with heat signs (red face or head, liver fire headaches, hypertension) can exacerbate these symptoms and can also cause insomnia.

Red Root *fresh root (Ceanothus americanus)* is an astringent useful for overactive mucosa with excessive mucous secretions. As a gargle it is effective for tonsillitis, aphthous stomatitis and periodontal disease. It is also indicated for lymphatic congestion, cystic breast disease, mononucleosis, lymphadenitis and hemorrhoids. Used with Fringe Tree and Milk Thistle, this herb was used by the Eclectic physicians for treating acute pancreatitis, hepatomegaly and splenomegaly.

Tincture - 20-30 drops (1-1.5 ml) TID.

Rehmannia *processed root (Rehmannia glutinosa)* or Shu Di Huang is a prominent blood (*xue*) tonic in TCM and is one of four herbs that make up the classic Women's Four Herb Tea (Si Wu Tang). It is useful for deficient blood patterns with pale skin, anemia, insomnia, dizziness, irregular menses and palpitations. The processed root is also a kidney *yin* tonic (nephroprotective) and helps reduce allergic response. Because of Processed Rehmannia's greasy nature, it is often combined with aromatic herbs to prevent digestive upset.

Tea - 1-2 tsp. of the dried root to 12 oz. water, decoct 20-30 minutes, steep 1/2 hour. Take 4 oz. 3 times per day.

Tincture - 30-40 drops (1.5-2 ml) TID.

CONTRAINDICATIONS: Diarrhea and indigestion.

Rehmannia *unprocessed root (Rehmannia glutinosa)* or Sheng Di Huang is used to clear heat and cool the blood. In Traditional Chinese Medicine it is used for fevers, abnormal bleeding, mouth and tongue sores, and dry mouth. It has also been shown to inhibit allergic and autoimmune response. It can be used along with other immunoregulatory herbs and immune amphoterics to treat conditions such as lupus, rheumatoid arthritis, psoriatic arthritis, Sjögrens syndrome and eczema.

Tea - 1-2 tsp. of the dried root to 12 oz. of water, decoct 20-30 minutes, steep 1/2 hour. Take 4 oz. 3 times per day.

Tincture - 30-40 drops (1.5-2 ml) TID.

Reishi *mushroom and mycelium (Ganoderma spp.)* also known as Ling Zhi, is an immune amphoteric indicated for immune deficiency (cancer, AIDS, chronic fatigue syndrome), autoimmune diseases (lupus, rheumatoid arthritis, Crohn's Disease, ankylosing spondylitis) as well as hyper-immune conditions such as allergies. In clinical trials Ganoderma inhibited development of colorectal adenomas (Oka, et al., 2010), reduced symptoms in men with lower urinary tract symptoms (Noguche, et al., 2008) and it inhibited endothelial cell cytotoxicity and proteinuria in people with proteinuric focal segmental glomerulosclerosis (FSGS) nephrosis (Futrakul, et al., 2004). Reishi also has hepatoprotective, cardiotonic, antioxidant and nervine activity. This "kingly remedy" is also used to treat altitude sickness (with Cordyceps and Rhodiola), insomnia, leukopenia, ADD/ADHD, and hypercholesterolemia.

Tea - 2 tsp. of the dried mushroom to 12 oz. water, gently decoct 1 hour. Take 2-4 cups per day.

Tincture - 60-100 drops (3-5 ml) TID.

CONTRAINDICATIONS: Mushroom allergies.

Rhodiola *root (Rhodiola rosea)*, or Rose root, is a stimulating adaptogen that has been extensively studied in Russia and Sweden. In human clinical trials Rhodiola has been found to enhance physical performance, memory and concentration and to alleviate mild to moderate depression, anxiety, and stress-induced fatigue (Hung, et al., 2011, Panossian, et al., 2010). It can also be used for "stagnant depression", erectile dysfunction, for altitude sickness, as a cardic tonic and for hypothyroidism (with Ashwagandha, and Bacopa).

Tea - 1 tsp. of the dried root to 8 oz. water, decoct 10 minutes, steep 1 hour. Take 1-2 cups per day.

Tincture - 20-40 drops (1-2 ml) QID.

CONTRAINDICATIONS: It is very drying and can increase dryness in people with deficient yin conditions. It can also overstimulate sensitive people and cause insomnia Do not use if you have bipolar disorder.

Roman Chamomile *flowers (Chamaemelum nobilis)* is more bitter tasting and stronger acting than its relative German Chamomile. It is an antispasmodic, anti-inflammatory and nervine/sedative. The flowers are used for muscle spasms,

intestinal cramping, or pain in the uterus and GI tract. I use it for treating dysmenorrhea, painful flatulence, IBS and diarrhea with bowel spasms.
Tea - 1 tsp. dried flowers to 8 oz. hot water, steep covered 20-30 minutes. Take 4 oz. 2-3 times per day.
Tincture - 20-40 drops (1-2 ml) TID.
CONTRAINDICATIONS: Not for use in pregnancy unless otherwise directed by qualified expert.

Rose *petals (Rosa spp.)* are a delight to the senses, especially the fragrant apothecary or cabbage roses. They look beautiful, smell wonderful, taste delightful in teas or jellies, and even feel soft and silky. Roses have long been given as a gift to ask forgiveness or indicate love and affection. Aromatherapists use attar of rose for depression, to "open the heart", and to comfort those in distress. Roses have antioxidant, anti-inflammatory, and antidepressant activity and I use them with Mimosa bark and Hawthorn flowers and fruit for "stagnant" depression (chronic situational depression), broken hearts, chronic grief and PTSD.
Tea - 1 tsp. of the dried petals to 8 oz. hot water, steep covered 20 minutes. Take 4 oz. 3 times per day.
Tincture - 20-40 drops (1-2 ml) TID.

Rosemary *herb (Rosmarinus officinale)* is a carminative, nervine, and cholagogue traditionally used in Europe for gas, nausea, liver headaches, and biliousness. Rosemary is also a powerful antioxidant making it of benefit for preventing arteriosclerosis and other types of oxidative damage. It also has been shown to promote cognitive function and memory (Pengelly et al., 2012), relieve mental fog and depression. I use it to treat stagnant depression (chronic situational depression) along with Lavender, Holy Basil, Damiana or Rhodiola.
Tea - 1/2-1 tsp. of the dried herb to 8 oz. hot water, steep covered 10-15 minutes. Take 4 oz. 2 times per day.
Tincture - 20-30 drops (1-1.5 ml) QID.
CONTRAINDICATIONS: Not for use in pregnancy unless otherwise directed by qualified expert.

Sage *herb (Salvia officinalis)* is not only a culinary herb, but a powerful antioxidant, carminative, antibacterial agent, diaphoretic, anti-inflammatory and antigalactogogue. Sage is used for digestive disturbances, colds, intestinal viruses, sore throats (gargle with Sage and Echinacea), laryngitis, tonsillitis, aphthous stomatitis and post nasal drip. It reduces excess secretions and is beneficial for menopausal hot flashes (Bommer, et al., 2011), to stop milk flow and for profuse sinus discharge. In clinical trials, Sage reduced hot flashes in men with prostate cancer undergoing androgen deprivation therapy (Vandecasteele, et al., 2012) and improved cognitive function in patients with mild to moderate Alzheimer's disease (Akhondzadeh, et al., 2003).
Tea - 1/2 tsp. of the dried herb to 8 oz. hot water, steep covered 10 minutes. Take 4 oz. 2 times per day.

Tincture - 30-40 drops (1.5-2 ml) QID.
CONTRAINDICATIONS: Not for use in pregnancy unless otherwise directed by qualified expert.

St. John's wort *flowering tops (Hypericum perforatum)* make a vivid dark red tincture or oil due to its dianthrones and flavonoids, which have broad-spectrum antiviral and anti-inflammatory activity. It is a trophorestorative to the nervous system and is useful for hepatic or GI-based depression, for seasonal affective disorder (with Lemon Balm), and as an anti-anxiety agent. St. John's wort is used locally and internally for nerve and spinal injuries, nerve pain, sciatica, shingles, reflex sympathetic dystrophy (RSD), and irritable bladder. The dark red infused oil is known as Hypericum oil. It can be applied topically for nerve pain, burns, shingles, rashes and to speed healing and prevent scarring with episiotomy incisions (Samadi, et al., 2010).
Tincture - 40-60 drops (2-3 ml) QID.
CONTRAINDICATIONS: Do not use this product while taking any prescription drugs without the advice of your prescribing physician. Avoid excessive exposure to UV irradiation (e.g., sunlight, tanning) when using this product.

Sarsaparilla *root (Smilax regelii and other Smilax spp.)* contains steroidal saponins which are anti-inflammatory. It is used for skin conditions that are red, hot and inflamed such as psoriasis and psoriatic arthritis. It is also appropriate for arthritis, gout, bursitis, rheumatoid arthritis and inflammation of connective tissue. Sarsaparilla binds endotoxins in the gut, thus enhancing excretions of metabolic wastes. It can be combined with Turmeric, Cat's Claw and Licorice to help heal leaky gut syndrome.
Tea - 1-2 tsp. of the dried rhizome to 10 oz. water, decoct 15-20 minutes, steep 1/2 hour. Take 4 oz. 3 times per day.
Tincture - 60-80 drops (3-4 ml) QID.

Saw Palmetto *berry (Serenoa repens)* is indicated in cases of benign prostatic hyperplasia (it is most effective when combined with Nettle root, Collinsonia, and White Sage) and interstitial cystitis. It is also a nutritive remedy and is especially useful for older, depleted people. Saw Palmetto can be used as a urinary antiseptic, an expectorant, for uterine fibroids, and with Chaste Tree, White Peony and Licorice for Polycystic Ovarian Syndrome (PCOS). I use Saw Palmetto along with Pulsatilla, Ashwagandha and Black Cohosh for andropausal depression.
Tincture - 40-60 drops (2-3 ml) TID.
Capsules (standardized extract) - 160 mg BID.

Schisandra *berry (Schisandra chinensis)* or Wu Wei Zi is an effective calming adaptogen. It strengthens the hypothalamic/pituitary/adrenal axis (HPA) and normalizes endocrine, nervous system and immune activity. Schisandra has hepatoprotective activity and can be used to protect the liver against environmental, viral or drug-induced damage (use it with Milk Thistle, Turmeric and Artichoke leaf). It enhances work and athletic performance while promoting mental clarity, focus, and a calm attitude. It astringes the *jing* - the vital essence and is used to treat urinary frequency, premature ejaculation and bladder prolapse. Schisandra is rich in anti-inflammatory flavonoids. and can be useful for mild asthma with wheezing (kidneys not grasping lung *qi*).

Tea - 1 tsp. of the dried berries to 8 oz. water, decoct 5 minutes, steep 1/2 hour. Take 2-3 cups per day.

Tincture - 30-60 drops (1.5-3 ml) QID.

Self Heal *fresh flowering tops (Prunella vulgaris)* is a little known herb in the West, but is used in Traditional Chinese Medicine for liver fire rising symptoms (red eyes, headaches, dizziness) and to clear heat and dissolve nodules. This latter use stems from Self Heal's effects as a lymphatic tonic used for swollen glands, lipomas and mastitis (use it with Figwort). It is also used for thyroid nodules and it has mild thyroxin-inhibiting activity. Prunella is an antiviral agent, anti-inflammatory, and astringent used for herpes lesions, gingivitis, and sore throats.

Tea - 2 tsp. of the dried herb to 8 oz. hot water, steep for 1/2 hour. Take 4-8 oz. 2-3 times per day.

Tincture - 30-60 drops (1.5-3 ml) TID.

Shatavari *root (Asparagus racemosus)* is one of the great Ayurvedic tonic herbs or rasayanas. It is a mild adaptogen, yin tonic, and female reproductive trophorestorative. It is especially useful for treating decreased fertility and libido in women, menopause-induced vaginal dryness, and for tired, deficient, and/or anemic women (it can be used with Amla and Ashwagandha for anemia). This nourishing root is also a galactogogue, enhancing milk flow in nursing mothers, and it is a soothing demulcent, relieving dry, ticklish coughs. It can also be used as a nutritive and immune tonic for deficient, asthenic people, to protect the stomach against aspirin-induced irritation, to help heal gastric ulcers, and to relieve irritation of the GI (IBS, gastritis, diarrhea) and GU tracts (burning cystitis, urinary calculi, urethritis). Preliminary research has also supported the use of this herb to relieve immunosuppression, neurodegenerative conditions, and alcohol withdrawal symptoms.

Tea - 1 tsp. of the dried, powdered root to 8 oz. water, decoct 10 minutes, steep 40 minutes. Take 8 oz. 2 times per day.

Tincture - 60-100 drops (3-5 ml) TID.

Shepherd's Purse *fresh herb (Capsella bursa-pastoris)* is a styptic and anti-hemorrhagic used for in menorrhagia, bleeding ulcers, excessive post partum bleeding, blood in the urine (hematuria) and bleeding hemorrhoids. It is also an astringent and diuretic indicated for cloudy, foul-smelling urine, urinary tract infections, urethritis, diarrhea and dysentery. The Eclectic physicians used Capsella for treating uterine fibroids, especially with heavy bleeding.

Tincture - 20-40 drops (1-2 ml) QID.

CONTRAINDICATIONS: Not for use in pregnancy unless otherwise directed by qualified expert. Individuals with a history of oxalate kidney stones should use this herb cautiously.

Shiitake *mushroom (Lentinula edodes)* has long been revered as both a food and a medicine. In Japan Shiitake is used as a dietary supplement for cancer, to lower cholesterol levels and to protect the liver from environmental toxins. This mushroom can be used to reduce respiratory inflammation, lower blood pressure and inhibit viral growth. Eating Shiitake can help lower unhealthy blood lipids, but its other medicinal effects are available only from an extract of the mushroom.
Tea - 2 tsp. of the dried fungi to 16 oz. water, decoct for 1-2 hours. Take 2-3 cups per day.
Tincture - 40-50 drops (2-2.5 ml) TID.
CONTRAINDICATIONS: Mushroom allergies.

Sichuan Teasel *root (Dipsacus asper)* is used in Chinese medicine as a kidney yang tonic. The root is astringent, styptic, anti-inflammatory and antispasmodic. It can be used internally and topically for low back pain, stiff joints, arthritis, sciatica, and trauma injuries. Some herbalists claim Teasel can cure Lyme disease. While it can help relieve Lyme arthralgia, it is not curative for this very serious disease. Dipsacus can also be of benefit for menorrhagia, leucorrhea, frequent urination, and impotence (use it with Suo Yang, Morinda root and Epimedium).
Tea - 1 tsp. of the dried root to 8 oz. water, decoct 15 minutes, steep 45 minutes. Take 4 oz. 3 times per day.
Tincture - 30-40 drops (1.5-2 ml) TID.

Skullcap *fresh herb (Scutellaria lateriflora)* is a superior nervine indicated for nervous exhaustion with spasticity (nervous tics, tardive dyskinesia). Is it also indicated for essential tremors, palsies, trigeminal neuralgia, mild Tourette's Syndrome, restless leg syndrome, as well as the tremors of Parkinson's disease. It strengthens a depleted nervous system and is especially useful for what are known in TCM as "liver wind" patterns. This would include stress-induced or fly off the handle anger, bruxism, muscle spasms and torticollis.
Tincture - 50-60 drops (2.5-3 ml) QID.
Glycerite - 80-120 drops (4-6 ml) QID.

Skunk Cabbage* *fresh root (Symplocarpus foetidus)* is a powerful antispasmodic and analgesic. It is most effective in treating spasms of the lungs, diaphragm and back muscles including asthma, back spasms, dry irritative coughs and pertussis. It works well with other antispasmodics such as Lobelia, Skullcap or Black Haw. Taking it with small amounts of Licorice can enhance its ability to stop coughing or asthma and helps prevent irritation of the mouth or throat that can be caused by this herb.
Tincture - 3-5 drops (.15-.25 ml) TID diluted in water or juice. (Undiluted, it can cause irritation of the mouth, tongue, and throat.)

CONTRAINDICATIONS: Pregnancy. Avoid use in people with a history of calcium oxalate kidney stones. Use under supervision of qualified practitioner.

Solomon's Seal *fresh root (Polygonatum biflorum)* is a soothing *yin* tonic used for dry coughs, sticky, hard to expectorate mucus and constant thirst. The root can also be used internally and topically for joint, tendon and cartilage injuries (mild tears of the ACL, meniscus or rotator cuff), as well as for compressed or bulging spinal discs.
Tea - 1 tsp. of the dried root to 10 oz. water, decoct 10-15 minutes, steep 1/2 hour. Take 4 oz. 2-3 times per day.
Tincture - 20-40 drops (1-2 ml) TID.

Spikenard *fresh root (Aralia racemosa)* is a diaphoretic, antibacterial, antiviral, and warming expectorant. This herb is indicated for colds, influenza, pneumonia, and bronchitis with wheezing coughs, irritation of mucous membranes and tough stringy mucus. Spikenard is also an emmenagogue and oxytocic used with Black Cohosh and Cotton root bark to stimulate productive contractions in labor. The root is also of benefit for amenorrhea or dysmenorrhea with a clotty, scanty flow and pain.
Tea - 1 tsp. of the dried root to 10 oz. water, decoct 10-15 minutes, steep 1/2 hour. Take 4 oz. 3 times per day.
Tincture - 30-40 drops (1.5-2 ml) TID.
CONTRAINDICATIONS: Not for use in pregnancy unless otherwise directed by qualified expert.

Spilanthes *herb (Spilanthes acmella, S. oleracea)* is also known as Paraguay Cress or Toothache plant. It is rich in phytochemicals known as isobutylamides which act as immune stimulants, antibacterial and antifungal agents. It can also be used as a local anesthetic to the mouth, gums, teeth and throat. Spilanthes is effective for treating urinary tract pain, gum disease, thrush and sore throats.
Tea - 1-2 tsp. of the dried herb to 8 oz. hot water, steep 20-30 minutes. Take 4 oz. three times per day.
Tincture - 20-25 drops (1-1.25 ml) TID.

Stinging Nettle *leaf (Urtica dioica)* Stinging Nettle is widely known for the rash it causes when you brush against the fresh plant. Once dry it becomes a highly nutritious herbal food rich in iron, magnesium, calcium, boron and carotenoids. It is an appropriate for treatment for "deficient blood" i.e. anemia and low iron levels during pregnancy. Urtica is a mild non-irritating, potassium-sparing diuretic (aquaretic), and it is a "kidney food" strengthening the function and tonus of the organ. Stinging Nettle is commonly used for kidney pain caused by low-grade chronic nephritis, especially with hematuria. It is also indicated for skin that feels like paper and tears or bruises easily. In human studies Nettle leaf has been found to have anti-inflammatory activity and was of benefit for arthritis (Anonymous, 2002) and inhibiting diabetes-induced oxidative damage (Namazi, et al., 2012).
Tea - 2 tsp. of the dried herb to 8 oz. hot water, steep 1/2 hour. Take 1-3 cups per day.
Tincture - 30-60 drops (1.5-3 ml) QID.

Stinging Nettle *root (Urtica dioica)* has anti-inflammatory activity and is used for treating benign prostatic hyperplasia (BPH). Its activity is believed to be due to inhibition of aromatase, sex hormone-binding globulin (SHBG), epidermal growth factor or possibly the prostate steroid membrane receptors. A combination of Urtica root, Saw Palmetto, Collinsonia, and White Sage, is vastly more effective than any one of these herbs alone for relieving BPH symptoms. Nettle root can also be used to slow the progression of prostate cancer.

Tea - 1-2 tsp. of the dried root to 8 oz. water, decoct 10-15 minutes, steep 1/2 hour. Take 2 cups per day.

Tincture - 40-60 drops (2-3 ml) TID.

Stinging Nettle *seed (Urtica dioica)* is a rich source of fatty acids and nephroprotective lectins. Stinging Nettle seed is currently being used in clinical practice as a trophorestorative for the kidneys. It can be used to treat chronic nephritis with loss of kidney function, glomerulonephritis and Berger's Disease (IgA nephropathy). In many cases of chronic degenerative kidney disease people taking nettle seed have shown improvement of renal function with increased creatinine excretion and reduced BUN levels. In old herbals, Stinging Nettle seed was also recommended for treating goiter, tuberculosis and malarial fevers.

Tincture - 30-40 drops (1.5-2 ml) TID.

Sweet Annie *herb (Artemisia annua)* is traditionally used in Chinese medicine for fevers, parasites (leptospirosis) and fungal infections (dermatomycoses). The specific indication is heat in the blood characterized by nosebleeds and rashes with bleeding under the skin. This intensely bitter herb has been found to inhibit malarial infections and can also be used to treat Dengue Fever (with Dogwood bark, Tree Peony and Lycium root) and amoebic infections.

Tincture - 20-30 drops (1-1.5 ml) TID.

CONTRAINDICATIONS: Not for use in pregnancy unless otherwise directed by qualified expert.

Thuja *leaf (Thuja spp.)* is a fragrant evergreen tree that grows in the Northern US and Canada. It has strong antiviral, diuretic, emmenagogue and expectorant activity. It is primarily used for immune stimulation and as an antiviral agent for treating bronchitis, influenza and cold/damp pneumonia. Small amounts of Thuja can be used for chronic prostatitis and uterine fibroids.

Tincture - 10-15 drops (.5-.75 ml) TID.

CONTRAINDICATIONS: Not for use in pregnancy unless otherwise directed by qualified expert. Not for long-term use; do not exceed recommended dose.

Thyme *herb (Thymus vulgaris)* is a flavorful spice and a powerful antibacterial, carminative, antiviral, expectorant, antifungal and antioxidant. Thyme is useful for lung congestion, respiratory tract infections, damp coughs, sinus congestion, pertussis, colds, influenza and PCP pneumonia. Due to its essential oil content, Thyme is also useful for digestive upset, nausea, diarrhea, intestinal viruses (noro virus) and flatulence.

Tea - 1 tsp. of the dried herb to 8 oz. hot water, steep covered 20 minutes. Take 2-3 cups per day.

Tincture - 40-60 drops (2-3 ml) QID.

Turmeric *fresh rhizome (Curcuma longa)* is a powerful anti-inflammatory, immunoregulator and mild analgesic useful for the treatment of musculoskeletal conditions such as osteoarthritis, rheumatoid arthritis and bursitis. It is also effective for inflammatory diseases of the GI tract including ulcerative colitis, Crohn's disease, celiac disease, gastritis and gastric ulcers. Turmeric mildly lowers blood pressure, reduces LDL cholesterol levels, and reduces oxidative damage to the liver, blood vessels (atherosclerosis), and eyes. Curcumin extracted from Turmeric has been found to down-regulate over 70 procancer cell signaling pathways and oncogenes. Regular intake of this herb may inhibit bowel and other cancers. Turmeric has hepatoprotective activity and can help prevent viral or chemical-induced liver damage, as well as enhancing hepatic glutathione levels and promoting Phase II liver detoxification.

Tincture - 40-60 drops (2-3 ml) QID.

CONTRAINDICATIONS: Not for use in pregnancy unless otherwise directed by qualified expert. Therapeutic quantities should not be taken by people with bile duct obstruction or gallstones.

Usnea *lichen (Usnea barbata)* is a lichen, a symbiotic life form composed of an algae and a fungus. Usnea is a powerful antibacterial agent inhibiting gram positive bacteria (Streptococcus, Staphylococcus, Pneumococcus, Mycobacterium tuberculosis). It is also an antifungal agent (ringworm, athlete's foot) and it also inhibits trichomonas and Candida albicans. Usnea is an antispasmodic to the lung and large intestine. It can be used in protocols to treat IBS, strep throat, bronchitis, pleurisy, hot/damp pneumonia and cystitis.

Tincture - 20-30 drops (1-1.5 ml) TID/QID.

Uva-Ursi *leaf (Arctostaphylos uva-ursi)* is also known as Bearberry, and it has a long history of use for urinary tract infections. It is a source of the phytochemical arbutin, which is metabolized by the kidneys and excreted as antibacterial hydroquinones. Hydroquinones are an active antimicrobial especially in alkaline urine (do not use with Cranberry juice). It is useful for cystitis, urethritis, bacterial prostatitis, and mild nephritis.

Tea - 1 tsp. of the dried herb to 8 oz. hot water, steep 20-30 minutes. Take 4 oz. 3 times per day.

Tincture - 20-40 drops (1-2 ml) TID.

CONTRAINDICATIONS: Not for use in pregnancy unless otherwise directed by qualified expert. Avoid use in kidney disease and gastric irritation. Not for prolonged use without consulting a practitioner.

155

Valerian *fresh root (Valeriana officinalis)* is one of the most popular herbs in Europe and is widely known as a sedative and carminative. Combined with nervines like Passionflower, Skullcap, Lemon Balm or fresh Oat, it is useful for insomnia, anxiety, nervousness, nervous stomach or bowel and headaches due to stress. In a recent clinical trial Valerian was found to be effective for relieving menstrual cramps (Mirabi, et al., 2011).
Tincture - 40-60 drops (2-3 ml) TID.
CONTRAINDICATIONS: In a small number of people, Valerian acts as a stimulant rather than a sedative. Avoid use in people with heat signs (red head, liver fire headaches, or hypertension)

Violet *fresh herb (Viola sororia)* is both edible and medicinal as well as an attractive woodland wildflower. The herb is an alterative, laxative, nutritive and demulcent. An excellent lymphatic herb, Violet is used for chronic lymphatic swellings and impaired lymph drainage especially associated with constipation. It can be utilized for mastitis, lymphedema, lymphadenitis and cystic breast disease. Violet also has a long history of use in alterative formulas for treating cancer, arthritis and it is used orally and topically for inflammatory skin conditions.
Tea - 1-2 tsp. of the dried herb to 8 oz. hot water, steep 30-40 minutes. Take 1-2 cups per day.
Tincture - 20-30 drops (1-1.5 ml) TID.
CONTRAINDICATIONS: Diarrhea.

Watercress *fresh herb (Rorippa nasturtium-aquaticum)* is an aquatic plant that is a nutritional powerhouse. It is a rich source of carotenoids (lutein, beta-carotene, zeaxanthin), minerals (iron, calcium, magnesium, iodine, potassium), Vitamins C, B Complex and K and anticancer glucosinolates. Watercress is a cholagogue, stimulating liver and gallbladder function and activity. It is used for stagnant liver *qi*, biliousness and poor fat digestion. Watercress also nourishes the lungs and acts as an antiseptic expectorant and mild antiasthmatic herb. In a human study watercress improved antioxidant status, reduced lymphocyte DNA damage and enhanced systemic detoxification. It was even more effective in smokers than in non-smokers (Gill, et al., 2007)
Extract - 30-40 drops (1.5-2 ml) QID.

White Pond Lily *fresh root (Nymphaea odorata)* is a demulcent, astringent and antiseptic, with a long history of use as a women's herb. This aquatic plant is used orally and intra-vaginally for cervicitis, leucorrhea, vaginal irritation and as part of Eli Jones's uterine cancer formula. White Pond Lily is also indicated for acute gastro-intestinal disorders (diarrhea, enteritis, dysentery) or chronic bowel problems such as irritable bowel syndrome (IBS).
Tincture - 20-30 drops (1-1.5 ml) TID.

White Sage *leaf (Salvia apiana)* is an aromatic sage that is a carminative, antimicrobial and analgesic. Used as a gargle it reduces pain and inflammation caused by Strep throat or sore throat. Internally it is used with Saw Palmetto, Nettle root and Collinsonia for benign prostatic hyperplasia. White Sage inhibits prolactin secretion and can be used to stop the production of breast milk when weaning a child. Like its relative garden sage, White Sage can be used for flatulence, to help heal gastritis and to stop excessive sweating.

Tea - 1 tsp. of the dried herb to 8 oz. hot water, steep covered 30 minutes. Take 4 oz. 3 times per day.

Tincture - 20-30 drops (1-1.5 ml) TID.

Wild Cherry *bark (Prunus spp.)* has long been known as a respiratory antispasmodic. It is used for coughs associated with bronchitis, chest colds, pneumonia and pertussis. It is a common ingredient in cough syrups combined with Licorice, Red Clover and Honey. Wild Cherry bark can also be used for spasms of the diaphragm (hiccoughs), vocal cords, hiatal hernia, and for intercostal pain (use it with Black Haw and Pleurisy root).

Tea - 1-2 tsp. of the dried bark to 8 oz. cool water, steep for four to six hours (do not heat the tea), strain. Take 4 oz. 3 times per day.

Tincture - 20-40 drops (1-2 ml) TID.

CONTRAINDICATIONS: Do not exceed recommended dosage.

Wild Lettuce *herb (Lactuca spp.)* is a mild sedative, respiratory antispasmodic and analgesic. It can be used along with other sedative herbs for insomnia, anxiety and nervous headaches. By itself, or combined with Wild Cherry bark and Khella, it is useful for spasmodic coughs and smoker's cough.

Tea - 1 tsp. of the recently dried leaf to 8 oz. hot water, steep 20-30 minutes. Take 4 oz. 3 times per day.

Tincture - 30-40 drops (1.5-2 ml) TID.

Wild Yam *fresh root (Dioscorea villosa)* is indicated for biliousness, abdominal, uterine, ovarian or hepatic pain, colic, gas pain, gallbladder spasms, menstrual cramps and IBS. It can also be used as a mild anti-inflammatory agent for rheumatoid arthritis. Wild Yam is a cholagogue and can be used along with Celandine, Khella and Fringe Tree for gallstones (use this formula only under a physician's supervision). Despite its popular reputation for being hormonally active, this herb has little or no effect on menopausal symptoms, and does not contain any human hormones or compounds that can be converted into them in a living organism.

Tea - 1 tsp. of the dried cut/sifted root to 10 oz. water, decoct 15-20 minutes, steep 30 minutes. Take 2-4 oz. 3 or 4 times per day.

Tincture - 30-40 drops (1.5-2 ml) TID/QID.

Willow *bark (Salix spp.)* contains salicin, an aspirin-like chemical, and it is used for reducing fevers and for relief of pain caused by arthritis, rheumatoid arthritis, bursitis, back pain and headaches. While it takes longer to work than aspirin, its effect lasts longer than the pharmaceutical drug. Willow also contains tannins which make it effective for diarrhea with intestinal spasms. Willow does not appreciably thin the blood as aspirin does, nor is it likely to cause gastric bleeding.

Tea - 1-2 tsp. of the dried bark to 10 oz. water, decoct 10-15 minutes, steep 20 minutes. Take 4 oz. 3 times per day.
Tincture - 40-60 drops (2-3 ml) TID.

Witch Hazel *fresh leaf (Hamamelis virginica)* is one of the most popular and enduring botanical medicines. Unlike simple astringents, Witch Hazel contains essential oils such as eugenol which stimulate circulation. This herb can be used internally (not the commercial distilled product) and externally. Topically it is appropriate for bruises, aphthous stomatitis (as a gargle), sprains, hemorrhoids, diaper rash, episiotomy incisions, and bleeding gums. Internally it can be used for acute diarrhea, hemoptyisis and mild gastric bleeding.
Tincture - 20-40 drops (1-2 ml) TID.

Wood Betony *fresh flowering tops (Pedicularis groenlandica)* is a small semi-parasitic plant that has nervine, antispasmodic and analgesic qualities. The specific indications are for sore muscles caused by overwork, spasm or trauma. It can also be useful for stress headaches, anxiety, torticollis and for fibromyalgia pain (with Black Cohosh, White Peony and Ashwagandha).
Tea - 2 tsp. of the dried herb to 8 oz. hot water, steep 30 minutes. Take 4 oz. 4 times per day.
Tincture - 30-40 drops (1.5-2 ml) TID.
CONTRAINDICATIONS: Pregnancy.

Wormwood *herb (Artemisia absinthium)* is an intensely bitter tasting herb that was used since ancient times to stimulate digestion, absorption and elimination. Wormwood increases bile secretion, pancreatic and small intestine enzyme production and gastric hydrochloric acid secretion. It is used for GI dysbiosis, dyspepsia, non-obstructive jaundice, anorexia and liver stagnation. In two human trials, Wormwood was found to reduce symptoms of IBD and depression (Krebs, et al., 2010, Omer, et al., 2007).
Tincture - 15-20 drops (.75-1 ml) TID.
CONTRAINDICATIONS: Not for use in pregnancy unless otherwise directed by qualified expert. Not to be used while nursing. Not for long term use. Do not exceed recommended dose.

Yarrow *flowering herb (Achillea millefolium)* is an effective anti-inflammatory indicated in cases of irritable bowel disorder and irritation of the bladder or urethra. Yarrow is a diaphoretic, useful for colds and influenza, it is often used with Elderflower. It is an effective styptic useful for treating menorrhagia, hematuria, hemoptysis, gastric ulcers and hemorrhoids (sitz bath). It is also useful for healing the mucosa of the GI tract and can be used for chronic diarrhea, leaky gut syndrome, ulcerative colitis, gastritis and diverticulitis.
Tea - 1-2 tsp. of the dried flowering herb to 8 oz. hot water, steep covered 40 minutes. Take 2-3 cups per day.
Tincture - 30-50 drops (1.5-2.5 ml) TID.
CONTRAINDICATIONS: Pregnancy (theoretical concern).

Yellow Dock *fresh root (Rumex crispus)* is indicated for chronic skin problems i.e. psoriasis, eczema and acne especially with a serous discharge. It is used for liver and gallbladder insufficiency, jaundice, and impaired iron absorption. Yellow Dock is also a cholagogue, improving bile secretion and excretion as well as liver and bowel function. The Eclectic physicians also used this herb to treat cachexia associated with cancer and in small doses for dry, irritative coughs.
Tea - 1 tsp. of the dried root to 8 oz. water, decoct 15 minutes, then steep 1/2 hour. Take 4 oz. 2 times per day.
Tincture - 20-30 drops (1-1.5 ml) TID.
CONTRAINDICATIONS: Contains calcium oxalate. Use cautiously if there is a history of oxalate kidney stones.

Yellow Root *rhizome (Xanthorhiza simplicissima)* is a common shrub of the southeastern US, that was originally used by the Cherokee people and then by European settlers. It contains a yellow alkaloid Berberine, which is antibacterial, antifungal and antiviral. The herb can be used to treat thrush (mouthwash), vaginal candidiasis, urinary tract infections, gastritis, sore throats, sinus infections (as a nasal douche) and as a topical antibacterial. Yellow Root can also be used as a digestive bitter, liver tonic, and aperient.
Tea - 1 tsp. of the dried rhizome to 10 oz. water, decoct 10-15 minutes, steep 30 minutes. Take 4 oz. 3 times per day.
Tincture - 20-40 drops (1-2 ml) TID.
CONTRAINDICATIONS: Pregnancy (theoretical concern).

Yellow Sweetclover *fresh flowering tops (Melilotus spp.)* is also known as Sweet Melilot. It is an antispasmodic, analgesic, anti-inflammatory and diuretic. The specific indication for this herb is sharp stabbing pain such as optic neuralgia, sciatica, brachial nerve pain, migraines or ovarian neuralgia. The herb also strengthens vascular integrity and reduces capillary leakage and can be used to treat edema, varicose veins and trauma injuries.
Tincture - 30-40 drops (1.5-2 ml) TID.
CONTRAINDICATIONS: Pregnancy.

Yerba Santa *leaf (Eriodictyon californicum)* is native to California and is used as an expectorant and antispasmodic. It is used for cold/damp coughs and lung conditions with excess mucus such as damp asthma, damp bronchitis, allergic rhinitis and damp pneumonia. One of its constituents Eriodictyol inhibits mast cell degranulation and helped to prevent allergic response. Yerba Santa is also a urinary antiseptic used for treating cystitis, urethritis and bacterial prostatitis.
Tea - 1 tsp. of the dried leaf to 8 oz. hot water, steep 30 minutes. Take 4 oz. 3 or 4 times per day.
Tincture - 20-40 drops (1-2 ml) TID.

TOPICAL OILS/OINTMENTS

ARNICA INFUSED OIL

Arnica montana or A. corifolia (fresh flowering tops), infused into extra-virgin olive oil. White Sage is added as a stabilizer.

INDICATIONS/ACTIVITY: Arnica has been used topically in European, Eclectic and Homeopathic traditions since the 1800s. It is a topical anti-inflammatory and antinociceptive especially indicated for bruised, strained or overworked muscles, tendons, or ligaments. Arnica oil is frequently applied to traumatic bruises, sprains, contusions, dislocations and whiplash injuries. In human trials Arnica used topically was effective at resolving bruising (Leu, et al., 2010), as well as relieving osteoarthritic pain in the hands (Wildrig, et al., 2007), and knees (Knuesel, et al., 2002).

SUGGESTED USE: Apply 2-3 times per day or as needed. Discontinue use if skin irritation or a rash develops.

CONTRAINDICATIONS: Avoid use on abraded or damaged skin and in people with Asteraceae allergies.

CALENDULA OIL

Calendula officinalis (dried flowers), infused into extra-virgin olive oil. Vitamin E added as a stabilizer.

INDICATIONS/ACTIVITY: Calendula is used in homeopathic and European traditions for enhancing wound healing. It is an anti-inflammatory and antibacterial agent that enhances collagen synthesis in the skin. The oil is used topically to speed healing of wounds, cracked nipples, chapped lips, abrasions and diaper rash. In human trials topical Calendula improved healing of venous leg ulcers (Duran, et al., 2005) and prevented acute dermatitis induced by radiation therapy for breast cancer (Pommier, et al., 2004). In a case report Calendula was effective for treating exfoliative cheilitis (Roveroni-Favaretto, et al., 2009).

SUGGESTED USE: Apply 2-3 times per day or as needed. Discontinue use if skin irritation or a rash develops.

COMFREY/CALENDULA OINTMENT™

CONTAINS: Comfrey root (Symphytum officinale) and Calendula flowers (Calendula officinalis) infused into extra-virgin olive oil, beeswax, lanolin, propolis extract and vitamin E.

INDICATIONS/ACTIVITY: This ointment is a soothing, healing vulnerary, useful for dry, chapped skin (including chapped lips), rashes, minor cuts and abrasions, eczema, dermatitis, vulvodynia, vaginal dryness, rectal fissures, minor sunburns and hemorrhoids. Comfrey contains allantoin and soothing mucilage which enhances tissue healing and cellular repair. Calendula has antibacterial activity as well as promoting healing of skin and mucous membranes. Lanolin enhances absorption of this ointment and propolis acts as an antioxidant preservative and antibacterial agent.

CONTRAINDICATIONS: Avoid using near the eyes. Discontinue use if a rash develops. Do not use on puncture wounds.

SUGGESTED USE: Apply 2-3 times per day or as needed.

COMPOUND ARNICA OIL™

CONTAINS: Arnica fresh herb in flower (Arnica spp.), St. John's wort fresh flowering tops (Hypericum perforatum), Lobelia seed (Lobelia inflata) and essential oil of Wintergreen. White Sage and Vitamin E are added as stabilizers.

INDICATIONS/ACTIVITY: This formula, which I call "trauma oil", is appropriate for sprains/strains, contusions, torticollis, whiplash, minor muscle tears, or tendon and ligament injuries. Arnica is a time-tested homeopathic/herbal remedy for acute trauma pain. It is an analgesic and anti-inflammatory. St. John's wort is indicated for nerve pain (spinal pain, TMJ pain). Lobelia seed is an antispasmodic and analgesic, relieving spasms, contractures, and tenesmus, as well as the associated pain. The essential oil of Wintergreen contains methyl salicylate which is used to relieve pain and inflammation.

ADDITIONAL HERBS: For oral administration: Muscle/Joint Tonic™ as an anti-inflammatory, J. Kloss Anti-Spasmodic Compound as an antispasmodic and analgesic. Fit Adapt™ for over-worked muscles, along with Wood Betony, Ashwagandha, or Aspirea for pain and inflammation.

CONTRAINDICATIONS: Avoid use on abraded skin or open cuts. Avoid using near the eyes or mucous membranes. Discontinue use if a rash occurs.

SUGGESTED USE: Apply 2-3 times per day or more as needed. Gently massage into the "traumatized" tissue and apply heat or cold as indicated.

COMPOUND MULLEIN OIL™

CONTAINS: Mullein flower (Verbascum thapsus), St. John's wort fresh flowering tops (Hypericum perforatum), Garlic fresh bulb (Allium sativum) and essential oil of Tea Tree. White Sage and Vitamin E are added as stabilizers.

INDICATIONS/ACTIVITY: This formula is effective for treating acute ear infections such as otitis media with pain (use only if the eardrum is intact). Mullein flower oil is a useful analgesic, reducing ear pain. St. John's wort is anti-inflammatory and, along with the Garlic and Tea Tree oil, has antiviral and antibacterial activity. This formula alleviates pain and inflammation, inhibits common pathogens (bacteria, viruses, and fungi) that cause ear infections, especially in children.

ADDITIONAL SUGGESTIONS: Children with chronic otitis media have lower serum levels of zinc, vitamin C, and antioxidants. All should be added as supplements. Exposure to second hand smoke is a contributing factor to ear infections and even more importantly, consumption of dairy is a major causative factor for many children. Eliminating dairy from the diet (milk, cheese, yogurt) can bring about major improvements in some children.

ADDITIONAL HERBS: Oral doses of Echinacea and Eyebright tinctures are useful, as is Elderberry syrup or tincture.

CONTRAINDICATIONS: Consult your physician if you have ear pain or infection. Do not use if eardrum is perforated.

SUGGESTED USE: Lean head to the side so that the ear is facing upward. Place 3-6 drops in the ear before bedtime. Do not insert the dropper directly into the ear. Gently insert a cotton ball into the ear to prevent leakage. Remove cotton in the morning. Repeat for 2-4 weeks as needed.

DRAGON'S DREAM™ OIL

CONTAINS: Ginger rhizome infused into extra virgin olive oil, essential oils of Camphor, Eucalyptus, Menthol, Black Pepper, Peppermint, and Wintergreen.

INDICATIONS/ACTIVITY: This oil is a deeply penetrating topical analgesic for sore muscles, bruises, sprains and strains, arthritis, lumbago, headaches (apply to temples), bursitis, and stiff joints. Also can be applied to chest as an herbal decongestant for sinus and bronchial congestion. Ginger is a warming herb that promotes circulation and is also anti-inflammatory. Menthol and Black Pepper Essential Oil provide a numbing sensation to the local nerve endings offering relief from itching and pain. The essential oils of Camphor, Eucalyptus, Peppermint and Wintergreen provide an intense and fast-acting analgesic effect to relieve pain, stimulate local circulation, and decrease nerve sensitivity.

ADDITIONAL USEFUL HERBS: For oral administration: Muscle/Joint Tonic™ as an anti-inflammatory. J. Kloss Anti-Spasmodic Compound as an antispasmodic and analgesic. Fit Adapt™ for over-worked muscles, along with Wood Betony, Ashwagandha, or Aspirea for pain and inflammation.

CONTRAINDICATIONS: Do not use near the eyes or mucous membranes. It may be too strong for an infant's tender skin. Discontinue use if skin irritation or a rash develops.

SUGGESTED USE: Shake well before using. Apply to skin with cotton gauze or massage into skin until well absorbed. Use 2-3 times per day or as needed.

HYPERICUM OIL (St. John's wort Oil)

Hypericum perforatum (fresh flowering tops), infused into pure extra-virgin olive oil. White Sage and Vitamin E added as stabilizers.

INDICATIONS/ACTIVITY: This oil is antiviral, antinociceptive (reduces sensitivity to pain) and anti-inflammatory. Hypericum or St. John's wort oil is traditionaly used for nerve pain. It can be gently massaged into area's with inflamed nerve tissue (sciatica, torticollis, post-herpetic neuralgia, back pain) or applied to cracked nipples, burns and trauma injuries in areas with many nerve endings (fingertips, genitalia, lips, etc.). In human studies, topical Hypericum enhanced wound healing and reduced pain and scarring in women with episiotomy incisions (Samadi, et al., 2010) as well as improving atopic dermatitis (Schempp, et al., 2003).

CONTRAINDICATIONS: Avoid using in areas that will receive significant sun exposure within 2-4 hours of application.

SUGGESTED USE: Apply 2-3 times per day or as needed. Discontinue use if skin irritation or a rash develops.

ST. JOHN'S WORT/SAGE OINTMENT™

CONTAINS: St. John's wort flowering tops and White Sage leaves infused into pure extra virgin olive oil, beeswax and lanolin. Propolis extract and vitamin E added as stabilizers.

INDICATIONS/ACTIVITY: This product is a topical ointment that combines herbs with anti-inflammatory, antioxidant, antibacterial and antiviral activities. It is a useful vulnerary/antiseptic for minor cuts, abrasions, insect bites or stings, acne, impetigo, acne rosacea, herpes lesions, shingles, Staph infections, psoriasis and athlete's foot. St. John's wort has anti-inflammatory and antiviral activity. It has a long history of use, especially for nerve pain and nerve injuries. White Sage is a powerful antioxidant and antibacterial/viral agent. It inhibits a wide array of pathogens including bacteria, viruses, and fungi. Lanolin increases dermal absorption of the herbs in the ointment. Vitamin E is antioxidant and helps heal the skin and prevent scarring. Propolis is a powerful preservative and antibacterial/viral agent which further enhances this ointment's activity.

CONTRAINDICATIONS: Avoid using near the eyes or mucous membranes.

SUGGESTED USE: Apply 2-3 times per day or as needed. Discontinue use if a rash develops.

Bibliography:

Abenavoli, L., Capasso, R., et al, Milk Thistle in liver disease: past, present, future. Phytother Res. 2010 Oct;24(10):1423-32.

Agrawal, AK., Rao, CV., et al, Effect of Piper longum Linn, Zingiber officianalis Linn and Ferula species on gastric ulceration and secretion in rats. Indian J Exp Biol. 2000 Oct;38(10):994-8.

Agrawal, P., Rai, V., et al, Randomized placebo-controlled, single blind trial of Holy Basil leaves in patients with noninsulin-dependent diabetes mellitus. Int J Clin Pharmacol Ther. 1996 Sep;34(9):406-9.

Ahmad, MK., Mahdi, AA., et al, Withania somnifera improves semen quality by regulating reproductive hormone levels and oxidative stress in seminal plasma of infertile males. Fertil Steril 2010:94(3):989-96.

Ahmad, N., Hassan, MR., et al, Effect of Momordica charantia (Karolla) extracts on fasting and postprandial serum glucose levels in NIDDM patients. Bangladesh Med Res Counc Bull. 1999 Apr;25(1):11-3.

Ahmed, MS., Hou, SH., et al, Treatment of idiopathic membranous nephropathy with the herb Astragalus. Am J Kidney Dis. 2007 Dec;50(6):1028-32.

Akhondzadeh, S., Kashani, L., et al, Comparison of Lavandula angustifolia Mill. tincture and imipramine in the treatment of mild to moderate depression: a double blind, randomized trial. Prog Neuropsychopharmacol Biol Psychiatry. 2003;27(1):123-7.

Akhondzadeh, S., Noroozian, et al, Salvia officinalis extract in the treatment of patients with mild to moderate alzheimer's disease: a double blind, randomized and placebo-controlled trial. J Clin Pharm Ther. 2003;28(1):53-9.

Akilen, R., Tsiami, A., et al, Glycated haemoglobin and blood pressure-lowering effect of Cinnamon in multi-ethnic Type 2 diabetic patients in the UK: a randomized, placebo controlled, double-blind clinical trial. Diabet Med. 2010 Oct;27(10):1159-67.

Aleksander, SK., Fidler, LM., et al, Effect of potassium iodide on tumor growth. Biull Eksp Biol Med. 1991 Jan;111(1):64-6.

Ali, MS., Ibrahim, et al, Ursolic Acid: A potent inhibitor of superoxides produced in the cellular system. Phytother Res. 2007;21(6):558-61.

Altman, RD., Marcussen, KC., Effects of a Ginger extract on knee pain in patients with osteoarthritis. Arthirits Rheum. 2001 Nov;44(11):2531-8.

Amagase, H., Nance, DM., A randomized, double-blind, placebo-controlled, clinical study of the general effects of a standardized Lycium barbarum (Goji) juice, GoChi. J Altern Complement Med. 2008 May;14(4):403-12.

Amagase, H., Nance, DM., Lycium barbarum increases caloric expenditure and decreases waist circumference in healthy overweight men and women: pilot study. J Am Coll Nutr. 2011 Oct;30(5):304-9.

Ament, PW., Bertolino, JG., et al, Clinically significant drug interactions. Am Fam Physician. 2000 Mar 15;61(6):1745-54.

Amsterdam, JD., Li, Y., et al, A randomized, double-blind, placebo-controlled trial of oral Matricaria recutita (Chamomile) extract therapy for generalized anxiety disorder. J Clin Psychopharmacol. 2009 Aug;29(4):378-82.

Anand, CL., Effect of Avena sativa on cigarette smoking. Nature. 1971; 233(5320):496.

Anbarasi, K., Vani, G., et al, Protective effect of Bacoside A on cigarette smoking-induced brain mitochondrial dysfunction in rats. J Environ Pathol Toxicol Oncol. 2005;24(3):225-34.

Anonymous, ESCOP Monographs, The Scientific Foundation For Herbal Medicinal Products, 2nd ed., New York, 2003.

Anonymous, General practive study with Nettle extract. Arthrosis patient need fewer non-steroidal anti-inflammatory drugs. MMW Fortschr Med. 2002 Jun 27;144(26):52.

Arck, P., Handjiski, B., et al, Is there a 'gut-brain-skin axis'?. Exp Dermatol. 2010 May;19(5):401-5.

Asgary, S., Sahebkar, A., et al, Clinical evaluation of blood pressure lowering, endothelial function improving, hypolipidemic and anti-inflammatory effects of Pomegranate juice in hypertensive subjects. Phytother Res. 2014;28:193-199.

Askari, F., Rashidkhani, B., et al, Cinnamon may have therapeutic benefits on lipid profile, liver enzymes, insulin resistance, and high-sensitivity C-reactive protein in nonalcoholic fatty liver disease patients. Nutr Res. 2014 Feb;34(2):143-8.

Auf'mkolk, M., Ingbar, JC., et al, Extracts and auto-oxidized constituents of certain plants inhibit the receptor-binding and the biological activity of Graves' immunoglobulins. Endocrinology. 1985 May;116(5):1687-93.

Babayigit, A., Olmez, D., Effects of Ginkgo biloba on airway histology in a mouse model of chronic asthma. Allergy Asthma Proc. 2009 Mar-Apr;30(2):186-91

Bai, W., Henneicke-von Zepelin, HH., et al, Efficacy and tolerability of a medicinal product containing an isopropanolic Black Cohosh extract in Chinese women with menopausal symptoms: A randomized, double blind, parallel-controlled study versus tibolone. Maturitas. 2007 Sep 20;58(1):31-41.

Bailey, DT., Dalton, C., et al, Can a concentrated Cranberry extract prevent recurrent urinary tract infections in women? A Pilot Study. Phytomedicine. 2007;14(4):237-41.

Balbir-Gurman, A., Fuhrman, B., et al, Consumption of Pomegranate decreases serum oxidative stress and reduces disease activity in patients with active rheumatoid arthritis: a pilot study. Isr Med Assoc J. 2011 Aug;13(8):474-9.

Bartram, T. Encyclopedia of Herbal Medicine, Dorset, 1998.

Baskaran, K., Kizar Ahamath, B., Antidiabetic effect of a leaf extract from Gymnema sylvestre in non-insulin-dependent diabetes mellitus patients. J Ethnopharmacol. 1990 Oct;30(3):295-300.

Basu, A., Lyons, TJ., Strawberries, Blueberries and Cranberries in the metabolic syndrome: clinical perspectives. J Agric Food Chem. 2012 Jun 13;60(23):5687-92.

Bell, DR., Gochenaur, K.. Direct vasoactive and vasoprotective properties of anthocyanin-rich extracts. J Appl Physiol. 2006;100(4):1164-70.

Bensky, D., Clavey, S., et al, Chinese Herbal Medicine - Materia Medica, 3rd ed.,

Seattle, 2004.

Boudjelal, A., Henchiri C, et al, Compositional analysis and in vivo anti-diabetic activity of wild Algerian Marrubium vulgare L. infusion. Fitoterapia. 2012 Mar;83(2):286-92.

Boericke, W., MD. Pocket Manual of Homeopathic Materia Medica, New Delhi, 1976.

Bommer, S., Klein, P., et al, First time proof of Sage's tolerability and efficacy in menopausal women with hot flushes. Adv Ther. 2011;28(6):490-500.

Bone, K., Clinical Applications of Ayurvedic and Chinese Herbs. Queensland, Australia, 1996.

Bone, K., Crataegus - more than the heart? Brit J. Phytother. 1991-2;(3):115-27.

Bortolotti, M., Coccia, G., et al, The treatment of functional dyspepsia with red pepper. Aliment Pharmacol Ther. 2002 Jun;16(6):1075-82.

Bradley, P. [ed.], British Herbal Compendium, vol. 1, Dorset, England, 1992.

Brattstrom, A., Long-term effects of St. John's wort (Hypericum perforatum) treatment: a year safety study in mild to moderate depression. Phytomedicine. 2009 Apr;16(4):277-83.

Briese, V., Stammwitz, U., et al, Black Cohosh with or without St. John's wort for symptom-specific climacteric treatment-results of a large-scale, controlled observational study. Maturitas. 2007 Aug 20;57(4):405-14.

Bright, JJ., Curcumin and Autoimmue Disease. Adv Exp Med Biol. 2007;595:425-51.

Bucheli, P., Vidal, K., et al, Goji berry effects on macular characteristics and plasma antioxidant levels. Optom Vis Sci. 2011 Feb;88(2):257-62.

Butterweck, V., Derendorf, H., et al, Pharmacokinetic herb-drug interactions: are preventive screenings necessary and appropriate? Planta Med. 2004 Sep;70(9):784-91.

Calabrese, C., Gregory, WL., et al, Effects of a Standardized Bacopa monnieri extract on cognitive performance, anxiety, and depression in the elderly: a randomized, double-blind, placebo-controlled trial. J Altern Complement Med. 2008; 14(6):707-13.

Chan, HC., Chang, RC., et al, Neuroprotective effects of Lycium barbarum Lynn on protecting retinal ganglion cells in an ocular hypertension model of glaucoma. Exp Neurol. 2007 Jan;203(1):269-73.

Chang, HM., But, PP.. Pharmacology and Applications of Chinese Materia Medica, Singapore, 1986. Vol. I & II.

Chatterjee, A., Yasmin, et al, Inhibition of Helicobacter pylori in vitro by various berry extracts, with enhanced susceptibility to clarithyromycin. Mol Cell Biochem. 2004;265(1-2):19-26.

Chen, CX., Kwan, CY., Endothelium-independent vasorelaxation by Leonurine, a plant alkaloid purified from Chinese Motherwort. Life Sci 2001;68(8):953-60.

Chen, J. & T., Chinese Medical Herbology and Pharmacology, City of Industry, CA, 2004.

Chen, JT., Tominaga, K., et al, Maitake mushroom (Grifola frondosa) extract induces ovulation in patients with polycystic ovary syndrome: A possible monotherapy and a combination therapy after failure with first-line clomiphene citrate. J Altern Complement Med. 2010;16(12):1295-9.

Chen, JZ., Clinical effect of chemotherapy combined with Chinese herbs and western drugs on leukocytes of gastric cancer patients. [article in Chinese] Zhong Xi Yi Jie He Za Zhi. 1990 Dec;10(12):717-9.

Chidrawar, VR., Patel, KN., et al, Antiobesity effect of Stellaria media against drug induced obesity in Swiss albino mice. Ayu. 2011 Oct;32(4):576-84.

Chong, NJ., Aziz, Z., A systematic review of the efficacy of Centella asiatica for improvement of the signs and symptoms of chronic venous insufficiency. Evid Based Complement Alternat Med. 2013;2013:627182

Chou, SC., Everngam, MC., et al, Antibacterial activity of components from Lomatium californicum. Phytother Res. 2006 Feb;20(2):153-6.

Chrubasik, S., Eisenberg, E., et al, Treatment of low back pain exacerbation with Willow Bark extract: a randomized double-blind study. Am J Med. 2000 Jul;109(1):9-14.

Chung, IW., Moore, NA., et al, Behavioural pharmacology of Polygalasaponins indicates potential antipsychotic efficacy. Pharmacol Biochem Behav 2002; 71(1-2):191-5.

Circosta, C., Pasquale, RD., et al, Estrogenic activity of standardized extract of Angelica sinensis. Phytother Res. 2006 Aug;20(8):665-9.

Conaway, CC., Yang, AYM., Isothiocyanates as cancer chemopreventive agents: their biological activities and metabolism in rodents and humans. Curr Drug Metab. 2002 Jun;3(3):233-55.

Dasgupta, A., Kidd, L., et al, Interference of Hawthorn on serum digoxin measurements by immunoassays and pharmacodynamic interaction with digooxin. Arch Pathol Lab Med. 2010;134(8):1188-92.

de Andrade, E., de Mesquita, AA., et al, Study of the efficacy of Korean Red Ginseng in the treatment of erectile dysfunction. Asian J Androl. 2007 Mar;9(2):241-4.

de Bock, M., Derraik, JG., et al, Olive (Olea europaea L.) leaf polyphenols improve insulin sensitivity in middle-aged overweight men: a randomized, placebo-controlled, crossover trial. PLoS One. 2013;8(3):e57622.

Degenring, FH., Suter, et al, A Randomised double blind placebo controlled clinical trial of a standardised extract of fresh Crataegus berries (Crataegisan) in the treatment of patients with congestive heart failure NYHA II. Phytomedicine. 2003;10(5):363-9.

Devra, DK., Mathur, KC., et al, Effect of Tulsi (Ocimum sanctum Linn.) on Clinical and Biochemical Parameters of Metabolic Syndrome. J Nat Remedies. 2012;12(1):63–7.

Dhanasekaran, M., Tharakan, et al, Neuroprotective mechanisms of ayurvedic antidementia botanical Bacopa monniera. Phytother Res. 2007;21(10):965-9.

Diener, HC., Pfaffenrath, V., et al, Efficacy and safety of 6.25 mg t.i.d. Feverfew CO2-extract (MIG-99) in mirgraine prevention-a randomized, double-blind, multicentre, placebo-controlled study. Cephalagia. 2005 Nov;25(11):1031-41.

Dimpfel, W., Suter, A., Sleep improving effects of a single dose administration of a valerian/hops fluid extract - a double blind, randomized, placebo-controlled sleep-EEG study in a parallel design using electrohypnograms. Eur J Med Res. 2008 May 26;13(5):200-4.

DiMartino, P., Agniel, R., et al, Reduction of Escherichia coli adherence to uroepithelial bladder cells after consumption of Cranberry juice: A double-blind randomized placebo-controlled cross-over trial. World J Urol. 2006;24(1).

Ding, CG., Tian, PX., et al, Clinical application and exploration on mechanism of action of Cordyceps sinensis mycelia preparation for renal transplantation recipients. [article in Chinese] Zhongguo Zhong Xi Yi Jie He Za Zhi. 2009 Nov;29(11):975-8.

Ding, C., Tian, PX., et al, Efficacy of Cordyceps sinensis in long term treatment of renal translplant. Front Biosci (elite ed.). 2011 Jan 1;3:301-7.

Dording, CM., Fisher, L., et al, A double blind, randomized, pilot dose-finding study of Maca root (L.meyenii) for the management of SSRI-Induced sexual dysfunction. CNS Neurosci Ther. 2008;14(3):182-91.

Dwoskin, LP., Crooks, PA., A novel mechanism of action and potential use for Lobeline as a treatment for psychostimulant abuse. Biochem Pharmacol. 2002; 63(2):89-98.

Duran, V., Matic, M., et al, Results of the clinical examinations of an ointment with Marigold (Calendula officinalis) extract in the treatment of venous leg ulcers. Int J Tissue React. 2005;27(3):101-6.

Eggeling, T., Regitz-Zagrosek, V., et al, Baseline severity but not gender modulates quantified Crataegus extract effects in early heart failure-a pooled analysis of clinical trials. Phytomedicine. 2011 Nov 15;18(14):1214-9.

Ellingwood, F., American Materia Medica, Therapeutics & Pharmacognosy, Evanston, IL, 1919.

Fan, C., Song, J., et al, A comparison of the hemostatic effects of Notoginseng and Yun Nan Bai Yao to placebo control. J Herb Pharmacother. 2005;5(2):1-5.

Felter, HW., The Eclectic Materia Medica, Pharmacology and Therapeutics, Cincinnati, 1922.

Felter, HW., Lloyd, JU., King's American Dispensatory, 19th edition, Cincinnati, 1905.

Finley, JW., Kong, AN., et al, Antioxidants in foods: state of the science important to the food industry. J Ag Food Chem. 2011 Jul;59(13):6837-46.

Futrakul, N., Panichakul, T., et al, Ganoderma lucidum suppresses endothelial cell cytotoxicity and proteinuria in persistent proteinuric focal segmental glomerulosclerosis (FSGS) nephrosis. Clin Hemorheol Microcirc. 2004;31(4):267-72.

Gaddam, A., Galla, C., et al, Role of Fenugreek in the prevention of type 2 diabetes mellitus in prediabetes. J Diabetes Metab Disord. 2015 Oct 2;14:74.

Gao, JL., He, TC., et al, A traditional Chinese medicine formulation consisting of rhizoma Corydalis and rhizoma Curcumae exerts synergistic anti-tumor activity. Oncol Rep. 2009 Nov;22(5):1077-83.

Gardner, Z. & McGuffin, M., (Eds.). Botanical Safety Handbook, Second Edition, Boca Raton, CRC Press, 2013.

Gastpar, M., Klimm, HD., Treatment of anxiety, tension and restlessness states with Kava special extract WS 1490 in general practice: a randomized placebo-controlled double-blind multicenter trial. Phytomedicine. 2003 Nov;10(8):631-9.

Geier, FP., Konstantinowicz, T., Kava treatment in patients with anxiety, Phytother Res. 2004 Apr;18(4):297-300.

Gettman, MT., Ogan, K., et al, Effect of Cranberry juice consumption on urinary stone risk factors. J Urol. 2005;174(2):590-4.

Ghosal, S., Prasad, BN., et al, Antiamoebic activity of Piper longum fruits against Entamoeba histolytica in vitro and in vivo. J Ethnopharmacol. 1996 Mar; 50(3):167-70.

Gill, CI., Haldar, S., et al, Watercress supplementation in diet reduces lymphocyte DNA damage and alters blood antioxidant status in healthy adults. Am J Clin Nutr. 2007;85(2):504-10.

Göbel, H., Heinze, A., et al, Effect of Harpagophytum procumbens LI 174 (devil's claw) on sensory, motor und vascular muscle reagilbility in the treatment of unspecific back pain. Schmerz. 2001 Feb;15(1):10-8.

Gossé, F., Guyot, S., et al, Chemopreventative properties of apple procyanidins on human colon cancer-derived metastatic SW620 Cells and in a rat model of colon carcinogenesis. Carcinogenesis. 2005;26(7):1291-5.

Gotteland, M., Andrews, M., et al, Modulation of Helicobacter pylori colonization with Cranberry juice and Lactobacillus johnsonii La1 in children. Nutrition. 2008;24(5):421-6.

Gupta, A., Gupta, R., et al, Effect of Trigonella foenum-graecum (fenugreek) seeds on glycaemic control and insulin resistance in type 2 diabetes mellitus: a double blind placebo controlled study. J Assoc Physicians India. 2001 Nov;49:1057-61.

Grzanna, R., Lindmakr, L., et al, Ginger-- An herbal medicinal product with broad anti-inflammatory actions. J Med Food. 2005;8(2):125-32.

Habs, M., Prospective, comparative cohort studies and their contribution to the benefit assessments of therapeutic options: heart failure treatment with and without Hawthorn special extracts WS 1442. Forsch Komplementarmed Klass Naturheilkd. 2004 Aug;11(Suppl 1):36-9.

Hasa, D., Perissutti, B., et al, Rationale of using Vinca minor Linne dry extract phytocomplex as a vincamine's oral bioavailability enhancer. Eur J Pharm Biopharm. 2013 May;84(1):138-44.

Hasanudin, K., Hashim, P., et al, Corn silk (Stigma maydis) in healthcare: a phytochemical and pharmacological review. Molecules. 2012 Aug 13;17(8):9697-715.

Hobbs, C., Medicinal Mushrooms, Capitola, CA, 1995.

Hobbs, C., Usnea: The Herbal Antibiotic, Capitola, CA, 1990.

Holm, K., Mäki, M., et al, Oats in the treatment of childhood coeliac disease: A 2-year controlled trial and a long-term clinical follow-up study. Aliment Pharmacol Ther. 2006;23(10):1463-72.

Holtmann, G., Adam, B., et al, Efficacy of Artichoke leaf extract in the treatment of patients with functional dyspepsia: a six-week placebo-controlled, double-blind, multicentre trial. Aliment Pharmacol Ther. 2003 Dec;18(11-12):1099-105.

Hong, B., Ji, YH., et al, A double-blind crossover study evaluating the efficacy of Korean Red Ginseng in patients with erectile dysfunction; a preliminary report. J Urol. 2002 Nov;168(5):2070-3.

Hung, SK., Perry, R., et al, The effectiveness and efficacy of Rhodiola rosea L.: A systematic review of randomized clinical trials. Phytomedicine. 2011;18(4):235-44.

Ihl, R., Tribanek, M., et al, Efficacy and tolerability of a once daily formulation of Ginkgo biloba extract EGb 761® in Alzheimer's disease and vascular dementia: results from a randomised controlled trial. Pharmacopsychiatry. 2012 Mar;45(2):41-6.

Ivanova, D., Vankova, D., et al, Agrimonia eupatoria tea consumption in relation to markers of inflammation, oxidative status and lipid metabolism in healthy subjects. Arch Physiol Biochem. 2013 Feb:119(1):32-7.

Jamshidi, N., Cohen, MM.. The Clinical Efficacy and Safety of Tulsi in Humans: A Systematic Review of the Literature. Evid Based Complement Alternat Med. 2017;2017:9217567.

Jang, DJ., Lee, MS., et al, Red ginseng for treating erectile dysfunction: a systematic review. Br J Clin Pharmacol. 2008 Oct;66(4):444-50.

Jawad, M., Schoop, R., et al, Safety and efficacy profile of Echinacea purpurea to prevent common cold episodes: A randomized, double-blind, placebo-controlled trial. Evid Based Complement Alternat Med. 2012;2012:841315.

Jeong, HG., Ko, YH., et al, Effect of Korean Red Ginseng as an adjuvant treatment for women with residual symptoms of major depression. Asia Pac Psychiatry. 2015 Sep;7(3):330-6.

Jepson, RG., Craig, JC., Cranberries for preventing urinary tract infections. Cochrane Database Syst Rev. 2008;23(1):CD 001321.

Jia, H., Jiang, Y., et al, Tenuigenin treatment decreases secretion of the alzheimer's disease amyloid beta-protein in cultured cells. Neurosci Lett. 2004;367(1):123-8.

Jiang, X-L., Cui, H-F., Different therapy for different types of ulcerative colitis in China. World J Gastroenterol. 2004 May 15;10(10):1513-20.

Jones, E., Cancer, Its Causes, Symptoms and Treatment. Boston, 1911.

Joseph, JA., Shukitt-Hale, B., et al, Reversals of age-related declines in neuronal signal transduction, cognitive and motor behavioral deficits with Blueberry, Spinach or Strawberry dietary supplementation. J Neurosci. 1999;19(18):8114-21.

Joshi, T., Sah, SP., et al, Antistress activity of ethanolic extract of Asparagus racemosus Willd roots in mice. Indian J Exp Biol. 2012 Jun;50(6):419-24.

Juliá Mollá, MD., Garcia-Sánchez, Y., et al, Cimicifuga racemosa treatment and health related quality of life in post-menopausal Spanish woman. Gynecol Endocrinol. 2009 Jan;25(1):21-6.

Jung, JH., Park, HT., et al, Therapeutic effect of korean red ginseng extract on infertility caused by polycystic ovaries. J Ginseng Res. 2011 Jun;35(2):250-5.

Kassaian, N., Azadbakht, L., et al, Effect of Fenugreek seeds on blood glucose and lipid profiles in type 2 diabetic patients. Int J Vitam Nutr Res. 2009 Jan;79(1):

34-9.

Kassi, E., Papoutsi, Z., et al, Greek plant extracts exhibit selective estrogen receptor modulator (SERM)-like properties. J Agric Food Chem. 2004,52(23):6956-61.

Kemppainen, T., Janatuinen, E., et al, No observed local immunological response at cell level after five years of Oats in adult coeliac disease. Scand J Gastroenterol 2007;42(1):54-9.

Kemppainen, TA., Heikkinen, MT., et al, Unkilned and large amounts of Oats in the coeliac disease diet: A randomized, controlled study. Scand J Gastroenterol. 2008;43(9).

Kim, EH., Shim, B., et al, Anti-inflammatory effects of Scutellaria baicalensis extract via suppression of immune modulators and MAP kinase signaling molecules. J Ethnopharmacol. 2009 Nov 12;126(2):320-31.

Kim, HG., Cho, JH., et al, Antifatigue effects of Panax ginseng C.A. Meyer: a randomised, double-blind, placebo-controlled trial. PLos One. 2013 Apr 17;8(4):e61271.

Kim, SY., Seo, SK., Effects of red ginseng supplementation on menopausal symptoms and cardiovascular risk factors in postmenopausal women: a double-blind randomized controlled trial. Menopause. 2012 Apr;19(4):461-6.

Kim, TH., Jeon, SH., et al, Effects of tissue-cultured mountain Ginseng (Panax ginseng CA Meyer) extract on male patients with erectlie dysfunction. Asian J Androl. 2009 May;11(3):356-61.

Knuesel, O., Weber, M., et al, Arnica montana gel in osteoarthritis of the knee: an open, multicenter clinical trial. Adv Ther. 2002;19(5):209-18.

Koetter, U., Schrader, E., et al, A randomized, double blind, placebo-controlled, prospective clinical study to demonstrate clinical efficacy of a fixed Valerian Hops extract combination (ZE 91019) in patients suffering from non-organic sleep disorder. Phytother res. 2007 Sep;21(9):847-51.

Koch, E., Malek, FA., Standardized extracts from Hawthorn leaves and flowers in the treatment of cardiovascular disorders--preclinical and clinical studies. Planta Med. 2011 Jul;77(11):1123-8.

Koo, H., Nino de Guzman, P., et al, Influence of Cranberry juice on glucan-mediated processes involved in Streptococcus mutans biofilm development. Caries Res. 2006;40(1):20-7.

Kort, DH., Lobo, RA.. Preliminary evidence that cinnamon improves menstrual cyclicity in women with polycystic ovary syndrome: a randomized controlled trial. Am J Obstet Gynecol. 2014 Nov;211(5):487.e1-6.

Krebs, S., Omer, TN., et al, Wormwood (Artemisia absinthium) Suppresses tumor necrosis factor alpha and accelerates healing in patients with crohn's disease - A controlled clinical trial. Phytomedicine. 2010;17(5):305-9.

Kreydiyyeh, SI., Usta, J., Diuretic effect and mechanism of action of Parsley. J Ethnopharmacol. 2002 Mar;79(3):353-7.

Krishnamurthy, S., Garabadu, D., et al, Asparagus racemosus modulates the hypothalamic-pituitary-adrenal axis and brain monoaminergic systems in rats. Nutr Neurosci. 2013 Nov;16(6):255-61.

Kuhn, M., Winston, D., Winston & Kuhn's Herbal Therapy & Supplements: A

Scientific & Traditional Approach. Philadelphia, 2007.

Kumar, SN., Mani, UV., et al, An open label study on the supplementation of Gymnema sylvestre in type 2 diabetics. J Diet Suppl. 2010 Sep;7(3):273-82.

Kuts-Cheraux, AW., Naturae Medicina and Naturopathic Dispensatory. Des Moines, 1953.

Lai, SW., Yu, MS., et al, Novel neuroprotective effects of the aqueous extracts from Verbena officinalis Linn. Neuropharmacology. 2006;50(6):641-50.

Lau, FC., Shukitt-Hale, B., et al, The beneficial effects of fruit polyphenols on brain aging. Neurobiol Aging. 2005 Dec;26 Suppl 1:128-32.

Lau, KM., Lai, KK., et al, Synergistic interaction between Astralgali radix and Rehmanniae radix in a chinese herbal formula to promote diabetic wound healing., J Ethnopharmacol. 2012 May;141(1):250-6.

Larramendi, CH., García-Abujeta, JL., et al, Goji berries (Lycium barbarum): risk of allergic reactions in individuals with food allergy. J Investig Allergol Clin Immunol. 2012;22(5):345-50.

Lavinge, JP., Bourg, G., et al, Cranberry (Vaccinium macrocarpon) and urinary tract infections: study model and review of literature. Pathol Biol. (Paris) 2007 Nov;55(8-9):460-4.

Lee, JY., Kim, KY., et al, Effects of BT-11 on memory in healthy humans. Neurosci Lett. 2009 Apr 24;454(2):111-4.

Leu, S., Havey, J., et al, Accelerated resolution of laser-induced bruising with topical 20% Arnica: a rater-blinded randomized controlled trial. 2010;163(3):557-63.

Li, MH., Zhang, HL., et al, Effects of Ginkgo leave [sic] concentrated oral liquor in treating asthma. [article in Chinese] Zhongguo Zhong Xi Yi Jie He Za Zhi. 1997 Apr;17(4):216-8.

Li, Shizhen, Compendium of Materia Medica (Bencao Gang Mu), Beijing, 2003.

Li, Y., Tran, VH., et al, Preventive and protective properties of Zingiber officinale (Ginger) in diabetes mellitus, diabetic complications, and associated lipid and other metabolic disorders: a brief review. Evid Based Complement Alternat Med. 2012;2012:516870.

Li, Y., Xue, WJ., et al, Clinical application of Cordyceps sinensis on immunosuppressive therapy in renal transplantation. Transplant Proc. 2009 Jun;41(5):1565-9.

Liao, HJ., Chen, XM., et al, Effect of Epimedium sagittatum on quality of life and cellular immunity in patients of hemodialysis maintenance. [article in Chinese] Zhongguo Zhong Xi Yi Jie He Za Zhi. 1995;15(4):202-4.

Liao, ZG., Liang, XL., et al, Correlation between synergistic action of Radix Angelica dahurica extracts on analgesic effects of Corydalis alkaloid and plasma concentration of dl-THP. J Ethnopharmacol. 2010 May 4;129(1):115-20.

Lien, HC., Sun, WM., et al, Effects of Ginger on motion sickness and gastric slow-wave dysrhythmias induced by circular vection. Am J Physiol, Gastrointest Liver Physiol. 2003 Mar;284(3):G481-9.

Lindenmuth, GF., Lindenmuth, EB., The efficacy of Echinacea compound herbal tea preparation on the severity and duration of upper respiratory and flu symptoms: a randomized double-blind placebo-controlled study. J Altern Complement

Med. 2000 Aug;6(4):327-34.

Liu, Y., Gallardo-Moreno, AM., et al, Cranberry changes the physiochemical surface properties of E. coli and adhesion with uroepithelial cells. Colloids Surf B Biointerfaces. 2008 Aug 1;65(1):35-42).

Liu, Z., Yang, ZQ., et al. Antiviral activity of the effective monomers from Folium Isatidis against influenza virus in vivo. Virol Sin. 2010 Dec;25(6):445-51.

Lloyd, JU. A Treatise on Cactus grandiflorus, Cincinnati, 1923.

Lloyd, JU. A Treatise on Collinsonia, Cincinnati, 1904.

Lloyd, JU. A Treatise on Crataegus, Cincinnati, 1917.

Lloyd, JU. A Treatise on Scutellaria, Cincinnati, 1908.

Lo, HY., Ho, TY., et al, Momordica charantia and its novel polypeptide regulate glucose homeostasis in mice via binding to insulin receptor. J Agric Food Chem. 2013 Mar 13;61(10):2461-8.

Locke, FJ., MD and Felter, HW., MD. Syllabus of Eclectic Materia Medica, Cincinnati, 1901.

Lockyer, S., Rowland, I., et al, Impact of phenolic-rich olive leaf extract on blood pressure, plasma lipids and inflammatory markers: a randomised controlled trial. Eur J Nutr. 2017 Jun;56(4):1421-1432.

Low Dog, T., Micozzi, M., Women's Health in Complementary and Integrative Medicine. St. Louis, MO, 2005.

Lu, T., Sheng, H., Cinnamon extract improves fasting blood glucose and glycosylated hemoglobin level in Chinese patients with type 2 diabetes. Nutr Res. 2012 Jun;32(6):408-12.

Lukas, SE., Penetar, D., et al, A standardized Kudzu extract (NPI-031) reduces alcohol consumption in nontreatment-seeking male heavy drinkers. Psychopharmacology (Berl). 2013 Mar;226(1):65-73.

Luo, Q., Cai, Y., et al, Hypoglycemic and hypolipidemic effects and antioxidant activity of fruit extracts from Lycium barbarum. Life Sci. 2004 Nov 26;76(2):137-49.

Masteiková, R., Muselík, J., et al, Antioxidant activity of tinctures prepared from Hawthorn fruits and Motherwort herb. Ceska Slov Farm. 2008;57(10):35-8.

Mazzanti, G., Battinelli, L., et al, Inhibitory activity of Melissa officinalis L. extract on Herpes simplex virus type 2 replication. Nat Prod Res. 2008;22(16);1433-40.

McKay, DL., Blumberg, JB., A review of the bioactivity and potential health benefits of Peppermint tea (Mentha piperita L.). 2006;20(8):619-33.

McKee, SA., Sinha, R., et al, Stress decreases the ability to resist smoking and potentiates smoking intensity and reward. J Psychopharmacol. 2011 Apr;25(4):490-502.

McQuade-Crawford, A., Herbal Remedies for Women, Rocklin CA, 1997.

McQuade-Crawford, A., The Herbal Menopause Book, Freedom, CA, 1997.

Melnikovova, I., Havlik, J., et al, Macamides and fatty acids content comparison in Maca cultivated plant under field conditions and greenhouse. Boletín Latinoamericano y del Caribe de Plantas medicinales y Armomáticas. 2012;11(5):420-427.

Milhowska-Leyck, K., Filipek, B., et al, Pharmacological effects of lavandulifolioside from Leonurus cardiaca. J Ethnopharmacol. 2002;80(1):85-90.

173

Mills, S., Bone, K., Principles and Practice of Phytotherapy, Edinburgh, 2000.

Mills, S., Bone, K., The Essential Guide To Herbal Safety, St. Louis, MO, 2005.

Mingji, P., Cancer Treatment With Fu Zheng Pei Ben Principle, Fujian, China 1992, 467pp.

Mirabi, P., Dolatian, M., et al, Effects of Valerian on the severity and systemic manifestations of dysmenorrhea. Int J Gynaecol Obstet. 2011 Dec;115(3):285-8.

Mitchell, W., ND. Plant Medicine in Practice, St. Louis, MO, 2003.

Miura, T., Chiba, M., et al. Apple procyanidins induce tumor-cell apoptosis through mitochondrial pathway activation of Caspase-3. Carcinogenesis. 2008;29(3):585-93.

Mohamed, DA., Al-Okbi, SY.. Evaluation of anti-gout activity of some plant food extracts. Pol J Food Nutr Sci. 2008;58(3):389-395.

Moore, M., Medicinal Plants of the Desert and Canyon West, Santa Fe, 1989.

Moore, M., Medicinal Plants of the Mountain West, Santa Fe, 2nd ed., 2003.

Moore, M., Medicinal Plants of the Pacific West, Santa Fe, 1993.

Morgan, A., Stevens, J., Does Bacopa monnieri improve memory performance in older persons? Results of a randomized, placebo-controlled double blind trial. J Altern Complement Med. 2010 Jul;16(7):753-9.

Morin, CM., Koetter, U., et al, Valerian-Hops combination and diphenhydramine for treating insomnia; a randomized placebo-controlled clinical trial. Sleep. 2005 Nov;28(11):1465-71.

Naito, R., Tohda, C., Characterization of Anti-neurodegenerative effects of Polygala tenuifolia in Abeta(25-35)-treated cortical neurons. Biol Pharm Bull. 2006;29(9):1892-6.

Namazi, N., Tarighat, A., et al, The effect of hydro alcoholic nettle (Urtica dioica) extract on oxidative stress in patients with type 2 diabetes: a randomized double-blind clinical trial. Pak J Biol Sci. 2012 Jan 15;15(2):98-102.

Nappi, RE., Maalvasi, B., et al, Efficacy of Cimicifuga racemosa on climacteric complaints: a randomized study versus low-dose transdermal estradiol. Gynecol Endocrinol. 2005 Jan;20(1):30-5.

Neto, CC., Cranberry and Blueberry: Evidence for protective effects against cancer and vascular diseases. Mol Nutr Food Res. 2007;51(6):652-64.

Ngan, A., Conduit, R., A double-blind, placebo-controlled investigation of the effects of Passiflora incarnata (passionflower) herbal tea on subjective sleep quality. Phytother Res. 2011 Aug;25(8):1153-9.

Niederkorn, J., MD, A Handy Reference Book, Cincinnati, 1905.

Noguchi, M., Kakuma, T., et al, Randomized clinical trial of an ethanol extract of Ganoderma lucidum in men with lower urinary tract symptoms. Asian J. Androl. 2008 Sep;10(5):777-85.

Oh, KJ., Chae, MJ., et al, Effects of Korean Red Ginseng on sexual arousal in menopausal women: placebo-controlled, double-blind crossover clinical study. J Sex Med. 2010 Apr;7(4 Pt 1):1469-77.

Oka, S., Tanaka, S., et al, A water-soluble extract from culture medium of Ganoderma lucidum mycelia suppresses the development of colorectal adenomas. Hiroshima J Med Sci. 2010 Mar;59(1):1-6.

Omer, B., Krebs, S., et al, Steroid-sparing effect of Wormwood (Artemisia absinthium) in Crohn's disease: A double-blind placebo-controlled study. Phytomedicine. 2007;14(2-3):87-95.

Panossian, A., Wikman, G., et al, Adaptogens stimulate neuropeptide y and hsp72 expression and release in neuroglia cells. Front Neurosci. 2012;6:6.

Panossian, A., Wikman, G., Evidence-based efficacy of adaptogens in fatigue and molecular mechanisms related to their stress-protective activity, Curr Clin Pharmacol. 2009;4(3):198-219.

Panossian, A., Wikman, G., et al, Rosenroot (Rhodiola rosea): Traditional use, chemical compostition, pharmacology and clinical efficacy. Phytomedicine. 2010;17(7):481-93.

Panossian, A., Wikman, G., Pharmacology of Schisandra chinensis Bail.: an overview of Russian research and uses in medicine. J Ethnopharmacol. 2008 Jul 23;118(2):183-212.

Park, CH., Choi, SH., et al, Novel cognitive improving and neuroprotective activities of Polygala tenuifolia Willdenow extract, BT-11. J Neurosci Res. 2002;70(3):484-92.

Park, HJ., Lee, K., et al, Effects of Polygala tenuifolia root extract on proliferation of neural stem cells in the hippocampal CA1 region. Phytother Res. 2008;22(10):1324-9.

Park, SJ., Chin, WH., Anthocyanins Inhibit airway inflammation and hyperresponsiveness in a murine asthma model. Food Chem Toxicol. 2007;45(8):1459-67.

Patel, R., Mahobia, N., et al, Analgesic and antipyretic activities of Momordica charantia Linn. fruits. J Adv Pharm Technol Res. 2010 Oct-Dec;1(4):415–418.

Pengelly, A., Snow, J., et al, Short-term study on the effects of Rosemary on cognitive function in an elderly population. J Med Food. 2012;15(1):10-7.

Perrinjaquet-Moccetti, T., Busjahn, A., et al, Food supplementation with an Olive (Olea europaea L.) leaf extract reduces blood pressure in borderline hypertensive monozygotic twins. Phytother Res. 2008 Sep;22(9):1239-42.

Pillai, AK., Sharma, KK., et al, Anti-emetic of Ginger powder versus placebo as an add-on therapy in children and young adults reciving high emetogenic chemotherapy. Pediatr Blood Cancer. 2011 Feb;56(2):234-8.

Piscoya, J., Rodriguez, Z., et al, Efficacy and safety of freeze-dried Cat's Claw in osteoarthritis of the knee: mechanisms of action of the species Uncaria guianensis. Inflamm res. 2001 Sep;50(9):442-8.

Pittler, MH., Ernst, E., Horse Chestnut seed extract for chronic venous insufficiency. Cochrane Database Syst rev 2012 Nov 14;11:CD003230.

Pizzorno, J., ND and Murray, M., ND, Textbook of Natural Medicine, 2 vol., New York, 2005.

Pole, S., Ayurvedic Medicine, The Principals of Traditional Practice, St. Louis, MO, 2009.

Pommier, P., Gomez, F., et al, Phase III randomized Trial of Calendula officinalis compared with Trolamine for the prevention of acute dermatitis during irradiation for breast cancer. J Clin Oncol 2004;15(22):1447-53.

Prasongwatana, V., Woottisin, S., et al, Uricosuric effect of Roselle (Hibiscus sabdariffa) in normal and renal-stone former subjects. J Ethnopharmacol. 2008 May 22;117(3):491-5.

Quettier-Deleu, C., Voiselle, G., et al, Hawthorn extracts inhibit LDL oxidation. Pharmazie. 2003;58(8):577-81.

Raffalt, GJ., Andersen, B., Treatment of cigarette smokers with an oat extract. Ugeskr Laeger 1975;137(38):2177-8.

Rafraf, M., Malekiyan, M., et al, Effect of Fenugreek Seeds on Serum Metabolic Factors and Adiponectin Levels in Type 2 Diabetic Patients. Int J Vitam Nutr Res. 2014;84(3-4):196-205.

Rahimi, R., Abdollahi, M., An update on the ability of St. John's wort to affect the metabolism of other drugs. Expert Opin Drug Metab Toxicol. 2012 Jun;8(6):691-708.

Rainer, M., Mucke, H., et al, Ginkgo bilboa extract EGb 761 in the treatment of dementia: a pharmacoeconomic analysis of the Austrian setting. Wien Klin Wochenschr. 2013 Jan;125(1-2):8-15.

Rajeswary, H., Vasuki, R., et al, Hepatoprotective action of ethanolic extracts of Melia azedarach Linn. and Piper longum Linn and their combination on CC14 induced hepatotoxicity in rats. Indian J Exp Biol. 2011 Apr;49(4):276-81.

Rechciski, T., Kurpesa, M., Oligomeric procyanidins from Hawthorn extract as supplementary therapy in patients with left ventricle systolic dysfunction. [article in Polish] Przegl Lek 2005;62(4):243-4.

Reid, G., Hsiehl, J., et al, Cranberry juice consumption may reduce biofilms on uroepithelial cells: pilot study in spinal cord injured patients. Spinal Cord. 2001;39(1):26-30.

Rietbrock, N., Hamel, M., et al, Actions of standardized extracts of Crataegus berries on exercise tolerance and quality of life in patients with congestive heart failure [Article in German]. Arzneimittelforschung. 2001 Oct;51(10):793-8.

Rigelsky, JM., Sweet, BV., Hawthorn: pharmacology and therapeutic uses. Am J Health Syst Pharm. 2002;59(5).

Rivera-Espinoza, Y., Muriel, P., Pharmacological actions of Curcumin in liver diseases or damage. Liver Int. 2009 Nov;29(10):1457-66.

Rondanelli, M., Giacosa, A., et al, Beneficial effects of artichoke leaf extract supplementation on increasing HDL-cholesterol in subjects with primary mild hypercholesterolaemia: a double-blind, randomized, placebo-controlled trial. Int J Food Sci Nutr. 2013 Feb;64(1):7-15

Rondanelli, M., Opizzi, A., et al, Metabolic management in overweight subject with naive impaired fasting glycaemia by means of a highly standardized extract from Cynara scolymus: a double-blind, placebo-controlled, randomized clinical trial. Phytother Res. 2014 Jan;28(1):33-41.

Roodenrys, S., Booth, D., et al, Chronic effects of Brahmi (Bacopa monnieri) on human memory. Neurophsychopharmacology. 2002;27(20).

Rose, P., Faulkner, K., et al, 7-Methylsulfinylheptyl and 8-methylsulfinyloctyl isothiocyanates from Watercress are potent inducers of phase II enzymes. Carcinogenesis. 2000 Nov;21(11):1983-8.

Roveroni-Favaretto, LH., Lodi, KB., et al, Topical Calendula officinalis L. successfully treated exfoliative cheilitis: a case report. Cases J. 2009;2:9077.

Roxas, M., Jurenka, J., Colds and Influenza: A review of diagnosis and conventional, botanical and nutritional considerations. Altern Med Rev. 2007;12(1):25-48.

Roy, S., Khanna, S., et al, Anti-angiogenic property of edible berries. Free Radic Res. 2002;36(9):252-7.

Russo, A., Izzo, AA., et al, Free radical scavenging capacity and protective effect of Bacopa monniera L. on DNA Damage. Phytother Res. 2003;17(8):870-5.

Saddiqe, Z., Naeem, I., et al, A review of the antibacterial activity of Hypericum perforatum L. J Ethnopharmacol. 2010 Oct 5;131(3):511-21.

Samadi, S., Khadivzadeh, T., et al, The effect of Hypericum perforatum on the wound healing and scar of cesarean. J Altern Complement Med. 2010;16(1):113-7.

Sandhu, JS., Shah, B., et al, Effects of Withania somnifera (Ashwagandha) and Terminalia arjuna (Arjuna) on physical performance and cardiorespiratory endurance in healthy young adults. Int J Ayurveda Res. 2010;1(3):144-9.

Santos Araújo Mdo, C., Farias, IL., et al, Uncaria tomentosa-adjuvant treatment for breast cancer: clinical trial. Evid Based Complement Alternat Med. 2012;2012:676984

Sarris, J., Kavanagh, DJ., et al, The Kava anxiety depression spectrum study (KADSS): a randomized, placebo-controlled crossover trial using an aqueous extract of Piper methysticum. Psychopharmacology (Ber). 2009 Aug;205(3):399-407.

Satapathy, S., Das, N., et al, Effect of Tulsi (Ocimum sanctum Linn.) Supplementation on Metabolic Parameters and Liver Enzymes in Young Overweight and Obese Subjects. Indian J Clin Biochem. 2017 Jul;32(3):357-363

Sawangjaroen, N., Sawangjaroen, K., et al, Effects of Piper longum fruit, Piper sarmentosum root and Quercus infectoria nut gall on caecal amoebiasis in mice. J Ethnopharmacol. 2004 Apr;91(2-3):357-60.

Schellekens, C., Perrinjaquet-Moccetti, T., et al, An extract from wild green Oat improves rat behaviour. Phytther Res. 2009 Oct;23(10):1371-7.

Schempp, CM., Windeck, T., et al, Topical treatment of atopic dermatitis with St. John's Wort cream - A randomized, placebo controlled, double blind half-side comparison. Phytomedicine. 2003;10 Suppl 4:31-7.

Schmid, B., Lüdtke, R., et al, Efficacy and tolerability of a standardized Willow bark extract in patients with osteoarthritis: randomized placebo-controlled, double blind clinical trial. Phytother. 2001 Jun;15(4):344-50.

Schmidt, U., Kuhn, U., et al, Efficacy of the Hawthorn (Crataegus) Preparation LI 132 in 78 patients with chronic congestive heart failure defined as NYHA Functional Class II. Phytomedicine. 1994;1:17-24.

Schoop, R., Klein, P., et al, Echinacea in the prevention of induced rhinovirus colds: a meta analysis. Clin Ther. 2006 Feb;28(2):174-83.

Scudder, JM., MD, A Practical Treatise on the Diseases of Women, Cincinnati, 1878.

Sell, EHH., MD, The Opium Habit: Its Successful Treatment by Avena sativa, Jersey City, NJ, 1883.

Sharon, N., Ofek, I., Fighting infectious diseases with inhibitors of microbial adhesion to host tissues. Crit Rev Food Sci Nutr. 2002;42(3 Suppl):267-72.

Shmuely, H., Yahav, J., et al, Effect of Cranberry juice on eradication of Helicobacter pylori in patients treated with antibiotics and a proton pump inhibitor. Mol Nutr Food Res. 2007;51(6):746-51.

Singer, A., Schmidt, M., et al, Duration of response after treatment of mild to moderate depression with Hypericum extract STW 3-VI, Citalopram and placebo: a reanalysis of data from a controlled clinical trial. Phytomedicine. 2011 Jun 15;18(8-9):739-42.

Somova, LI., Shode, FO., et al, Antihypertensive, antiatherosclerotic and antioxidant activity of triterpenoids isolated from Olea europaea, subspecies africana leaves. J Ethnopharmacol. 2003 Feb;84(2-3):299-305.

Stoeken, JE., Paraskevas, S., et al, The long term effect of a mouthrinse containing essential oil on dental plaque and gingivitis: a systematic review. J Periodontol. 2007 Jul;78(7):1218-28.

Stothers, L., A randomized trial to evaluate effectiveness and cost effectivness of naturopathic Cranberry products as prophylaxis against urinary tract infection in women. Can J Urol. 2002 Jun;9(3):1558-62.

Stough, C., Lloyd, J., et al, The chronic effects of an extract of Bacopa monnieri (Brahmi) on cognitive function in healthy human subjects. Psychopharmacology. 2001;156(4):481-4.

Stull, AJ., Cash, KC., et al, Bioactives in Blueberries improve insulin sensitivity in obese, insulin-resistant men and women. J Nutr. 2010;140(10):1764-8.

Sunila, ES., Kuttan, G., Protective effect of Piper longum fruit ethanolic extract on radiation induced damages in mice: a preliminary study. Fitoterapia. 2005 Dec;76(7-8):649-55.

Susalit, E., Agus, N., et al, Olive (Olea europaea) leaf extract effective in patients with stage-1 hypertension: comparison with Captopril. Phytomedicine. 2011 Feb 15;(4):251-8.

Suter, A., Niemer, W., et al, A new Ginkgo fresh plant extract increases microcirculation and radical scavenging activity in elderly patients. Adv ther. 2011 Dec;28(12):1078-88.

Takahashi, S., Hamasuna, R., et al, A randomized clinical trial to evaluate the preventive effect of Cranberry juice (UR65) for patients with recurrent urinary tract infection. J Infect Chemother. 2013 Feb;19(1):112-7.

Tang, T., Targan, SR., et al, Randomised clinical trial: herbal extract HMPL-004 in active ulcerative colitis - a double blind comparison with sustained release Mesalazine. Aliment Pharmacol Ther. 2011 Jan;33(2):194-202.

Tao, Y., Pinzón-Arango, PA., et al, Oral consumption of Cranberry juice cocktail inhibits molecular-scale adhesion of clinical uropathogenic Escherichia coli. J Med Food. 2011 Jul-Aug;14(7-8):739-45.

Tarkkey, S., & Pyles, T., An Herbal (1525), New York Botanical Garden, NY 1941

Tauchert, M., Efficacy and safety of Crataegus extract WS 1442 in comparison with placebo in patients with chronic stable New York Heart Association class-III heart failure. Am Heart J. 2002 May;143(5):910-5.

Tayyab, F., Smith Lal, S., Comparative study on supplementation effect of

Momordica charantia Linn. and Emblica officinalis Gaertn. on lipid profile of type II diabetic patients in Allahabad, Uttar Pradesh, India. Annals of phyto-medicines. 2016;5(1):40-42.

Tillotson, A., The One Earth Herbal Sourcebook. New York, 2001.

Thompson, R., Ruch, W., et al, Enhanced cognitive performance and cheerful mood by standardized extracts of Piper methysticum (Kava-kava). Hum Psychopharmacol. 2004 Jun;19(4):243-50.

Tobyn, G., Denhan, A., Whitelegg, M. The Western Herbal Tradition: 2000 years of Medicinal Plant Knowledge. Edinburgh, 2011.

Tong, GH., Zhang, Y., Effect of Celery Seed extract on hyperuricemia in rats. Food Science. 2008;29(12):641-4.

Treasure, J., Urtica semen reduces creatinine levels. J Am Herb Guild. 2003;4(2):22-5.

Tripathi, DM., Gupta, N., et al, Antigiardial and immunostimulatory effect of Piper longum on Giardiasis due to Giardia lamblia. Phytother Res. 1999 Nov;13(7):561-5.

Tsai, CH., Chen, EC., et al, Wild bitter gourd improves metabolic syndrome: a preliminary dietary supplementation trial. Nutr J. 2012 Jan 13;11:4.

Upton, R. [Ed.] American Herbal Pharmacopoeia and Therapeutic Compendium, Ashwagandha Root, Santa Cruz, CA, 2000a.

Upton, R. [Ed.] American Herbal Pharmacopoeia and Therapeutic Compendium, Astragalus Root, Santa Cruz, CA, 1999a.

Upton, R. [Ed.] American Herbal Pharmacopoeia and Therapeutic Compendium, Black Haw Bark, Santa Cruz, CA, 2000b.

Upton, R. [Ed.] American Herbal Pharmacopoeia and Therapeutic Compendium, Chaste Tree, Santa Cruz, CA, 2001a.

Upton, R. [Ed.] American Herbal Pharmacopoeia and Therapeutic Compendium, Cramp Bark, Santa Cruz, CA, 2000c.

Upton, R. [Ed.] American Herbal Pharmacopoeia and Therapeutic Compendium, Cranberry Fruit, Santa Cruz, CA, 2002.

Upton, R. [Ed.] American Herbal Pharmacopoeia and Therapeutic Compendium, Dang Gui, Santa Cruz, CA, 2003a.

Upton, R. [Ed.] American Herbal Pharmacopoeia and Therapeutic Compendium, Echinacea angustifolia, Santa Cruz, CA, 2010a.

Upton, R. [Ed.] American Herbal Pharmacopoeia and Therapeutic Compendium, Echinacea purpurea root, Santa Cruz, CA, 2004.

Upton, R. [Ed.] American Herbal Pharmacopoeia and Therapeutic Compendium, Ginkgo leaf, Ginkgo leaf dry extract, Santa Cruz, CA, 2003b.

Upton, R. [Ed.] American Herbal Pharmacopoeia and Therapeutic Compendium, Goldenseal Root, Santa Cruz, CA, 2001b.

Upton, R. [Ed.] American Herbal Pharmacopoeia and Therapeutic Compendium, Hawthorn berry, Santa Cruz, CA, 1999b.

Upton, R. [Ed.] American Herbal Pharmacopoeia and Therapeutic Compendium, Reishi Mushroom, Santa Cruz, CA, 2000d.

Upton, R. [Ed.] American Herbal Pharmacopoeia and Therapeutic Compendium,

Schisandra Berry, Santa Cruz, CA, 1999c.

Upton, R. [Ed.] American Herbal Pharmacopoeia and Therapeutic Compendium, Stinging Nettle leaf, Santa Cruz, CA, 2009.

Upton, R. [Ed.] American Herbal Pharmacopoeia and Therapeutic Compendium, Stinging Nettle root, Santa Cruz, CA, 2010b.

Upton, R. [Ed.] American Herbal Pharmacopoeia and Therapeutic Compendium, Valerian, Santa Cruz, CA, 1999d.

Upton, R. [Ed.] American Herbal Pharmacopoeia and Therapeutic Compendium, Willow Bark, Santa Cruz, CA, 1999e.

Upton, R. [Ed.] American Herbal Pharmacopoeia, St. John's wort - Hypericum perforatum, Binghamton, NY, 1997.

Vandecasteele, K., Ost, P., et al, Evaluation of the efficacy and safety of Salvia officinalis in controlling hot flashes in prostate cancer patients treated with androgen deprivation, Phytother Res. 2012 Feb;26(2):208-13.

Vendrame, S., Guglielmetti, S., et al, Blueberry powder may boost beneficial gut bacteria: Study. J Agric Food Chem. 2011 Dec 28;59(24):12815-20.

Vidlar, A., Vostalova, J., et al, The effectiveness of dried Cranberries (Vaccinium macrocarpon) in men with lower urinary tract symptoms. BR J Nutr. 2010 Oct;104(8):1181-9.

Vyas, SR., et al, Leaf concentrate as an alternative to iron and folic acid supplements for anaemic adolescent girls: A randomised controlled trial in India, Pub Health Nutri, 2009 Sept;13(3):418-23.

Walker, AF., Marakis, G., et al, Promising hypotensive effect of Hawthorn extract: A randomized double-blind pilot study of mild, essential hypertension. Phytother Res. 2002;16(1).

Walker, AF., Marakis, G., et al, Hypotensive effects of Hawthorn for patients with diabetes taking prescription drugs: A randomised controlled trial. Br J Gen Pract. 2006;56(527):437-43.

Wang, Y., Chang, CF., et al, Dietary supplementation with Blueberries, Spinach, or Spirulina reduces ischemic brain damage. Exp Neurol. 2005;193(1):75-84

Warnock, M., McBean, D., Effectiveness and safety of Devil's Claw tablets in patients with general rheumatic disorders. Phytother Res. 2007 Dec;21(12):1228-33.

Weber, W., Taylor, JA., et al, Echinacea purpurea for prevention of upper respiratory tract infections in children. J Altern Complement Med. 2005 Dec;11(6):1021-6.

Webster, H., MD. Dynamical Therapeutics, San Francisco, 1898.

Weiss, R., Weiss' Herbal Medicine, Classic Edition, NY, 2001.

White, CM., Fan, C., et al, An evaluation of the hemostatic effects of hydrophilic, alcohol, and lipophilic extracts of Notoginseng. Pharmacotherapy. 2001 Jul;21(7):773-7.

Wichtl, M., Herbal Drugs and Phytopharmaceuticals. Stuttgart 3rd ed. 2004.

Widrig, R., Suter, A., et al, Choosing between NSAID and Arnica for topical treatment of hand osteoarthritis in a randomised double-blind study. Rheumatol Int. 2007;27(6):585-91.

Williamson, E., Major Herbs of Ayurveda, Edinburgh, 2002.

Winston, D., Differential Treatment of Depression and Anxiety with Botanical and Nutritional Medicines. DWCHS. Washington, NJ, 2020.

Winston, D., Saw Palmetto - For Men and Women. Pownal, VT, 1999.

Winston, D., Botanic Materia Medica. DWCHS Washington, NJ, 2020.

Winston, D., Maimes, S., Adaptogens, Herbs For Strength, Stamina and Stress Relief, Rochester, VT, 2019.

Winterhoff, H., Gumbinger, HG., et al, Endocrine effects of Lycopus europaeus L. following oral application. Arzneimittelforschung. 1994 Jan;44(1):41-5.

Wojtyniak, K., Szymański, M., et al, Leonurus cardiaca L. (Motherwort): A review of its phytochemistry and pharmacology. Phytother Res. 2013 Aug;27(8):1115-20.

Wolfson, P., Hoffman, DL., An investigation into the efficacy of Scutellaria lateriflora in healthy volunteers. Altern Ther Health Med. 2003 Mar-Apr;9(2):74-8.

Wu, X., Gu, L., et al, Characterization of anthocyanins and proanthocyanidins in some cultivars of Ribes, Aronia, and Sambucus and their antioxidant capacity. J Agric Food Chem. 2004;52(26):7846-56.

Wu, Y., Li, JQ., et al, In vivo and in vitro antiviral effects of Berberine on influenza virus. Chin J Inter Med. 2011 Jun;17(6):444-52.

Xiuying, P., Jianping, L., et al, Therapeutic efficacy of Hypericum perforatum L. extract for mice infected with influenza A virus. Can J Physiol Pharmacol. 2012 Feb;90(2):123-30.

Yance, D., Herbal Medicine, Healing and Cancer. New York: McGraw-Hill, 1999.

Yang, M., Lee, HS., et al, Effects of Korean red ginseng (Panax Ginseng Meyer) on bisphenol A exposure and gynecologic complaints: single blind, randomized clinical trial of efficacy and safety. BMC Complement Altern Med. 2014 Jul 25;14:265.

Yang, QY., Lu, S., et al, Effects of astragalus on cardiac function and serum tumor necrosis factor-alpha level in patients with chronic heart failure. Zhongguo Zhong Xi Yi Jie He Za Zhi. 2010 Jul;30(7):699-701.

Yang, QY., Chen, KJ., et al, Research progress on mechanism of action of Radix Astragalus in the treatment of heart failure. Chin J Integr Med. 2012 Mar;18(3):235-40.

Ying, J-Z., Mao, X-L., et al, Icones of Medicinal Fungi from China, Beijing, 1987.

Zafra-Stone, S., Yasmin, T., et al, Berry anthocyanins as novel antioxidants in human health and disease. Mol Nutr Food Res. 2007;51(6):675-83.

Zakay-Rones, Z., Thom, E., et al, Randomized study of the efficacy and safety of oral Elderberry extract in the treatment of influenza A and B virus infections. J Int Med Res. 2004;32(2):132-40.

Zakay-Rones, Z., Varsano, N., et al, Inhibition of Several strains of influenza virus in vitro and reduction of symptoms by an Elderberry extract (Sambucus nigra L.) during an outbreak of influenza B Panama. J Altern Complement Med. 1995;1(4):361-9.

Zapfe jun G., Clinical efficacy of Crataegus extract WS1442 in congestive heart failure NYHA class II., Phytomedicine. 2001 Jul;8(4):262-6.

Zenico, T., Cicero, AF., et al, Subjective effects of Lepidium meyenii (Maca) extract on well-being and sexual performances in patients with mild erectile dysfunction: A randomised, double-blind clinical trial. Andrologia.

2009;41(2):95-9.

Zhang, L., Ma, J., et al, Efficacy of Cranberry juice on Helicobacter pylori infection: A double-blind, randomized placebo-controlled trial. Helicobacter. 2005;10(2):139-45.

Zhang, Z., Wang, X., et al, Effect of Cordyceps sinensis on renal function of patients with chronic allograft nephropathy. Urol Int. 2011;86(3):298-301.

Ziegenfuss, TN., Hofheins, JE., et al, Effects of a water-soluble Cinnamon extract on body composition and features of the metabolic syndrome in pre-diabetic men and women. J Int Soc Sports Nutr. 2006 Dec 28;3:45-53.

NOTES: